What Your Colleagu

"This book is so much more than a "few great strategies to try on." Rather, it explains the science of how our reading brains work, so that we acknowledge all that the brain does when making sense of text. *How to Prevent Reading Difficulties* can benefit both new and seasoned practitioners in two ways: First, these powerful strategies detail specific yet practical activities, routines, and techniques that teachers can use to teach *all* children the basics of reading, and second, because these practices focus on establishing a strong foundation, they also help teachers to prevent reading difficulties through strong Tier 1 instruction."

—Hilda Martinez
NBCT, RTI Coordinator
2020 San Diego County Teacher of the Year

"Master teacher Mark Weakland serves up a smorgasbord of evidence-based best teaching practices in *How to Prevent Reading Difficulties, Grades PreK–3*, presented with the science of reading in ways you will understand. This smart and fun-to-read teaching guide gives you the bread, butter, cheese, meat and potato routines for ensuring that virtually all students learn to read, write, and spell."

—J. Richard Gentry
Researcher, Author, and Educational Consultant
Co-author, *Brain Words: How the Science of Reading Informs Teaching*
Mobile, AL

"I will be suggesting this title to all of my preservice and early career teachers who are searching for a comprehensive guide to the science of reading and an understanding of how the reading brain works. Not only does Mark Weakland provide a thorough explanation of literacy development and skills, he also helps us understand reading difficulties, how to support students who struggle, and the related research basis. With practical suggestions and engaging vignettes, Mark Weakland helps inform teachers on best practices to support all students."

—Molly Ness
Associate Professor at Fordham University
Author, *Every Minute Matters*
New York, NY

"From brain research to building better readers, Mark Weakland's *How to Prevent Reading Difficulties, Grades PreK–3—Proactive Practices for Teaching Young Children to Read* provides a very readable and actionable approach to overcoming reading difficulties in young children. This is definitely a book worth reading and having on hand as a guide for developing reading instruction that works."

—Timothy Rasinski
Professor of Literacy Education, Kent State University
Rebecca Tolle and Burton W. Gorman Chair in Educational Leadership
Stow, OH

"In *How to Prevent Reading Difficulties, Grades PreK–3,* Mark Weakland begins by taking you on a tour of the inner workings of the reading brain. With this landscape as your backdrop, he showcases five highly effective teaching techniques to weave into your repertoire. The chapters that follow offer a helpful collection of proactive practices and activities that will boost readers' understanding of the dynamic interplay among meaning, sounds, and spelling."

—Maria Walther
Traveling Teacher, Literacy Consultant
Author, *The Ramped-Up Read Aloud*
Aurora, IL

"In *How to Prevent Reading Difficulties, Grades PreK–3: Proactive Practices for Teaching Young Children to Read,* Mark Weakland offers a wealth of practical instructional activities and routines to maximize student learning in phonological awareness, phonics, spelling, vocabulary, comprehension, and more. This resource is grounded in the latest research drawn from multiple sciences examining how children learn to read. It's a valuable addition to any teacher's bookshelf."

—Wiley Blevins
Author, *A Fresh Look at Phonics*
New York, NY

"I am so excited and grateful for Mark Weakland's latest work. *How to Prevent Reading Difficulties, Grades PreK–3* is a must-read filled with "must dos" for new and experienced elementary educators, coaches, and interventionists. As educators, we often learn the mechanics of how to work with students who are reading at or above grade level, and then later struggle to find the resources and materials needed to support students with greater needs. Mark Weakland does an amazing job bringing us from the mechanics of brain functioning all the way to practical implementation."

—Melissa Black
District of Columbia Public Schools
Washington, DC

How to Prevent Reading Difficulties, Grades PreK–3

To the teachers, 2020.

How to Prevent Reading Difficulties, Grades PreK–3

Proactive Practices for Teaching Young Children to Read

Mark Weakland

FOR INFORMATION:

Corwin
A SAGE Company
2455 Teller Road
Thousand Oaks, California 91320
(800) 233-9936
www.corwin.com

SAGE Publications Ltd.
1 Oliver's Yard
55 City Road
London EC1Y 1SP
United Kingdom

SAGE Publications India Pvt. Ltd.
B 1/I 1 Mohan Cooperative Industrial Area
Mathura Road, New Delhi 110 044
India

SAGE Publications Asia-Pacific Pte. Ltd.
18 Cross Street #10-10/11/12
China Square Central
Singapore 048423

Acquisitions Editor: Tori Bachman
Editorial Development Manager: Julie Nemer
Associate Content Development Editor: Sharon Wu
Project Editor: Amy Schroller
Copy Editor: Amy Hanquist Harris
Typesetter: C&M Digitals (P) Ltd.
Proofreader: Caryne Brown
Indexer: Integra
Cover Designer: Candice Harmann
Marketing Manager: Deena Meyer

Printed in the United States of America

Library of Congress Cataloging-in-Publication Data

Names: Weakland, Mark, author.

Title: How to prevent reading difficulties, grades preK–3 : proactive practices for teaching young children to read / Mark Weakland.

Description: Thousand Oaks, California : Corwin, 2021. | Series: Corwin literacy | Includes bibliographical references and index.

Identifiers: LCCN 2020052561 | ISBN 9781071823439 (paperback) | ISBN 9781071844038 (epub) | ISBN 9781071844045 (epub) | ISBN 9781071844052 (pdf)

Subjects: LCSH: Reading (Early childhood) | Reading (Primary) | Reading, Psychology of.

Classification: LCC LB1140.5.R4 W43 2021 | DDC 372.4—dc23
LC record available at https://lccn.loc.gov/2020052561

This book is printed on acid-free paper.

21 22 23 24 25 10 9 8 7 6 5 4 3 2 1

CONTENTS

ACKNOWLEDGMENTS

I wish to thank everyone at Corwin Literacy, especially Tori Bachman; the teachers and administrators at Divine Mercy Catholic Academy in Johnstown, Pennsylvania, especially Miss Sonja Gable, Miss Kathy Marano, and Mrs. Patty Gable; the teachers and administrators at St. Stephen's Episcopal School in Harrisburg, Pennsylvania, especially Ms. Emily Hand and Ms. JoAnn Baldwin; the parents and children who helped me with book pictures and writing samples, especially Lydia and Kirby Shaffer and their children, Abram, Eliza, and Amelia, and Arthur and Christine Manalang and their daughter, Anneliese; teacher friends Katrina Kimmel and Jennifer Jones; friends in literacy Terry Thompson, Richard Gentry, Ellen McHugh, and Michael Herzberg, who have been helpful in my quest to understand dyslexia; my mother, Lynne Weakland, who taught me so much and continues to nerd out with me over all things reading and writing; my sisters, Melissa and Rachael Weakland, who give words of encouragement but also egg me on; my wife Beth, a most excellent teacher; and the many dedicated teachers I meet everywhere—you are a constant source of knowledge, inspiration, and hope.

Publisher Acknowledgments

Corwin gratefully acknowledges the contributions of the following reviewers:

Melissa Black
Associate Dean
Progressive Education Institute, Harlem Village Academy
Washington, DC

J. Richard Gentry, PhD
Author, Educational Consultant, Former Professor
J. Richard Gentry, Inc.
Mobile, AL

Meghan Schofield
Teacher
Wiscasset School Department
Wiscasset, ME

INTRODUCTION

"No single truth does not mean no truth."

—Iain McGilchrist

This book describes the science and art of teaching in action. It focuses first on knowledge and then on specific techniques, activities, strategies, and routines that teachers can do in Tier 1 classroom settings. The goal it sets is to help teachers teach reading in ways that prevent reading difficulties from developing.

The mission of preventing reading difficulties is one close to my heart. As a reading specialist and special education teacher, I taught dozens of upper-elementary-aged children who had profound reading and writing deficits. For these students, the opportunity for prevention had passed. My job was to help them overcome full-blown difficulties. But when I began classroom teaching in 1991, I was ill equipped to do this. My special education teacher preparation program provided me with one—that's right, ONE—reading course, and I knew very little about the fundamentals of the reading process, why children developed reading difficulties, and what specific instructional practices were especially effective in helping kids overcome their reading, writing, and spelling challenges.

Thankfully, I learned a lot about both reading theory and instructional practice from my classroom experiences, reading initiative workshops, training in the Wilson Reading System, and eventually a reading specialist certificate. By 2011, when assigned to teach a literacy block for my school's lowest-achieving third-grade readers, I felt confident and knowledgeable enough to design and then run (with a coteacher) a specialized program. This program was a great success: In each of three consecutive years, with only one exception, every low-achieving third-grader who went through the program made moderate-to-large gains in oral-reading fluency, significant gains in writing achievement, and at least one-year's worth of growth on schoolwide assessments.

Even after this experience, however, I still didn't deeply understand how reading occurs in the brain or what the root causes of various reading disabilities were. It wasn't until later, when I started my own literacy business and dived into reading research, that I gained much needed knowledge on how the reading process works and why some instructional practices are more effective than others.

Research Base and Bedrocks of Belief

My conviction that certain classroom practices are superior to others is built upon evidence and experience. First, decades of research point to types of instruction that are especially effective for teaching children to read, write, and spell. I call this body of knowledge the "golden threads." Second, I have worked for more than 29 years in public and nonpublic education systems, teaching hundreds of kids, discussing literacy with dozens of administrators, and working with scores of teachers. Every experience teaches me something, and as the years go by, I more clearly see how science and art intersect and interact, and I more clearly understand what can be done to help children learn how to read, write, and spell.

It was Dr. Richard Gentry who kick-started my deep exploration of how science illuminates the foundational reading process and the instructional practices we use to teach it. For that, I am grateful. Richard was the one who told me that to write a book about spelling instruction (which I was working on at the time), I had to understand how reading arises at a fundamental level. And so I dug in.

In scholarly journals and books, I found studies, articles, and chapters authored by brilliant researchers, including Linnea

Ehri, Marilyn Adams, Bruce McCandliss, Usha Goswami, and Anne Castles. Their research and writing were illuminating and influencing.

- "Learning to Read and Learning to Spell: Two Sides of a Coin" by Linnea Ehri in *Topics in Language Disorder*, 2000; also, "Phases of Word Learning: Implications for Instruction With Delayed and Disabled Readers" by Linnea Ehri and Sandra McCormick in *Theoretical Models and Processes of Reading*, 1989
- "The Three-Cueing System" by Marilyn Adams in *Literacy for All Issues in Teaching and Learning*, 1998
- "Hemispheric Specialization for Visual Words Is Shaped by Attention to Sublexical Units During Initial Learning" by Yuliya N. Yonchevaa, Jessica Wise, and Bruce McCandliss in *Brain and Language*, 2015
- "Educational Neuroscience for Reading Researchers" by George Hruby and Usha Goswami in *Theoretical Models and Processes of Reading*, 2013
- "Ending the Reading Wars: Reading Acquisition From Novice to Expert" by Anne Castles, Kathleen Rastle, and Kate Nation in *Psychological Science in the Public Interest*, 2018; also, "Helping Children With Reading Difficulties: Some Things We Have Learned So Far" by Genevieve McArthur and Anne Castles in *npj Science of Learning*, 2017

Equally enlightening was the information I found in books beautifully written by literacy scholars who make use of neuroscience insights. Here are a few that were (and still are) especially important to me:

- *Language at the Speed of Sight: How We Read, Why So Many Can't, and What We Can Do About It* by Mark Seidenberg, 2017
- *Proust and the Squid: The Story and Science of the Reading Brain* and *Reader, Come Home: The Reading Brain in a Digital World* by Maryanne Wolf, 2008/2018
- *Reading in the Brain: The New Science of How We Read* by Stanislas Dehaene, 2009
- *Overcoming Dyslexia: A New and Complete Science-Based Program for Reading Problems at Any Level* by Sally Shaywitz, 2003/2020

- *Brain Words: How the Science of Reading Informs Teaching* by Richard Gentry and Gene Ouellette, 2019
- *Essentials of Assessing, Preventing, and Overcoming Reading Difficulties* by David Kilpatrick, 2015

Viewed through the lens of reading instruction, the quote that kicks off this introduction speaks to two ideas: (1) There is no single best way of teaching children to read, and (2) no single best way does *not* mean no best ways at all. In fact, some instructional practices are better than others, and by *better*, I mean more effective at teaching students to read. But what are these effective practices? And when and where do we use them?

Determining what practice to use in any given situation or classroom involves the art of balancing research knowledge and professional judgement. Someone once asked me, "What gives you the authority to write about reading difficulties? And how will you decide what practices to include in a book?" My reply was to point to the researchers and writings I previously mentioned. Each has contributed to my understanding of the reading process and the instructional practices that effectively bring it about; collectively, the research and writings describe a bedrock of knowledge (truths, if you will) that provides the foundation for this book.

The Science and Art of Reading Instruction

Researchers know a lot about how kids learn to read. The science is established, and the theory that flows from it is increasingly defined, stable, and predictive. But although scientists are skilled at pointing out what types of instruction work best, they are less accomplished at turning their elemental insights into practices that teachers can do in their classrooms on Monday morning. This may be one reason the field of teaching still isn't moving large numbers of students to the point of proficient reading (National Assessment of Educational Progress [NAEP], 2019). Societal issues, such as poverty, addiction, and inequity, can also be blamed for stagnant reading scores. Or perhaps the sheer scope of bringing millions of teachers to proficiency on reading theory and best instructional practice slows the progress of our nation's children.

Uninformed and ideological thinking in the field of education might be a limiting factor, too. Sadly, even in the face of ever-accumulating evidence, a more fully realized way to teach reading has yet to take root in all classrooms. By this, I mean that many educators, from primary grade teachers to professors of education, have not completely integrated the empirically derived information that cognitive science and neuroscience have revealed regarding how reading arises and develops in the brain.

In some cases, educators haven't even learned the basics. More than a decade ago, studies found that teacher preparation programs lacked attention to concepts put forth in 2000 by the National Reading Panel and that those involved in training preservice and inservice teachers were not well acquainted with the concepts of phonemic awareness, phonics, fluency, vocabulary, and comprehension (Joshi et al., 2009a; Joshi et al., 2009b). Fast-forward a few years and things weren't much better. A 2019 survey found more than 25 percent of teachers teach students to use decoding strategies as a last resort rather than a first line of attack (Loewus, 2019). The survey also found 1 in 5 professors confused phonemic awareness with letter–sound correspondence. And a 2016 *Journal of Childhood & Developmental Disorders* article stated the following:

> Although the Science of Reading provides considerable information with regard to the nature of dyslexia, its evaluation and remediation, there is a history of ignorance, complacency, and resistance in colleges of education with regard to disseminating this critical information to pre-service teachers. (Hurford et al., 2016, para. 1)

This book aims to provide information on what is known about the science of reading (i.e., the information empirical study has revealed about the reading process) and to describe and explore the instructional practices that flow from it. Thus, upcoming chapters present facts on how reading arises in the brain as well as techniques, activities, and routines that lead to lots of learning in the areas of phonology, orthography, and language comprehension.

Here, I want to clearly state that teaching phonic skills and fostering a love of reading are in no way antithetical. Also, framing reading instruction as a war between two opposing armies—one waving the banner of code-first, the other flying the flag of meaning-first—is misleading and unhelpful, and I strongly disagree when professors (or any educators, for that matter) define the reading process in binary terms. For me, the metaphor of warring camps is heard primarily in higher-ed haggling and media reporting, not in discussions between classroom teachers. The most skillful teachers I know are not rigidly ideological but rather flexible, open-minded, and—above all—practical, constantly striving to figure out what instructional practices will best teach their students to read.

Reading is a complex, multifaceted activity that arises from a convergence of numerous subprocesses. Although researchers have identified many of its discrete features, I think it is a mistake to go too far down the path of reductionism, for the act of reading has an *emergent* quality to it; a fluent reader is something far greater than the sum of his neural parts, and the reading process is holistic and interactive, with many pieces influencing each other in myriad ways. Because the reading process is complex and because readers develop in different ways for different reasons, I believe it is best to have a teaching stance that is inclusive, not exclusive, as well as flexible. We can instruct large groups *and* small. Our instruction can be direct and explicit, *as well as* expansive and creative. We should teach decoding and encoding (in some cases, a lot of it) *as well as* metacognition and meaning (in some cases, a lot of it). And we can set up our classrooms so children are learning to read *and* reading to learn, which can be done if we program extended reading opportunities that allow students to pull it all together, building critical word recognition skills *as well as* increasing their ability to derive meaning from text.

Finally, although I've used a good deal of "both-sides-now" language in the previous paragraphs, I do not advocate instruction that is "balanced" at all times. There are times to focus on one skill more than another. Capable readers who are ready to explore genre, authors' purpose, and metacognition strategies can be given these things. Meanwhile, those students who are still trying to "break the code" should receive higher doses of systematically taught encoding and decoding. But we don't want to go overboard! Reading is always about meaning, and rich literature and comprehension activities should always be part of the reading curriculum (Shanahan, 2017a).

The Components of Reading Success

The instructional practices included in this book are grouped into four categories. I think of these categories as the components of effective reading instruction, Grades preK to 3. Because each component reinforces the other, literacy instruction works best when all these components are firmly in place:

- **Teacher-used instructional techniques,** such as wait time, distributed practice, direct and explicit instruction, activating multiple senses, and instant error correction.
- **Activities and strategies that build language comprehension,** which includes background, topical, and vocabulary knowledge, as well as metacognition, grammar, and syntax. Practices such as shared reading, interactive read-alouds, teaching metacognition strategies, and vocabulary word sorts fall into this category.
- **Activities and strategies that build word recognition,** which include phonological awareness, letter combinations and sounds, spelling and phonics (from basic patterns to multisyllabic words), and the study of morphemes, from affixes to roots (English, Greek, and Latin). Activities in this category also include shared, guided, and independent reading.
- **Extended and extensive reading** (meaning bouts of reading, 15 or more minutes in length, in a wide variety of books), which often occurs during guided and independent reading time and which gives students opportunities to practice both language comprehension and word recognition.

Each component can be taught through any number of techniques, activities, routines, and/or strategies, which I collectively call practices. The practices in this book straddle the science of reading and my ongoing work with classroom teachers. Additionally, they are useful for teaching low-achieving readers *as well as* typically achieving readers, and they are effective with young children *and* many older children. Also, I hope you find my choices to be logical, easy to implement, and removed from the pendulum swings and paradigm shifts that plague education. Finally, none of the practices in this book is programmatic, meaning all practices can be integrated (to varying degrees) into Tier 1 classroom instruction, reading interventions, and any number of instructional frameworks, from balanced literacy and reader's workshop to basal reading programs such as Reading Street and Wonders.

Regarding instructional frameworks from balanced to basal and beyond, I leave many aspects of integrating the practices in this book up to your professional judgement. After all, each of you is teaching within a specific educational ecosystem. For example, one reviewer of this book has expertise in a dual-immersion classroom. Her thought is that if you teach this type of classroom, "you may want to hover in comprehension lessons a little longer" because vocabulary and language structures are still at the emergent level in primary grades. I couldn't agree more. Meanwhile, if you teach in a balanced-literacy classroom, you may want to give certain students more practice with phonics-spelling-morphology, which could come about by using decodable text, extra bouts of rereading, and additional activities that explicitly and directly teach phonics–spelling patterns. Conversely, if your classroom is basal-based, you may want to slice away ineffective workbook pages, too much shared reading, and time-consuming summative assessments in order to make room for more guided and independent reading, as well as guided writing.

When best practices are used, many students with problems in their early years do not have long-term difficulties. This is wonderful news! If we identify areas of concern early and instruct specifically and effectively, many serious reading difficulties might never arise. As research states, interventions can greatly reduce the number of children with continuing difficulties in reading, perhaps even below 2 percent (Torgesen et al., 2003; Vellutino et al., 2000). But this does not mean that reading difficulties that stem from neurological differences do not exist. On the contrary, I fully acknowledge that some readers need further, specialized instruction, especially those with diagnoses such as dyslexia and dysgraphia.

This book's ultimate purpose is to have more kids reading on their own. We will start by learning about the brain and then move to how reading takes place through the interactions of brain areas and circuitry. Our examination of foundational reading will be via the models of "the Eternal Triangle" and "the Simple View of Reading." Both will help us quickly grasp how reading difficulties arise. The rest of the book is then devoted to instructional practices that give all students the foundational reading skills they need and prevent reading difficulties from occurring. Thank you for joining me in the important action of teaching children to read!

THE READING BRAIN

CHAPTER 1

The human brain: What better place to begin an understanding of how we read? Weighing only three pounds, our brain contains approximately 85 billion branching neurons, each firing between five to 50 times per second. Because neurons form links with one another, brain cells connect and communicate across more than 100 trillion synapses. Some sources estimate up to 1,000 trillion! An Olympic-sized fireworks display dims in comparison to the electrical storm crackling inside our skulls. No wonder humans are capable of sustained contemplation, verbal flights of fancy, and surprising leaps of creativity.

From discretely occurring thoughts to extended bouts of cognition, the activities of our brain occur in the time frame of milliseconds. Yet for all its billions of neurons, trillions of connections, and gazillions of synaptic firings, the brain requires only 20 watts of energy to run, barely enough to power a small incandescent light bulb. To put that in perspective, a single supercomputer, which can neither write a sonnet nor cook a decent stir-fry, requires enough electricity to power a small city.

Our brain's neuronal connections are not static. In fact, they change as the months and years go by. Change occurs because the more two neurons communicate, the stronger their connection becomes. As the saying goes, "Neurons that fire together, wire together." The end result is that each time an event or fact is remembered, the physical structure of the brain is slightly altered. Given strong enough learning and regular remembrances over long periods of time, a brain's rewiring can be quite profound.

The incredible connectivity and nonstatic nature of a human brain equates to great plasticity. After an accident or illness, damage to a specific brain area may cause significant behavioral deficits, but over months and years, an injured or ill person can regain lost abilities when undamaged areas of the brain take over for injured ones. For example, people born blind use brain areas normally devoted to processing sight to instead process sound, giving them the ability to orient and navigate in spaces they cannot experience visually. And people who lose physical and cognitive functioning (such as swallowing, walking, or recalling words) due to a traumatic stroke often regain their lost skills when given specialized therapy over time. Brain plasticity is a great gift to the reading process, too, because it enables teachers, through their instruction, to connect the disparate parts of the brain that lead to reading. Plasticity also provides a path forward for students who have brain circuitry differences that make learning to read difficult.

The human brain processes sensory data, calls for the release of hormones, regulates circulatory and respiratory systems, controls appetite and sleep cycles, and brings about blunt emotions like fear and surprise, among other actions. But what truly makes a human brain unique is its ability to leverage sensory information into extraordinary levels of conscious thought and knowledge acquisition. In addition to such high-powered intellectual acts as logical decision making, associational thinking, and numeric computation, our brains are capable of reading, an advanced cognitive achievement.

From Lizard to Linnaeus

How did the brain get to be a titan of cognition, able to leap to a logical conclusion and read a bound book in a single sitting? In a word: evolution. To grasp the human brain's advancement over millions of years, let's think of it as three brains in one.

The first brain within the brain is the reptilian one. Evolutionarily very old, reliable but rigid in its operation, and consisting of the brain stem and cerebellum, our "lizard brain" sits in back of the skull and above the spinal cord, automatically controlling vital body functions such as heart rate, breathing, and body temperature.

Second is the limbic brain, which evolved in the first mammals. Buried deep in the folds of the cortex and sitting just above the brain stem, its main structures are the hippocampus, amygdala, and hypothalamus. Our limbic system enables us to move spatially through the world. It's also responsible for transferring episodic memories into long-term storage and connecting sensory input to memories. If the smell of a pumpkin pie makes you think of Thanksgiving dinner, the Detroit Lions, and awkward political conversations with rarely seen relatives, thank your hippocampus. Because the limbic system records behavioral memories, as well as any agreeable or disagreeable experiences associated with them, it generates our emotions, from joy and delight to disgust and fear.

The crowning glory of the human brain is the neocortex, which first arose in the primates. The modern-day human neocortex consists of two large hemispheres, each divided into four folded lobes: frontal, temporal, parietal, and occipital. In terms of structure and how information is processed, each lobe is similar to the other but with important differences. As we shall see, each of the hemispheres, and the lobes demarcated within them, plays an important part in the reading process.

Halves and Wholes

The left hemisphere, excellent at noticing and processing details and thinking in a linear fashion, allows us to make fine discriminations and to reason logically. Is that bird a yellow warbler or a goldfinch? Does that word begin with the letter *b* or the letter *d*? Should I look for a new job or stick with one I have? Top-notch at isolating particulars from context, our left hemisphere gives us the ability to focus on specific aspects of the world before us, understand them, and then try to control them.

If we engaged only in left-hemisphere thinking (details, focus, control), the world would be a drab, analytical place. Thankfully, we are capable of broad, holistic, and integrated thought. This is due, in large part, to the workings of our right hemisphere, the brain half that enables us to feel and understand aspects of other being's lives (empathy), "read between the lines" (infer), form big pictures and overarching trends, and keep several uncertain outcomes in mind so that, in the end, some of our choices are mature and well-considered (McGilchrist, 2019a).

When both sides of our brain are connecting and communicating with each other through a thick band of neurons called the corpus callosum, our perceptions and ideas are much richer, emotional, and even spiritual. In the words of writer and brain researcher Iain McGilchrist, "Our talent for division, for seeing the parts, is of staggering importance—second only to our capacity to transcend it, in order to see the whole" (McGilchrist, 2019b, p. 93).

The hemispheres of our neocortex—divided into lobes, packed with neurons, unbelievably rich in synapses, communicating within themselves and between each other at lightning-fast speeds—give us much of what it means to be human: complex language, music and song, abstract thought, imagination, and elevated levels of consciousness. They also enable reading, for the left hemisphere is an important language processing center and storehouse for correct word spellings, while the right is important for integrating word forms and the sounds of language with semantic and syntactic information, as well as synthesizing pieces of information into a wider landscape of understanding.

Reflecting on what happens when we read a novel, I am astounded. Strings of visual symbols are registered as whole words and associated with meaning. Our eyes track back and forth through descriptive sentences and paragraphs, discerning and integrating syntax, vocabulary, and context. And our feelings and past experiences are pulled in, too, helping us to understand nuance, unearth deeper meaning, and uncover emotional content infused in the writing. Because our brain can synthesize a complex mix of words, text structure, meanings, feelings, sound, and memory, when we read we may find ourselves magically transported to a dusty barn where we sit beside Fern and listen as geese and sheep talk and a clever spider named Charlotte spins a wordy web to save Wilbur's life.

Circuits and Lobes

It was 8,000 to 9,000 years ago that humans first started using their brains to read (Wolf, 2008). That's a drop in the bucket, evolutionarily speaking. While our brains have dedicated neural pathways for abilities such as sight, emotion, and spoken language (created over hundreds of thousands of years), they have not yet developed an "intrinsic" reading pathway. There simply hasn't been enough time for evolution to build it. This means that to read text, various parts of our historically nonreading brain must be pressed into action. When teachers teach students to read and write, they are, in effect, commandeering brain structures in order to make these actions happen. But this takeover is a good thing, not a bad thing, for we live in a world of words, and if no one took the time in our childhood to wire our brains for reading, we simply would not and could not become reading adults.

Our brain's overarching reading circuit spreads within and throughout each of its four lobes. What does each lobe do? Here are examples gleaned from the book *Brain Words* by Richard Gentry and Gene Oullette (2019, p. 36). Notice how they describe old structures being repurposed to accomplish the relatively new act of reading.

- The occipital lobe, which processes visual information and is critical for behaviors such as recognizing faces, is involved in scanning text and recognizing letter shapes.
- The temporal lobe, where hearing and auditory information is processed and language is based, takes on the processing of the individual sounds of language (phonemes). It also makes connections to syntax and meaning.
- The parietal lobe, responsible (in part) for handling and integrating sensory information and forming body awareness, makes connections to meaning. It processes sound sequences as well.
- The frontal lobe, important for thought, self-regulation, and motor control, assumes the role of speech planner and manages grammar functions.

Concerning reading, here's an amazing thing: All of this scanning, recognizing, handling, managing, and connecting must be taught. Sometimes, it takes only a little teaching. Sometimes, it takes a lot. Today, teachers everywhere are engaged in actions that wire the reading brains of millions of kids. It is a large and serious responsibility.

Questions and Answers

If we are going to teach all children to read, including readers who can learn only via the most effective instructional practices carried out by masterful teachers, we must be able to answer these important questions:

- How does reading arise in the brain?
- What types of reading instruction teach children to read?
- What specific types of instruction prevent reading difficulties from occurring?

Fortunately, we live in an age in which many reading questions can be easily answered. For 35 years or more, reading researchers, cognitive scientists, and neuroscientists have been putting their heads together to create a cohesive, evidence-based theory on how humans read. To a great extent, these folks know what brain areas and circuits are used for reading and how reading arises from their interactions. In turn, this knowledge can be used to invent instructional practices that effectively teach children.

These practices, and the skillful teachers who use them, are especially important to children who find it difficult to learn how to read. The reasons that reading difficulties arise are many and varied. We will spend some time on them in upcoming paragraphs and pages. But for now, the important point is this: Because we know so much about how the process of reading occurs and because we have identified instructional practices that work for most children, we can engage in classroom practices that prevent reading difficulties from arising in the first place.

The Eternal Triangle

For me, nothing beats "the Eternal Triangle" as a way to begin understanding how reading arises in the brain. Coined by cognitive neuroscientist Mark Seidenberg and described in his book *Language at the Speed of Sight* (2017), the triangle describes the brain areas and circuitry that humans press into use in order to read text.

Like all good triangles, it consists of three points and three lines (see Figure 1.1). We can think of the points as areas of brain processing and the lines as the pathways (or circuitry) of language and reading. When connected, the three areas of processing that lead to reading are, in no specific order, as follows:

- **Semantics** or meaning
- **Phonology** or sound
- **Orthography** or spelling

Here is a brief description of each:

- Semantics: Regarding reading, it means word meanings. Some use the term *lexical semantics* to more closely connect it to the reading process.
- Phonology: The study of the sounds in language. Going a bit deeper, phonology is the study of how speech sounds of a language (here, we are talking about English) are organized and categorized in the mind, parsed and blended, and ultimately used to create words that have meaning.
- Orthography: The conventional spelling system of a language. Put another way, orthography is the study of how every word (which by definition has meaning) has a correct letter sequence.

Figure 1.1

The Eternal Triangle

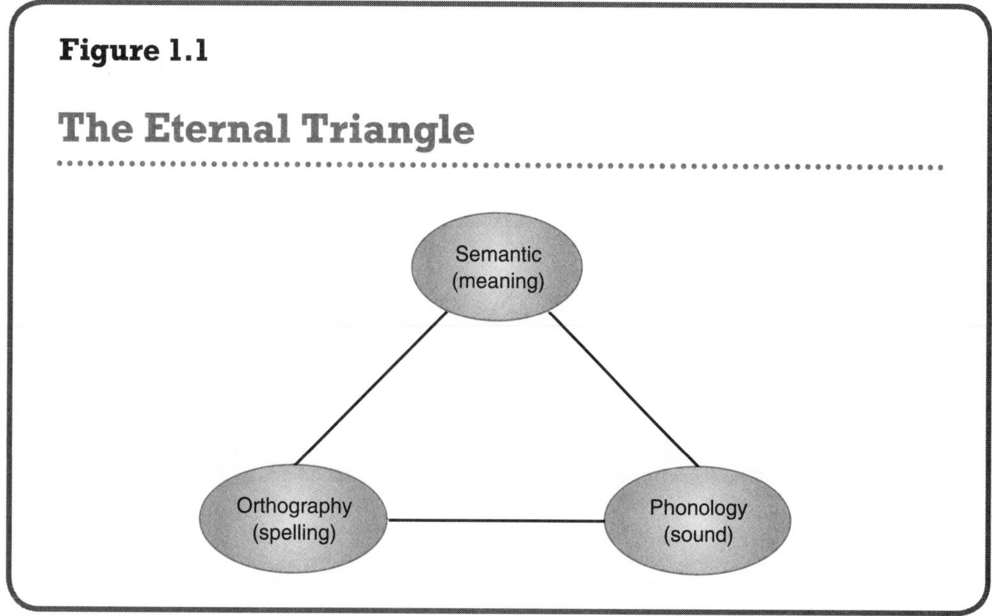

We will come back to this trio—**semantics**, **phonology**, and **orthography**—over and over again. For me, the catchy way to say them is **meaning**, **sound**, and **spelling**. Meaning, sound, and spelling; meaning, sound, and spelling . . . when repeated, it becomes an important mantra for literacy instruction.

Knowing the three essential points of the reading process, we can connect them with lines, which we can think of as pathways. One line denotes the pathway of spoken language comprehension. Another is the pathway of fluent reading. A third, which is actually two lines connecting three points, describes a second reading pathway, one that is less efficient. In this pathway, decoding plays a major role. But let's consider the language pathway first.

The Language Pathway: Linking Semantics and Phonology

The sound of a spoken word is stored via phonological processing, while the meaning of that word is stored through semantic processing (see Figure 1.2). The two are inextricably linked in the pathway of spoken language comprehension (Seidenberg, 2017). As infants and very young children, we hear words spoken by others and learn their meanings through associations made mostly

Figure 1.2

The Language Pathway

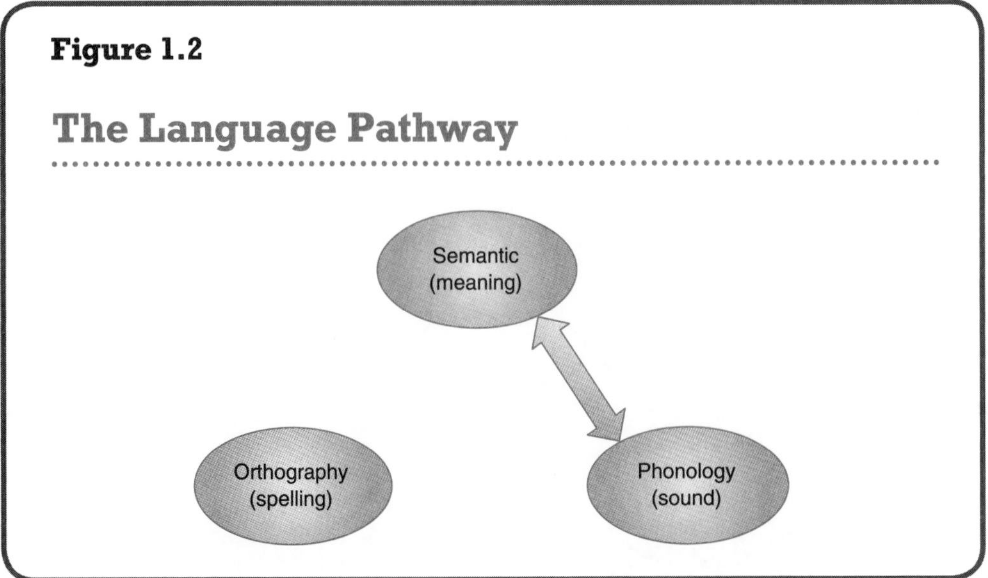

on our own. Through this hearing, observation, and cognition, we come to understand that the spoken word /mama/ refers to one specific person, /dada/ refers to another, and /doggy/ is a thing with four sturdy legs, a slobbering tongue, and a wagging tail.

Here's one amazing thing about the language pathway: It wires itself. Young children are constantly taking in the world, including listening to the sounds of spoken words, and then deriving word meaning by connecting that language to the sights, smells, tastes, and touches they experience. Although this language comprehension happens on its own, it can get a boost from outside agents. Once I was at a Panera Bread, writing and answering emails. Across the room, a group of women were focused on a toddler. One woman appeared to be the child's grandmother. Putting aside my work, I watched the group for a few moments. The conversation went something like this: "Where's your nose?" asked Grandma. The little kid touched her nose. "Good for you!" grinned Grandma. "Where's your chin?" she asked next. The child touched her mouth. "That's not your chin!" she exclaimed. "Where's your chin?" The little girl touched her chin. "Good girl," said Grandma. "You are so smart!"

Grandma was helping her granddaughter strengthen her brain's language comprehension pathway. Preschool and preK teachers join in the effort by engaging young children in rich classroom discussions, singing songs, reciting poetry, reading out loud to students, and constantly tying spoken words to their meanings.

Like any spoken language, English is made-up words. Each word is a "blob" of sound that has meaning. For example, *worm* means a wriggling, ropelike creature that lives in the ground and eats dirt. Another sound blob—*hop*—means a mild up-and-down action (much less than a *leap* and perhaps done on one leg). Sometimes, a word's meaning is specific and narrow; at other times, it is rich and multifaceted. Each spoken word—*nose, chin, worm, hop*—consists of coarticulated sounds, meaning the sounds are blended together into a seamless whole (Wolf, 2008). When we are young and have not yet learned to read, we don't think in terms of the individual sounds of word (phonemes). But amazingly, even very young brains accurately register the small differences between speech sounds. According to researchers Janet Werker and Richard Tees (1999, 2002), infants less than one year old not only distinguish the sounds of speech from environmental sounds (birds chirping, cups clinking), but they also hear the differences between speech sounds, regardless of the language being used and even when the sounds are similar.

Although children can discriminate between the minute sounds of a language, they do not grasp their importance. Kids are not in the business of labeling and understanding sounds as words, syllables, chunks, or phonemes. Phonemes (the individual sounds of words) are an artificial construct. Nonetheless, the construct is very important. In fact, it is foundational to the act of reading because phonology anchors written-word learning and enables the act of word reading (Kilpatrick, 2015). For this reason, it is important that teachers in preK classrooms engage young children with songs that feature rhymes and alliteration, games that involve breaking words into sound chunks, and activities that feature counting the number of words in spoken sentences.

The Lexical Pathway: The Importance of Orthography

So far, we have discussed two points of the triangle: phonology (sound) and semantics (meaning). To complete the brain's reading circuitry, we must bring in the third, orthography, which can be defined as the sounds of language represented as written symbols or the conventional spelling system of a language.

Orthography ultimately has to do with entire written words. But the term also encompasses "chunks," or word families (both rimes, such as *ank* and *ide*, and morphemes, such *as dis* and *ful*), as well as single letters and letter combinations that represent single sounds. In a letter-based writing system, the individual phonemes of a language are represented by letters, which are then sequenced to create written words that can be read. We call this letter–sound association the **alphabetic principle**, and it is a HUGE part of learning how to read. If children don't master the alphabetic principle, their reading is greatly impaired or nonexistent.

The alphabetic principle encompasses both encoding and decoding. Encoding (spelling) is the flip side of decoding (phonics); thinking of spelling and phonics as two sides of an inseparable whole helps us to understand how the reading process works. As a starting point, children in preK, kindergarten, and even first grade learn to name and then identify letters. Simultaneously, they are learning that words are made up of sounds, from big chunks like syllables to the smallest chunks, which are phonemes. When children put these two pieces together via instruction such as *Letter-a-Day* (Chapter 6) and singing a *Letter–Sound Song* (Chapter 3), they have taken steps toward mastering the alphabetic principle.

Once our brain masters letter–sound associations, it can begin to encode and decode entire words. For example, the spoken word/ pat/ is represented with the letter combination *p-a-t*, while the spoken word /tap/ is represented by *t-a-p*. Conversely, when we read the written words *pat* and *tap*, we hear the sound blobs /pat/ and /tap/ in our mind. With continued use (repetition), the spellings of entire words are stored in a lexicon of our brain. Stocked with the correct spelling representations of every word we "know" and completely connected to the sound and meaning (or meanings) of the word, this lexicon is part of the very essence of reading.

With the addition of orthography, we have a third point on our reading triangle. Now, we can discuss how reading in the brain occurs along, and between, two basic pathways (Seidenberg, 2017). The first reading pathway is the one that mature, competent readers use *most* of the time. Known as the **lexical pathway** (or whole-word pathway), it is dependent upon only two points of the triangle: semantics and orthography (see Figure 1.3).

To understand how this pathway works, let's more deeply define *orthography*. *Ortho* means "straight, true, correct." Thus, *ortho*pedics

Figure 1.3

The Lexical Reading Pathway

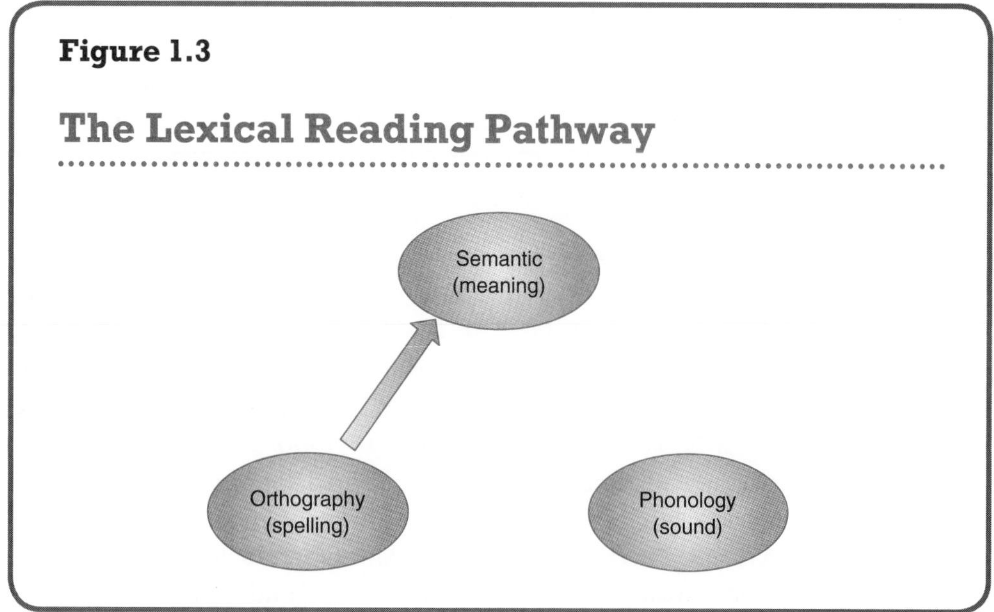

has to do with correct bones, *ortho*dontics has to do with straightening teeth, and *ortho*dox relates to the true or correct way to think about an established doctrine. Meanwhile, *graphy* has to do with recording. Typically, we think of it as a written recording, as in a bio*graphy* or autobio*graphy*. But the recording can also be with photons, as in photo*graphy*, or through movement, as in choreo*graphy*.

In terms of reading, orthography is all about the recording of the correct (straight and true) letter sequences of English words. Our brain's orthographic system simultaneously moves words into permanent storage and acts as the area of storage. This area, along with the meaning and sound areas, functions as a brain dictionary. Stored in the orthographic part are the correct letter spellings of thousands of words. So if I hear someone tell me I am "*third* in line," I can see the letter sequence *t-h-i-r-d* in my mind's eye, and I can then write the word *third* on a piece of paper.

The correct letter sequences of words are stored in our brain dictionary through a process known as orthographic mapping. This process moves word spellings into brain areas once used for nonreading purposes (thanks, brain plasticity!). Later, to read, we visually register the letter sequences of text and match them to brain dictionary information: correct spelling sequences in our orthographic storage system and their associated meanings and sounds stored in our semantic and phonological systems.

Using our previous example, when we see *third*, we know it is spoken as /third/. In fact, when we see it, we also internally hear it! We also know that the word 100 percent matches the orthographic representation t-h-i-r-d. Finally, we know that specific letter sequence means the number three in a sequence, next after second, and one of three equal parts.

If, however, we were to see the letter sequences *thurd*, we might feel confused. Because we have the letter–sound chunks *th* and *urd* stored in our lexicons, we can combine these letter sequences to speak (or internally hear) a sound blob that says /thurd/. But unless your name happens to be *Thurd Winkler* or you live in *Thurdsville*, the letter sequence *t-h-u-r-d* won't match any letter sequence stored in your brain. Thus, *thurd* is not an English language letter sequence. In other words, it is not a word. Finally, because we *do* have real English words in our lexicon analogous to *thurd* in sight and sound (such as *curd* and *turd*), we might feel a tinge of laughter or revulsion (or both) when we read the word *Thurdsville*.

The big ideas here are these: (1) In the reading process, meaning is invoked, but it is not the first thing that "comes to mind;" (2) words are not encoded in our brains by the complex attribute of meaning but rather by the simpler characteristics of shape and sound; and (3) when we read, we instantly see each word as a kind of picture while almost simultaneously hearing each word spoken inside our heads (Glezer et al., 2015; Sutherland, 2015). This automatic action of instantly matching a spelling sequence to a pronunciation is known as **word recognition**, and word recognition is at the heart of a reading process made of seamless and unending cycles of meaning, sound, and spelling.

The Sublexical Pathway: Sounding It Out

Because you are a mature reader, you are using the lexical reading pathway to read most, if not all, of the words on this page. You would certainly use it to read this sentence: "The big dog ran after the red ball." But even competent readers like yourself use a second reading pathway when encountering unfamiliar words, like the ones in this sentence from *The Washington Post* (2019): "Nursultan Nazarbayev, the President of Kazakhstan, has resigned."

The second reading pathway, called the **sublexical pathway**, is the sounding out or decoding pathway (Ehri, 2005, 2017; Gentry & Oullette, 2019; Seidenberg, 2017). Decoding can occur at the level of letters and sounds, but in more advanced readers, it occurs at the "chunking" level (see Figure 1.4). We break apart a word (Nur-sultan or Nur-sul-tan) to read it. And we may chunk it in different ways (Ka-zak-hstan, Ka-zakh-stan, Kaz-akh-stan) and compare the various pronunciations, all the while searching our brain's semantic center to see if one of them matches a known word. Finally, using context and background knowledge, we attach meaning to the decoded word. With enough practice, the word (made up of its sound, spelling, and meaning) becomes fully stored in our brain dictionary.

Young readers rely on the sublexical pathway a great deal. Picture how a kindergarten reader who is just learning to "break the code" would read the sentence "Mom and Dad like the cat." At first, the sounding-out pathway is the exclusive pathway for reading. But as readers become more accomplished, they use the more efficient lexical pathway more often. The two pathways, however, are not binary (either/or). Rather, they are both/and. This means they function at varying levels of coactivation according to a reader's level of reading ability, as well as a text's level of reading difficulty, which varies according to each reader (Gentry & Oullette, 2019).

Figure 1.4

The Sublexical Reading Pathway

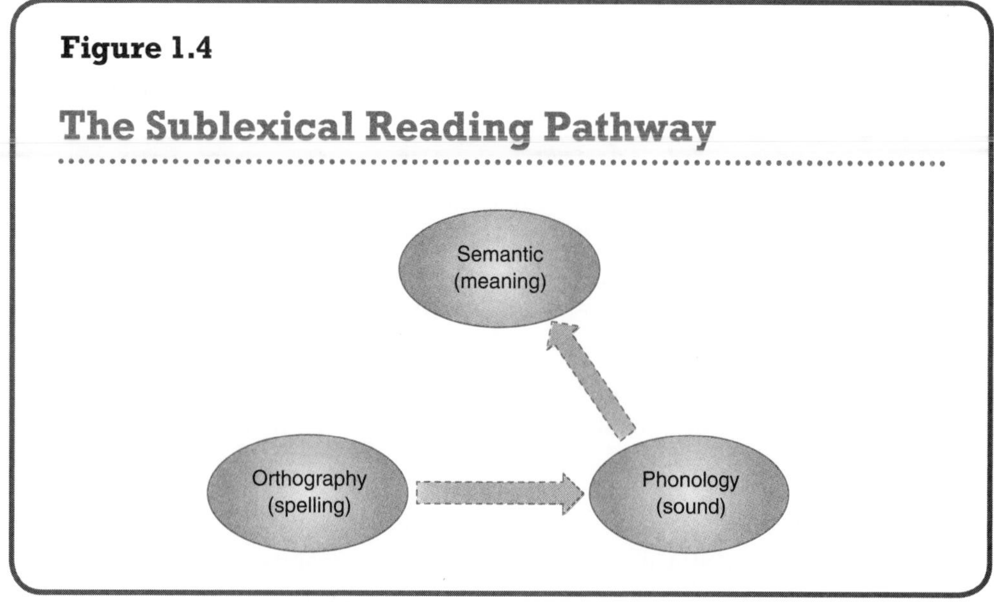

Problems With the Points and Pathways

The Eternal Triangle provides a way to understand reading at its most fundamental level. It also starts us on our journey to understand why children sometimes struggle to read. When the areas of semantics, orthography, and phonology are well developed and connected, the reading process unfolds with few glitches. But if one or more areas are weak or if the connections between them are underdeveloped, reading, writing, and spelling become more difficult.

Consider, for example, the students who fluently read this sentence but don't understand its meaning: "Of the many national parks in America, Glacier National Park contains the most dramatic scenery." How is it that they can fluently read the sentence but not know what it means? One reason could be a strength in word recognition (orthography) but a weakness in semantics, such as a lack of background knowledge, vocabulary knowledge, syntactic understanding, or some combination thereof. Perhaps the semantic weakness stems from a dearth of language-rich conversations at home. Or maybe the students lack background knowledge because they have never traveled outside of their town, never read books about national parks or glaciers, and/or don't know the meanings of the words *scenery* and *dramatic.*

In comparison, some children have a strong ability to understand text when it is read aloud but lack the ability to read sentences fluently. Their difficulty in comprehending is not based in semantic processing. Rather, their lack of understanding arises from deficits or problems in orthographic and/or phonological processing. Remember that the sublexical reading pathway relies on the workings of both the orthographic and phonological systems (see Figure 1.5). If this pathway is functioning poorly due to an inability to distinguish phonemes within a word or a dearth of spelling representations stored in the brain's lexicon of words, teachers will see any number of reading difficulties, including slow reading, error-prone reading, difficulty with phonemic analysis tasks, poor spelling, and slow and labored writing.

Reading is a wonder. According to Maryann Wolf, "Whenever you read a single word, you activate thousands upon thousands of neuronal working groups" (2018, p. 34). These groups, containing

Figure 1.5

Components of the Sublexical Pathway

	Phonology	Orthography
Reading skills that can be observed and assessed	• Identifying syllables or words in a sentence • Identifying rhymes • Phonemic tasks, such as blending phonemes into words, identifying like or dissimilar phonemes, or deleting phonemes from a word ("Say slip. Now take out the /l/ sound.")	• Rapid letter naming • Letter names–sounds • Knowledge of word spellings • Spelling in writing • Generating spellings • Seeing how words are the same

multitudes of interconnected neurons communicating at lightning-fast speeds, are associated with vision, speech, language, memory, attention, word meaning, grammatical meaning, background knowledge and life experience, and more. In total, they form the meaning–sound–spelling circuit that is the reading brain.

How this incredibly complex reading-brain circuit comes to be is "influenced by three key environmental factors: specifically, *what it reads* (both the particular writing system and the content), *how it reads* (the particular medium . . . and its effect on the way we read), and *how it is formed* (methods of instruction)" (Wolf, 2018, p. 19, italics added). And so we can see how teachers become the essential builders of every child's reading-brain circuit. The books we provide, the materials we use, and the ways in which we instruct all have an impact on how completely and strongly reading circuity comes into being. We will discuss particulars of Wolf's factors, specifically content, materials, ways of reading, and methods of instruction, deeply in Chapters 3 through 7. But first, let's examine reasons why the reading circuit might become underdeveloped or compromised—in other words, why reading difficulties develop. To do this, we'll look through the lens of another reading model: the Simple View of Reading.

WHAT ARE READING DIFFICULTIES?

CHAPTER 2

Some experts say as many as 20 percent of our nation's children experience reading difficulties (Hurford et al., 2016). Others express the problem as a cardinal number, as in "about 10 million children have difficulties learning to read" (Drummond, 2020). Still others give a fraction, such as the National Assessment of Educational Progress (NAEP) report that tells us one-third of America's fourth graders read below a basic level (NAEP, 2019). Regardless of how the number is expressed, the problem is real: Too many kids are not reading adequately.

The good news is that many reading difficulties can be prevented and even overcome. Dr. David Kilpatrick, reading authority and professor of psychology, says research studies indicate the number of struggling readers can be reduced by 70 percent to 80 percent. Others are even more optimistic. In a Reading Rockets article, Dr. Kathryn Drummond states that "90 to 95 percent of reading-impaired children can overcome their difficulties if they receive appropriate treatment at early ages" (Drummond, 2020). And the International Literacy Association (ILA), citing the research of Frank Vellutino and others, goes further, asserting that appropriate interventions can "reduce the number of children with continuing difficulties in reading to below 2% of the population" (ILA, 2016, p. 3).

These statistics, however, don't say much about the "what, how, and why" of reading difficulties. What exactly are the difficulties these experts and organizations mention? What do they look like in the classroom? How do they differ from one another? And why do they arise in the first place? Let's work through these questions, one by one.

A Range of Behaviors

Casually observe a classroom during independent reading time and you'll easily spot the students who enjoy reading. Sprawled in bean bags and comfy chairs or hunched over their desks, these readers are engrossed, reading for long periods of time and focusing intently as they pore over paragraphs and pages. After reading, they happily discuss their thoughts and feelings about all they have read. And then they're ready for the next book.

Other children are not so involved and contented. You might see them staring out of windows, fiddling with objects, or trying to avoid books altogether. Some may act the class clown or become painfully shy when asked to read. And when they read out loud, they exhibit a wide range of deficit behaviors. Problems crop up in spelling and writing, too, from misspelled words to a lack of word variety. Figure 2.1 provides a list gathered from the writings of Seidenberg (2017), Wolf (2018), and Kilpatrick (2015). Which of these have you seen in your classroom?

Figure 2.1

Reading and Writing Behaviors That Indicate a Reading Difficulty

In students who have reading difficulties, these reading and writing behaviors are exhibited:

- Slow and labored reading aloud
- Reading aloud quickly but filled with many errors, such as substitutions, omissions, and insertions
- Reading aloud lacks appropriate stress or intonation (prosody)
- Poor at sounding out unfamiliar words (*strove, jolt*) and pseudo-words (*mave, trask*)
- Makes many spelling errors while writing
- Reverses or transposes letters in writing
- Reverses or transposes letters while reading (reads *stop* for *pots*, *saw* for *was*)
- Struggles to learn phonic patterns
- Struggles to learn letter names–sounds
- Cannot generate rhyming words
- Slow to learn sight words
- Does not recognize frequently occurring words
- Does not understand what was read
- Unable to make inferences or identify the main idea of a passage
- Cannot effectively summarize a passage
- Cannot remember (retell) what was read

Some children show only a few signs of struggle. Others show many. Some have only mild reading impairments. Others have severe ones. For some students, reading difficulties are easily corrected and relatively short lived. But others have problems that are tenacious, long-lasting, and debilitating.

Terms to Describe Difficulties

Behind each observable difficulty is an underlying weakness or deficit in one or more parts of the reading process. In other words, there is a reason, or a combination of reasons, that a child makes spelling errors, fails to accurately decode words, cannot remember what has been read, or doesn't understand the meaning of the text that has just been read. We'll discuss the causes of reading difficulties, from lack of meaning to slow word recognition, in just a bit. But let's first acknowledge a few terms.

Some students are formally diagnosed as having a reading *disability* or *disorder*. Typically, disabilities and disorders are rooted in biology, although the reading problems that flow from them can be exacerbated by poverty, a lack of appropriate instruction, low proficiency in English, and other educational and societal factors (Snow & Strucker, 1999). Always, a reading disability or disorder is identified by carefully examining and weighing a number of indicators. For example, to determine if a child has dyslexia, a diagnostician would consider factors such as chronically poor spelling, difficulty with phoneme deletion tasks, an inability to remember sight words, slow rates of object naming and word reading, and a sluggish response to robust reading interventions, as well as strengths, such as a strong to excellent ability to comprehend text when it is read aloud.

For special education purposes, a struggling reader might be identified with a specific learning disability, an intellectual disability, a health impairment, or a speech-language impairment. Each of these can moderately to greatly impact a student's ability to learn to read. Meanwhile, in the clinical realm a child might be diagnosed with a learning disorder. The American Psychiatric Association (APA) categorizes dyslexia as a specific learning disorder (Petretto & Masala, 2017), one that is neurodevelopmental in nature, begins at school age (APA, 2019), and is the reason for severe and persistent reading problems in perhaps 5 percent of all children (McArthur & Castles, 2017).

It is important to look below the terms *disability* and *disorder* and find out what deficits in the reading process are actually causing the reader to struggle. As David Kilpatrick (2015) says, disability categories "do not cause reading difficulties—specific reading-related skill deficits cause reading difficulties" (p. 77). This is an especially important point because understanding reading difficulties in terms of specific skill deficits enables teachers to first grasp the unique needs of each reader and then focus instruction on the appropriate places. If our question is "Why is this student with a behavior disorder struggling to read," and we answer it with "Because he has a behavior disorder," then we have nothing to instruct on. A skill-based answer, however, is useful: "This student with a behavior disorder lacks word recognition skills, specifically with vowel-team decoding and multisyllable word decoding. He also has deficits in vocabulary knowledge and self-monitoring strategies." This skill-based answer provides us with specific areas of instruction.

Of course, reading difficulties arise for reasons other than an identified disability or diagnosed disorder. Sometimes, a child struggles to read because of a deficit in instruction, a specific challenge that keeps them away from school, or a piece of the reading puzzle that just hasn't yet come into focus. Also, young children stepping into primary grade classrooms are diverse in their interests, experiences, and abilities. All of these factors affect current and future reading performance. So do these, which Catherine Snow and John Strucker (1999) have identified: chronically low-achieving schools, low proficiency in English, and living in a community of poverty.

More and more, research is helping teachers pinpoint the underlying cause or causes of reading difficulties and what to do to prevent them. For example, focusing on the discrete preliteracy differences young children bring to schools and the possible reasons a reading difficulty might arise, one study looked at over 1,200 prekindergarten and kindergarten students in New England (Ozernov-Palchik et al., 2017). Investigating their performance on tasks that tested phonemic awareness, rapid automatic naming, letter knowledge, and verbal short-term memory, the study found that children fell into six developmental profiles: high performers, average performers, below-average performers, phonemic awareness (PA) risk, rapid automatic naming (RAN) risk, and double-deficit risk (both PA and RAN).

Knowing which profile a student falls into can help a teacher program for specific needs. According to one of the authors of the study, children in the first two profiles need merely "good" instruction to succeed (Wolf, 2018). This does not mean that for teachers "good" is good enough, but simply that these students will succeed in reading without specialized efforts. Further parsing showed that the below-average performers had difficulty with sounds and letters; their needs will be relatively easy to address. Children falling into the last three performance profiles will "go on to be diagnosed with some form of reading disability or dyslexia" (Wolf, 2018, p. 155). This, however, is not a prediction of lifelong reading failure. On the contrary, knowing early on that a particular child has a phonemic awareness risk, a rapid automatic naming risk, or a double-deficit risk can and should lead to targeted interventions that prevent reading difficulties, even in the face of a disability or disorder.

To help distinguish between a reading disability/disorder that arises mostly from biology and a reading difficulty due to instructional and/or societal factors, let's look at two case studies.

Two Case Studies

As an example of a child with a reading difficulty severe enough to be labeled a *learning disability*, I offer Robert (not his real name). His story was recently recounted to me by his mother, a pediatrician and friend of my family. We'll call her Dr. M.

Born a healthy baby into an educated, middle-class family, Robert was a verbose and curious child when Dr. M enrolled him in a full-day Montessori kindergarten. In first grade, he transferred to the small elementary school near his home and the dairy farm his father ran. In November of that year, his mother received a phone call from the first-grade teacher, Mrs. B, who said Robert was receiving extra help in the reading resource room because of problems with spelling and reading.

Robert's difficulties continued as he started second grade. In the words of Dr. M., "*The Cat in the Hat* was too hard for him to read. But when I read books to him, like the *Chronicles of Narnia*, he could understand and recall events beautifully." Meanwhile, as second grade unfolded, Robert showed persistent confusion about left and right, failed to accurately recall letter and number sequences, and often had to exert great effort to retrieve mental images of simple sight words. Experiencing these difficulties during homework, he would sometimes exclaim to his parents, "I'm having a brain block" or "I'm going into the black hole!"

Thankfully, Robert remained optimistic, engaged, and social, even as his reading deficits made the start of third grade very difficult. Growing concerned that her son was still not achieving, even when provided with three-times-a-week "reading resource room" interventions, Dr. M took him to a developmental psychologist for an evaluation. Afterward, Robert was identified with a specific learning disability and given an IEP (individual education program). This was the late fall of his third-grade year. Still, he failed to make appreciable gains toward grade-level reading benchmarks as the year went on.

At the beginning of fourth grade, Dr. M, now very knowledgeable about reading difficulties, came to understand her son had dyslexia. She also knew the school district's well-meaning teachers lacked knowledge of and training in instructional practices that could produce significant reading ability growth. And so she hired an after-school tutor trained in Ruth Warden Frank's Phonetic Reading Chain, a reading intervention program that employs overlearning, explicit and sequential phonics instruction, phonological analysis, and multisensory instruction, among other practices.

For almost three years, Robert received one-on-one tutoring three times a week after school. Additionally, he was repeatedly told two things: You are smart and capable, *and* you have to work much harder than most children to learn how to spell and read. Finally, in the middle of seventh grade, Robert said to his mom, "You don't have to read to me anymore. I can do it myself!" And he did. With a 504 plan that spelled out subject area modifications and testing accommodations—and after barely passing Spanish but scoring a 99 percent in physics—Robert graduated from high school. He was accepted to Cornell University, graduated with an electrical engineering degree, went on to obtain a master's, and even earned an internship at Elon Musk's Space X campus. As of this writing, he lives in Moscow, is still a poor speller, practices stand-up comedy, works for himself and earns a living through software programming, and avidly but slowly reads all manner of books.

In contrast, I offer my niece Morgan, who has graciously given me the go-ahead to tell her story. In kindergarten and first grade, Morgan was a typically achieving student, quiet, attentive, and hardworking, neither struggling nor high flying. Her progress in reading, however, took a turn for the worse in second grade when, at the beginning of the school year, she came down with mononucleosis. For over seven weeks, she was mostly at home. Thanksgiving and Christmas breaks added to her days out of school. By January, she was experiencing significant reading difficulties.

Because I volunteered in Morgan's school, I knew the system was ill-equipped to help children who were low achieving but not in special education. Second-grade instruction was basal-based and mostly whole group, with lots of workbook assignments, little differentiated instruction, and no guided reading. Additionally, non–special ed reading intervention groups met only twice a week for 30 minutes. At a parent–teacher meeting, Morgan's mother was shown her daughter's reading scores. The school suggested Morgan be assessed for special education, but Morgan's mom was dead set against that option. Instead, she asked me to help.

Before I began tutoring Morgan, I listened to her read. Her reading was hesitant and full of errors, and she failed to understand large portions of the stories she had just read. She didn't appear to be doing much self-monitoring or employing metacognition strategies. And when I gave her both a phonics and a spelling inventory, it was obvious she lacked decoding and encoding skills.

Over the next five months, I tutored my niece two to three times a week in 60- to 75-minute sessions. She studied phonic patterns, built words with the patterns, read word lists, practiced applying word attack strategies while reading sentences, and worked on fluency through repeated readings of passages. While reading, I made sure she looked at every word and employed decoding strategies consistently. Morgan read for an extended amount of time in books that were on her independent and instructional levels, and we discussed how she could fix up her mistakes, as well as make connections, predict, and ask and answer questions. Each session ended with me reading aloud from a chapter book of her choosing.

Over the summer, Morgan read a lot with her mom, and I continued to see her once or twice a week. By the time third grade began, she was back to her old reading self. She has had no significant problems since. Morgan recently told me that, as a college student, she feels she works harder than others to achieve. Also, she's not much of a recreational reader. Still, she's an excellent student, and she just earned a master's degree in education.

Both Morgan and Robert experienced reading difficulties. Robert's were severe and long-lasting. Morgan's were moderate and short lived. Both sets of difficulties, however, were lessened by specific instructional practices. In Morgan's case, specific types of instruction helped her completely overcome her problems. In Robert's case, they enabled him to conquer the most difficult aspects of his reading disorder. But because his dyslexia is fundamental to how he processes information, reading and spelling will always be demanding tasks for him.

All readers who demonstrate reading difficulties require instruction that speaks to the underlying causes of the difficulties. To better understand what these causes are, let's examine reading through the lens of the Simple View of Reading, a theoretical model that succinctly describes the components of the reading process and helps us more clearly understand the skill deficits that cause problematic reading behaviors.

The Simple View of Reading

Reading involves identifying letters, mastering letter–sound combinations, combining letters into phonic "chunks," learning word meanings, reading through every word on a page, making connections between text ideas, understanding genre, integrating background knowledge, employing strategies to stay on task, and much more. In other words, reading is complex! In Chapter 1, the Eternal Triangle described the foundations of this complex process with just three terms: semantics, phonology, and orthography (meaning, sound, and spelling). Amazingly, the reading process can be expressed in an even more distilled form.

The formula that is the Simple View of Reading was put forth more than 30 years ago in a seminal article titled "Decoding, Reading, and Reading Disability." Then, reading researchers Philip Gugh and William Tunmer proposed this equation to describe what reading is: $R = D \times C$. Translated, the formula reads "reading equals the product of decoding and comprehension" (Gough & Tunmer, 1986).

Over time, because the foundational reading process has come to be understood in increasingly complex and nuanced ways, Gough and Tunmer's original formulation of reading changed slightly. For example, shortly after the National Reading Panel released its report in 2000, Dr. Hollis Scarborough (2001) presented the Simple View as a braided rope, constructed of two main strands each consisting of numerous threads. Her innovative and illuminating graphic was built upon a slightly tweaked Simple View of Reading formula: $SR = LC \times WR$, in which *SR* is skilled reading, *LC* is language comprehension, and *WR* is word recognition. In Figure 2.2, I reimagine the rope as a reading river, created when vital headwater streams flow into two tributaries that then mix to become one powerful, smoothly flowing waterway.

More than a decade later, David Kilpatrick wrote the Simple View's equation as $R = D \times LC$, where *R* is reading comprehension, *D* is decoding (or word-level reading), and *LC* is linguistic comprehension (Kilpatrick, 2015). He then unpacked the two variables—linguistic comprehension and decoding (or word-level reading)—to show their components and subcomponents, all of which overlap and interact in complex and interesting ways.

In all versions of the Simple View's equation, reading comprehension is the *product* of decoding and language comprehension, not the sum. This is important because zero times even the highest number is still zero. Thus, if a student has great ability to comprehend language but zero ability to decode, his reading comprehension is zero. Of course, the opposite is also true; if a student is a decoding champ but understands no language, his reading comprehension will be zero.

There are many narrowly defined skills underpinning the Simple View, and each influences the development and ultimate strength of the two broad variables. Thus, small reading difficulties can lead to bigger ones. For example, if children fail to develop strong phonological skills, especially in the area of phoneme analysis, their ability to map letters onto sounds is diminished. In turn, word-level reading is diminished, which ultimately leads to deficits in reading comprehension. Likewise, if children lack knowledge about words (vocabulary knowledge) and the world (background knowledge), their language comprehension is diminished. In the end, this too leads to deficits in reading comprehension.

Figure 2.3 provides a synthesis and a summary of many, but not all, of the components and subcomponents of the Simple View of Reading, according to Scarborough (2001) and Kilpatrick (2015). Ironically, the Simple View of Reading is not simple at all! Nonetheless, Scarborough's and Kilpatrick's organizational schemes can help us in our quest to understand why many children experience varying degrees of reading difficulties.

Figure 2.2

The Reading River

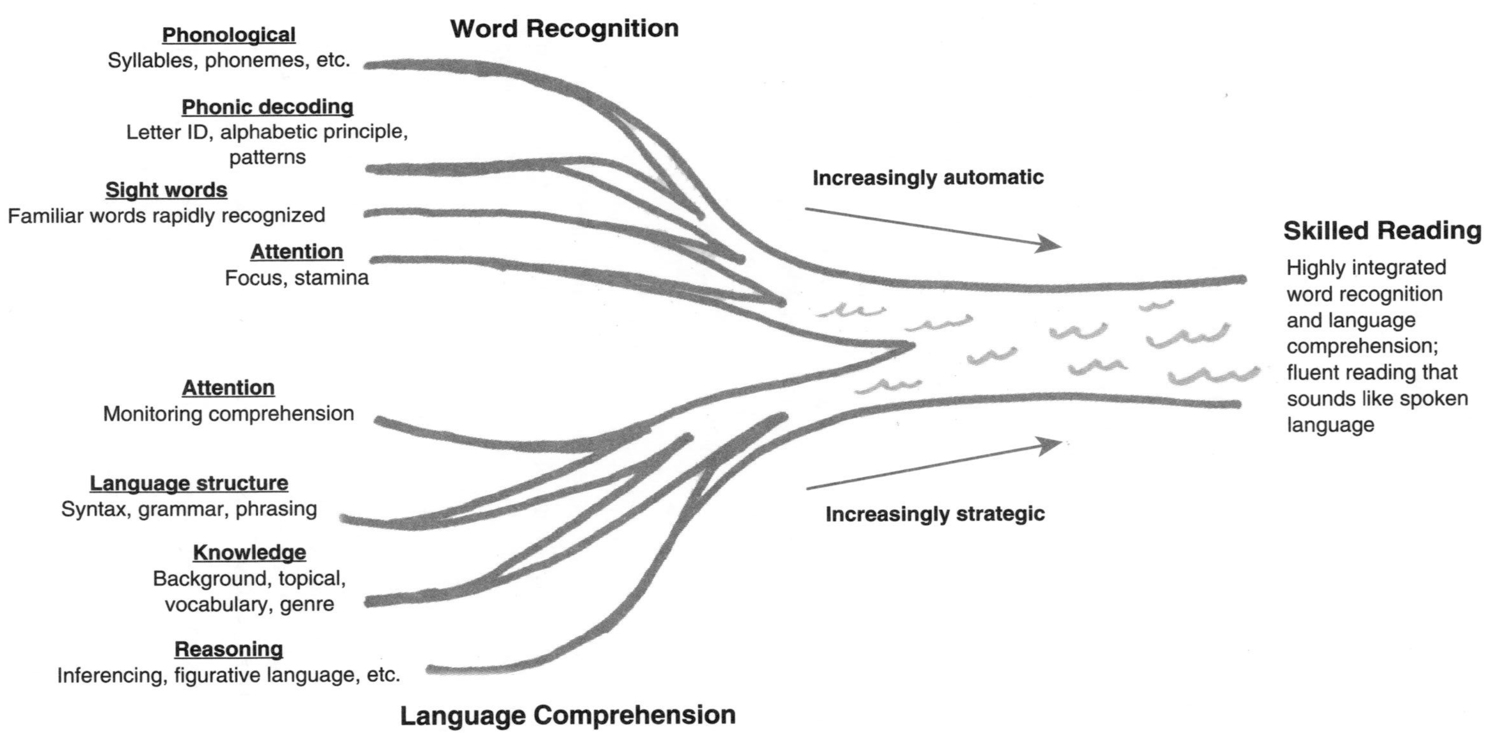

Source: Adapted from original graphic that was published in Scarborough, H. S. (2001). Connecting early language and literacy to later reading (dis)abilities: Evidence, theory, and practice. In S. Neuman & D. Dickinson (Eds.), *Handbook for research in early literacy* (pp. 97–110). New York, NY: Guilford Press.

Figure 2.3

Components and Subcomponents of the Simple View of Reading

$R = LC \times WR$		
Skilled Reading	**Language Comprehension** (or Linguistic Comprehension)	**Word Recognition** (or Word-Level Reading)
Skilled reading is the "fluent execution and coordination of text comprehension and word recognition" (Scarborough, 2001). Said another way, skilled reading is a combination of highly strategic reading and automatic word-level reading.	**Attention** • Comprehension monitoring **Language Skills** • Inferencing • Vocabulary knowledge • Grammatical and syntactical knowledge **Background Knowledge** • General knowledge • Topical knowledge • Genre and text structure knowledge	**Phonic decoding** • Phonological skills • Letter ID knowledge • Letter–sound knowledge • Rapid naming **Word-specific knowledge** (knowing words on sight) • Orthographic knowledge (having the correct letter sequences of every word) • Phonological long-term memory • Sight recognition of specific words

I love the Simple View of Reading for a number of reasons:

1. Research has widely supported the ideas inherent in it; Figure 2.5 lists just a few of the studies that support this statement.
2. The Simple View beautifully reflects the reading process as described by the Eternal Triangle. The two illuminate each other, as demonstrated in Figure 2.4.
3. The equation is a clean, straightforward way for teachers like me to enter the intricate world of reading theory, including how reading works and how it can be assessed and taught.
4. The Simple View helps me to quickly and easily conceptualize and organize my classroom reading practices so that they prevent reading difficulties from happening in the first place.

Figure 2.4

Comparing the Eternal Triangle and the Simple View of Reading

The Eternal Triangle Processing Areas Associated With Terms From the Simple View	**The Simple View of Reading** Variables Associated With Terms From the Eternal Triangle
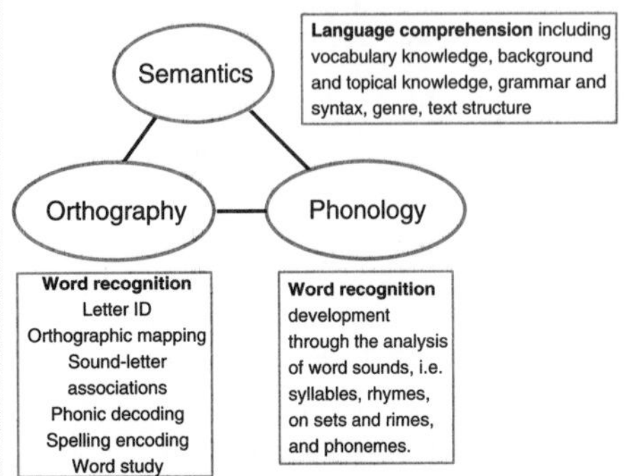	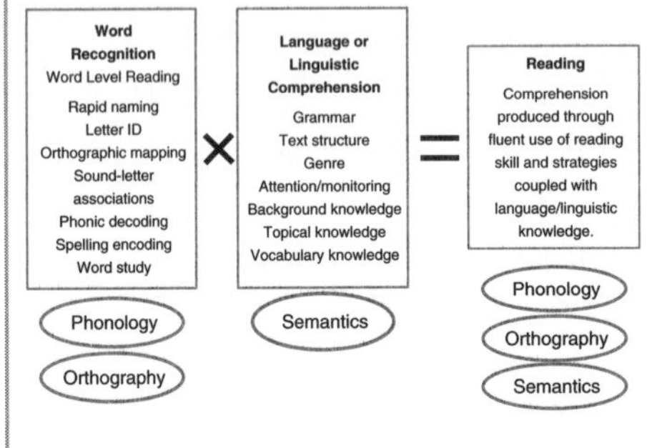
Phonology refers to the study of sounds within the words of language. When children have advanced phonological awareness, they are not only aware of the sounds at the most discrete level (phonemes), but they are also able to manipulate the sounds (segment, blend, delete, add, and substitute).	Word recognition has its roots in **letter–sound knowledge**. Letter–sound knowledge arises from the pairings of known letters and known sounds. **Phonology** is the study of these sounds. For orthographic mapping to occur, the sounds of language must be understood as sounds within words, from large chunks to the smallest discrete sounds, phonemes.
Orthography refers to correct letter sequences of words or the correct spelling of words. The orthographic processing area of the brain stores correct letters and letter sequences, from single letters (*a, s, t, w*) and chunks that range from digraphs to rimes (*sh*, *ay*, *ow*, *aight*) to thousands of entire words. These letters, chunks, and words are used for reading and writing.	**The crux of word recognition is automatically reading words**, which are mapped and stored through **orthographic processing**. An effortlessly recalled word is familiar (a sight word) because its particular orthographic representation (correct letter sequence) is stored in the "brain dictionary" and thus instantly available for reading and writing. Students' ability to recognize words vary from little to no difficulty to great difficulty.
Semantics, with regard to reading, refers to **meaning**. There are many elements of meaning that come to bear in the reading process, such as vocabulary meaning, background knowledge, and understanding of text structure. Reading words without generating meaning is not really reading because reading implies comprehension of text, at the word level and beyond.	**Language or linguistic comprehension** is all about having understanding and making meaning. Readers have differing levels of all types of language elements, from background and vocabulary knowledge to grammar and syntax. Attention and monitoring also play a part in language comprehension. They are typically taught through metacognition, from self-monitoring to employing strategies such as visualizing and predicting.

Source: Adapted from Seidenberg (2017), Kilpatrick (2015), and Dehaene (2009).

Figure 2.5

A Sample From Three Decades of Research That Supports the Simple View of Reading (SVR)

Catts, Hogan, & Fey, 2003
Catts et al., 2006
Harlaar et al., 2010
Hoover & Gough, 1990
Kendeou, Savage, & van den Brock, 2009
Kim et al., 2019
Language and Reading Consortium, 2015
Munger & Blachman, 2013
Ripoll Salceda, Alonso, & Casilla-Earls, 2014

Source: Adapted, in part, from Kilpatrick, 2015, p. 47.

To Better Understand Difficulties, Graph the Simple View

The Simple View of Reading describes the constant interaction between two dynamic processes: language comprehension and word recognition. Graphing the two processes makes the interaction easier to see. To create a graph of the Simple View, first think of each process as a line that runs from great difficulty to great ease. Next, graph the Simple View's two processes as perpendicular intersecting lines. Viola! You now have a graph with quadrants of reading variability (as shown in Figure 2.6).

We can use the graph's four quadrants to frame our observations and assessments of any child's reading behaviors. Information from reading words lists, running records, and oral reading fluency probes give information on word recognition. Assessments that measure vocabulary, metacognition skills, inferencing, and background knowledge give information on language comprehension. A body of assessment information helps us place each reader

Figure 2.6

Graphing the Simple View of Reading

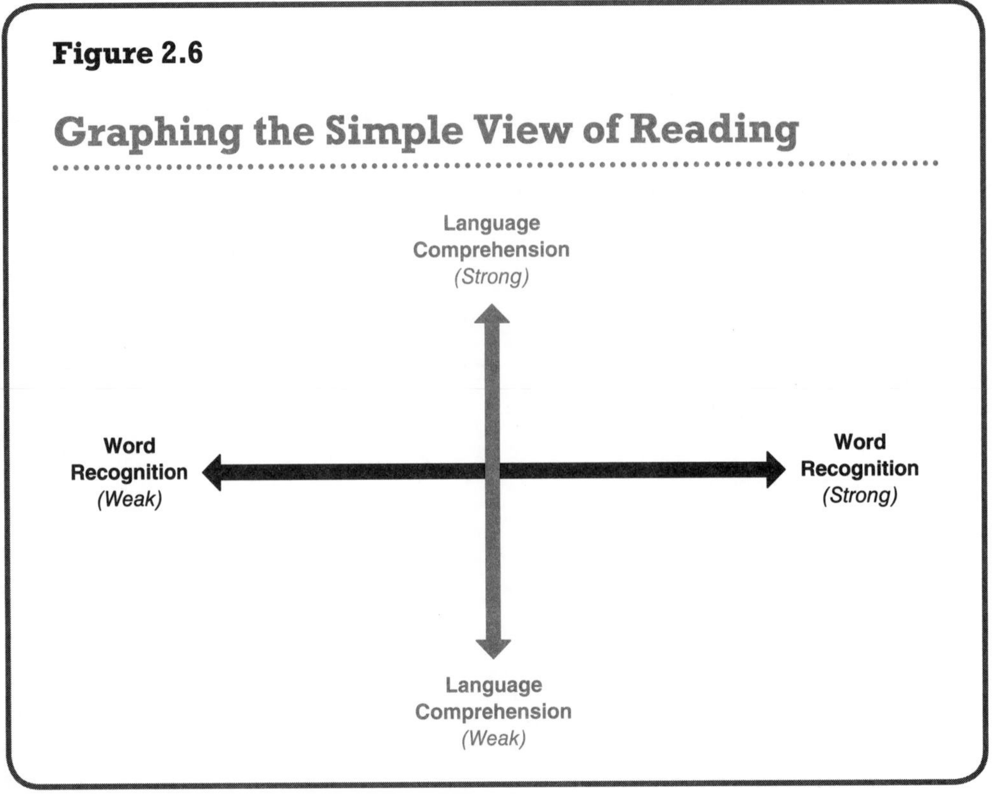

at some point on the graph. For instance, a point on the far left of the word recognition line represents great difficulty in decoding, a point somewhere toward the middle shows decoding is only somewhat difficult (or somewhat easy), and a point on the far right denotes automatic and effortless word recognition. The same holds true for the language comprehension continuum.

Plotting the intersection of the two points of the two processes yields a graph that gives a student's general reading profile (Kilpatrick, 2015, p. 54). Any reader not in the "typical reader" quadrant can be said to have some type of regularly occurring reading difficulty. Figure 2.7 shows and defines categories of readers as described by their position in the quadrants, while Figures 2.8 and 2.9 show scatter plots from a hypothetical general education classroom (20 students) and a reading remediation classroom (10 students).

Keep in mind that because reading comprehension is the *product* of two variables, it is only well developed when there is strength in *both* variables. Conversely, reading comprehension is always

Figure 2.7

General Categories of Readers

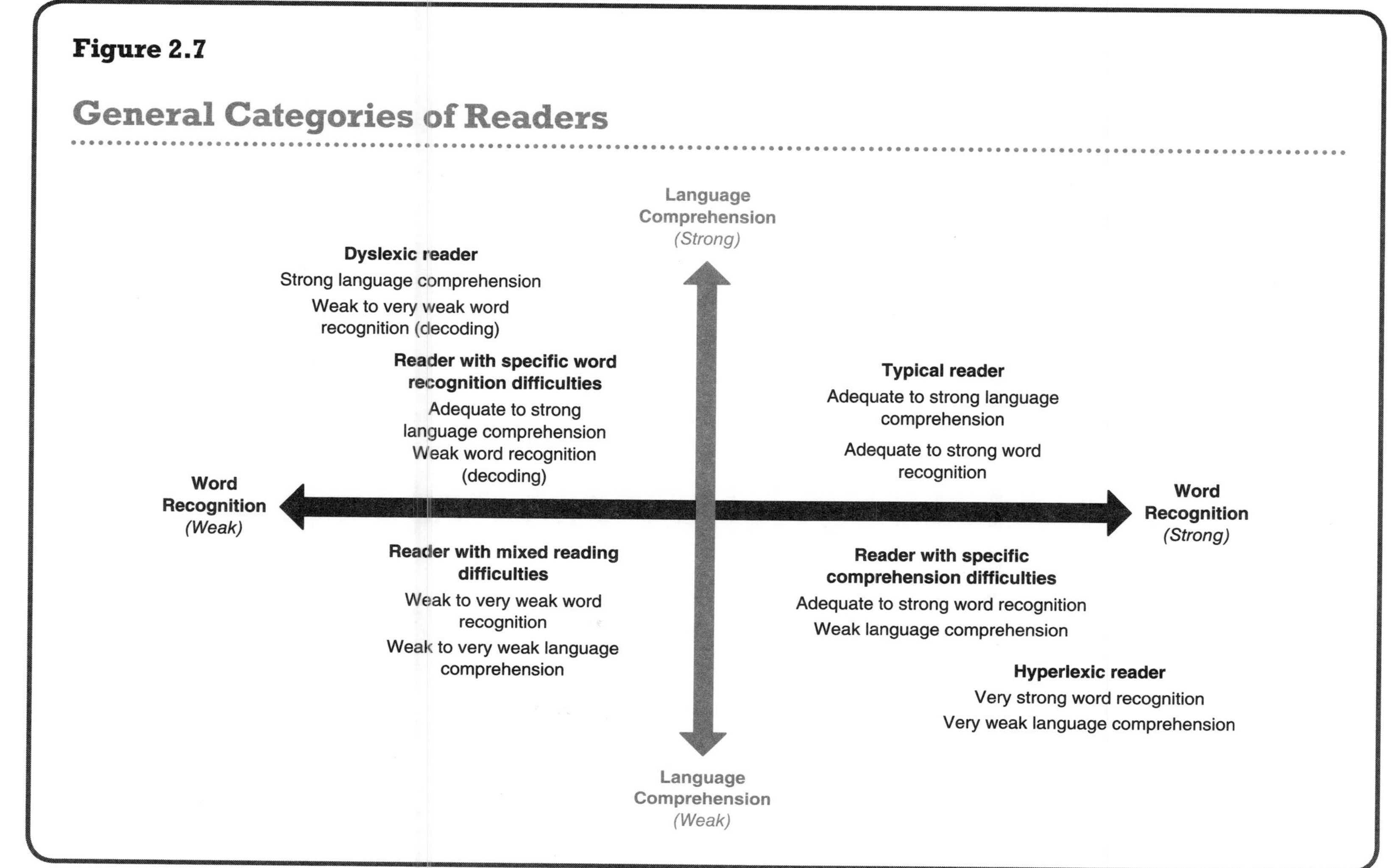
Language Comprehension (Strong)
Dyslexic reader
Strong language comprehension
Weak to very weak word recognition (decoding)
Reader with specific word recognition difficulties
Adequate to strong language comprehension
Weak word recognition (decoding)
Typical reader
Adequate to strong language comprehension
Adequate to strong word recognition
Word Recognition (Weak)
Word Recognition (Strong)
Reader with mixed reading difficulties
Weak to very weak word recognition
Weak to very weak language comprehension
Reader with specific comprehension difficulties
Adequate to strong word recognition
Weak language comprehension
Hyperlexic reader
Very strong word recognition
Very weak language comprehension
Language Comprehension (Weak)

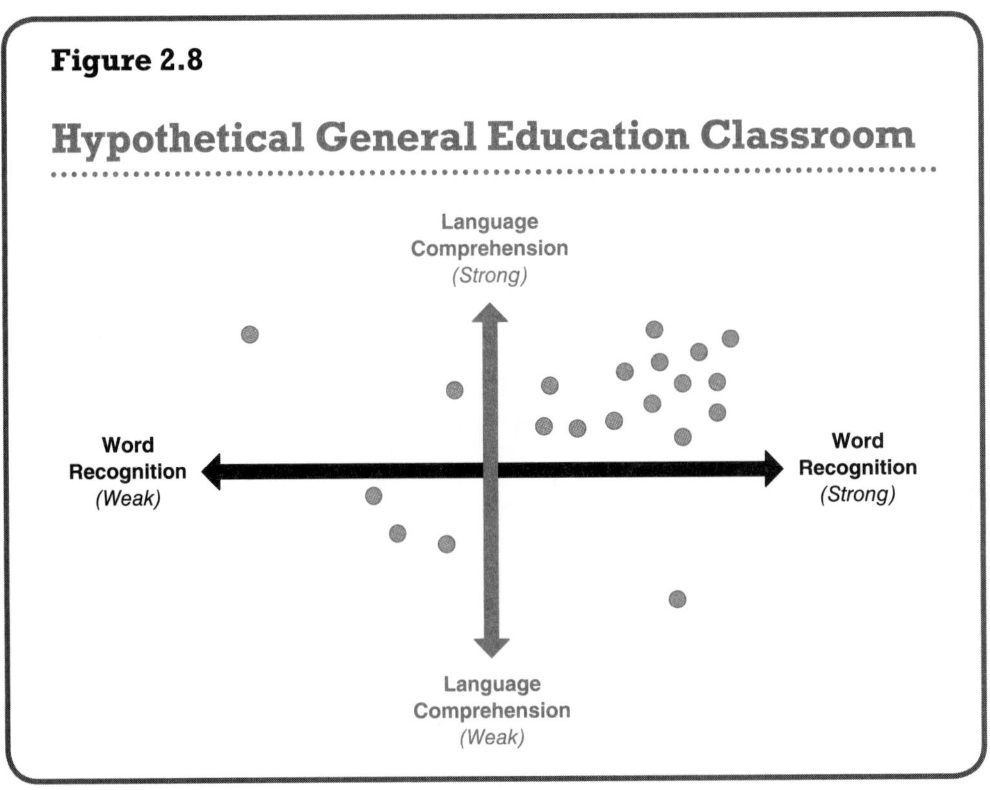
Figure 2.8
Hypothetical General Education Classroom
Language
Comprehension
(Strong)
Word
Recognition
(Weak)
Word
Recognition
(Strong)
Language
Comprehension
(Weak)

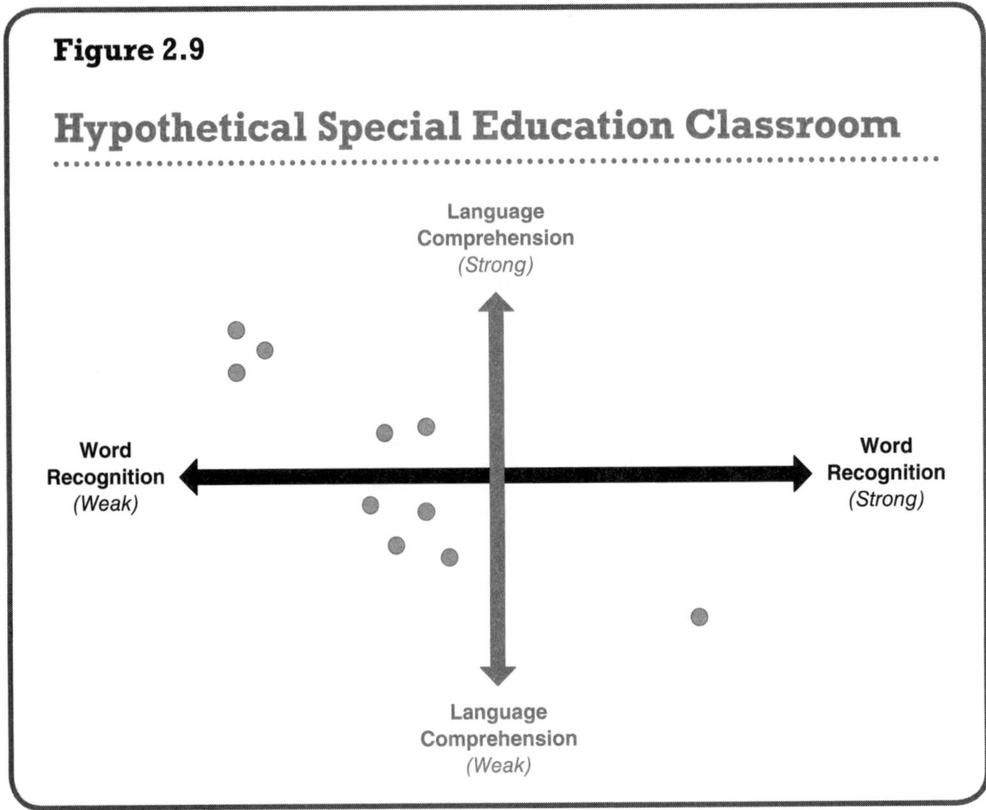
Figure 2.9
Hypothetical Special Education Classroom
Language
Comprehension
(Strong)
Word
Recognition
(Weak)
Word
Recognition
(Strong)
Language
Comprehension
(Weak)

reduced when there is a weakness in *either* of the two variables. Thus, even though students may have a high degree of language comprehension, they could still show a low degree of *reading* comprehension. In this case, lack of word recognition (decoding) keeps them from accessing meaning. If you were to read this sentence to such students—"A volcanic eruption was imminent"—they would know just what it meant. But if you asked them to read it independently, they would struggle through the words *volcanic*, *eruption*, and *imminent*, and in the end, they would have little to no idea of the sentence's meaning.

FOR FURTHER STUDY •••

- "Learning to Read: Should We Keep Things Simple?" by the Language and Reading Consortium in the April/May/June 2015 issue of *Reading Research Quarterly*, pp. 151–169.
- "The Simple View of Reading" by Linda Farrell, Michael Hunter, Marcia Davidson, and Tina Osenga, www.readingrockets.org/article/simple-view-reading
- Orton Gillingham Online Academy: *The Simple View of Reading*
- Maria S. Murray, PhD. *What Is the Simple View of Reading? What It Means for Meaning-Making.*

www.readingrockets.org/article/simple-view-reading

ortongillinghamonlinetutor.com/the-simple-view-of-reading-svr-part-1/

www.youtube.com/watch?v=stHW2Sfi3ho&t=6s

We Can Prevent Problems

When I think of how the Eternal Triangle and the Simple View of Reading inform one another, my takeaway is this: Successful and happy readers effortlessly recognize words as they read, as well as exist in a constant state of language comprehension and meaning-making. On the other hand, unsuccessful readers have a limited ability to break the code, cannot effortlessly recognize words as they read, and/or lack the skills and knowledge that generate high degrees of language comprehension.

Knowing the ultimate cause of a reading difficulty can be helpful. If a student's lack of text comprehension is due to poor word recognition, we use specific types and amounts of instruction to address this difficulty. If, however, a deficit of text comprehension is due to deficits of background and vocabulary knowledge, we use other instructional practices.

According to the Simple View of Reading, we can generally put our instructional efforts into three baskets: (1) practices that help kids "break the code" and effortlessly recognize words; (2) practices that develop a child's ability to make meaning and comprehend language before, during, and after reading; and (3) a combination of practices that promotes both abilities in varying amounts. There are, of course, additional levels of specificity within each basket. For example, when looking at the meaning-making basket, we can differentiate between instruction that builds background knowledge and instruction that increases strategic reading through the use of metacognition strategies. Each category and subcategory of the Simple View performs a different function within the reading process, and each can be taught through different classroom practices. These practices are the focus of the rest of this book.

Reading is a complex process, and managing a classroom of young learners is tricky. Thus, preventing reading difficulties from occurring is a challenge. I bet you know this! Many things can go wrong during classroom teaching and learning. Still, many reading problems can be prevented. One way to accomplish this is to employ general classroom Tier 1 instruction that engages students and offers all of them many opportunities to learn and practice important skills *while* simultaneously supporting struggling readers and writers with targeted types of instruction. These general-practice ideas are not onerous or esoteric, and they don't necessarily have to be at the intensity of a Tier 2 or Tier 3 intervention. They may be, however, different from or in addition to what your reading program typically provides. Let's get to them.

HIGHLY EFFECTIVE TEACHING TECHNIQUES

CHAPTER 3

Techniques are specific ways of carrying out particular tasks. As we tackle our daily duties and chores, we employ any number of them. A landscaper applies techniques when pruning shrubs. A surgeon uses them to suture skin. My technique for making a pizza crust involves vigorously stretching the dough and then flamboyantly tossing it high in the air. My wife, Beth, has a technique, too: She carefully slides a ready-made shell of a Mama Mia's pizza crust onto a pan. The situation determines which technique is more effective. If we are starving and want to eat sooner rather than later, Beth's is the superior one.

In classrooms, teachers use techniques to educate students. Perhaps you employ a few in your lessons already, such as using humor, organization, and gradual release. Because time is limited and content demands are great, it makes sense to carefully choose the most effective teaching techniques. The ones in this chapter are included because they

- Have a well-established research record,
- Complement each other and can be used in combination,
- Are appropriate for all grade levels, and
- Can be used within any framework of literacy instruction, from balanced literacy to a basal reading series.

In addition, I have seen firsthand how they lead to more learning in classrooms. As part of my consulting work, I teach model literacy lessons. Sometimes, my instruction is more like a sputtering tractor than a purring Lamborghini. I lose my train of thought, trip over my tongue, misplace materials, forget the names of students . . . I could go on. And kids being kids, some give me a run for my money. But on most days, my lessons unfold smoothly. Afterward, during our debriefing session, teachers who have watched me teach often comment on how well I held their students' attention through the entire lesson. There's no doubt this is partly due to my being a classroom novelty. But I'm able to engage students for another reason: the powerful nature of my teaching techniques, which I have worked diligently to master over many years.

Simply put, some teaching techniques are more effective than others. Effective ones hold the attention of more students for longer periods of time, increase opportunities to participate and process, and generally lead to greater rates of learning and retention (Benjamin & Tullis, 2010; Deci, 2014; Hindman & Wasik, 2018). This is why I use certain techniques constantly, including a brisk pace, varying voice volume, descriptive feedback, positive reinforcement, repetition, direct and explicit instruction, wait time, and turn and talk, among others.

Teaching is inherently hard work. To make it easier, I suggest using these five techniques every day and week: (1) repetition and distributed practice, (2) direct and explicit instruction, (3) instant error correction, (4) wait time, and (5) sensory activation. If you are not familiar with any of them, start with one and then add another and another. Once their use becomes habit, your job gets easier because a habit is one less thing to think about! The trick is to make sure habits, whether personal or professional, are helpful, not harmful.

The techniques we are about to explore can be used to teach any content, from math to music. In this chapter, however, they are tools for teaching vocabulary words, spelling strategies, phonic patterns, reading routines, the individual sounds of words, and more. When used consistently, they help to bring about greater gains in learning (Archer & Hughes, 2011; Rosenshine, 2012). Best of all, they are especially supportive for students who are struggling to learn and can play a big part in your efforts to prevent reading difficulties.

Use Repetition and Distributed Practice

To truly master information, be it fact, spelling pattern, or vocabulary word, students must be exposed to it multiple times. Some students need just a few exposures. Others need many. Motivation, prior knowledge, attention to the task, and ability to remember are a few factors that determine how many encounters are needed to move information from working memory to long-term memory.

Due to the many variables, it's impossible to give the definitive number of repetitions it takes a student to move a letter and its associated sound, a spelling pattern, or a vocabulary word into long-term memory. Regarding the acquisition of a vocabulary word—both recognizing it on sight and instantly knowing its meaning—it may take as few as one to four exposures (Kilpatrick, 2015) or as many as 10 to 15 (McKeown et al., 1985; Webb, 2007). And if we are talking about kindergarten students who are just beginning to understand the alphabet, some may need dozens if not hundreds of repetitions to associate specific letters with specific sounds (Kilpatrick, 2015; Pressley & Allington, 2014).

It pays to assume that some students will need many exposures to the information being taught. This is especially true if you are working with children who have or may have a reading disability such as dyslexia. As Dr. Richard Gentry writes, one way to easily support children with dyslexia is to "embrace repetition" in their instruction, "because the brain 'loves' repetition for developing automaticity in almost every skill" (Gentry & Oullette, 2019, p. 137).

Effectively using repetition means more than repeating words and sentences over and over again. Rather, it means giving learners multiple chances to actively practice skills in multiple ways. To program for the number of exposures some students need, it helps if you know how to differentiate, use gradual release, and present content in multiple ways. What follow are examples of instructional routines that use repetition:

- *I Say, We Say, You Say* and *I Do, We Do, You Do* combine repetition with gradual release. Here's an example using poetry (mentioned in Chapter 7) and *I Read, We Read, You Read*: When reading a poem, say to the students, "First, I will read the poem. Next, we will read the poem together. Finally, you read the poem without me. I read, we read, you read!" Another example is found in *Sky Writing* (mentioned later in this chapter): "Students, I will show you how to Sky Write the word *said.* Then, we will Sky Write the word *said* together. Finally, you will Sky Write the word *said.* I Sky Write, we Sky Write, and then you Sky Write."

- Gentry's *Hear It, Say It, Write It, Read It,* in which the target word is presented at least four times in multiple forms, is explained later in this chapter.
- Take two minutes to sing your alphabet sound chart every day (presented in Chapter 6). Later, when some children have mastered letter–sound relationships (but others haven't), move the activity to an intervention group that includes students who still need to work on this skill.
- Trace the sandpaper letter *m* three times, writing it three times on a whiteboard, noticing the letter during shared reading, and writing the letter during authentic writing time.

Learning the letter *m* is a perfect segue to *distributed practice*, a form of repetition. Skills are learned more perfectly and permanently when the skill practice is repeated in concentrated doses that are distributed over time (Benjamin & Tullis, 2010). Distributed practice occurs frequently in sports and music. For example, as part of your Monday piano practice, you play your C minor scale for four minutes, first slowly and then at increasing speeds. You do the same during Wednesday and Friday's practices. Then, before your Saturday concert you warm up by playing the scale for one minute. That's distributed practice. It's also what is described in the previous bullet: tracing the letter *m*, then writing it on a whiteboard, later noticing it during shared reading, and finally writing it again during authentic writing. Here are other primary education examples:

- Lead students in phonemic awareness activities every day for eight minutes in the morning and five minutes in the afternoon (rather than a 20-minute session every Tuesday and Thursday).
- Teach students in guided-reading groups on Monday, Wednesday, and Friday, rather than running them only once a week.
- Break a 30-minute phonics lesson into 20 minutes of whole-group instruction and 10 minutes at the start of some guided-reading groups.
- Point out spelling patterns not just during 20 minutes of dedicated spelling time but also during writing lessons, for a minute or two during shared reading, and for three or four minutes during a guided-reading lesson.

- Each day, give students two or three 15-minute bouts of independent reading. These bouts could occur during independent work time (during guided-reading groups), a dedicated 15-minute independent reading time, and a social studies or science lesson. See Chapter 7 for ideas on how to set up leveled browsing bins, science book bins, independent reading bags, and the *I Can List*.

Teach Directly and Explicitly

When teaching critical literacy elements, from phonic patterns and vocabulary words to writing genres and comprehension strategies, be direct and explicit in your teaching. In other words, avoid circuitous routes and take the shortest paths possible to learning. For example, when I first present information on letter sounds, spelling patterns, and vocabulary words, I do my best to avoid asking students questions such as these: "Who knows what sound this letter makes," "Do any of you know how to spell the /shun/ sound," and "Who knows what this word means?" Likewise, when teaching students who are at risk of developing reading difficulties, I steer clear of presenting discovery first (as in, "Let's discover what patterns exist in these words). Instead, I do direct and explicit instruction (see Figure 3.1).

Figure 3.1

Direct and Explicit Instruction Is . . .

1. Analyzing the information or action you will present.
2. Breaking the information or action into simple, discrete parts.
3. Specifically telling and showing the students each part of what you want them to know and do.
4. Guiding them as they practice saying and doing.
5. Watching them independently say the information and do the task. Reteaching and re-modeling if they make a mistake or give an incomplete action or answer.

Researchers and clinicians have been pointing out the great power of direct and explicit instruction for years (Archer & Hughes, 2011; Carnine et al., 1997; Gentry & Graham, 2010). It's a technique that is easy to use, time efficient, and highly effective in getting kids to initially learn basic information. It often involves specifically telling students what you want them to learn, explicitly modeling actions, and then having them immediately repeat the information and actions with you. What follow are some examples of the technique in action.

Imagine a second-grade classroom. The setting is a 15-minute afternoon spelling lesson. It's the beginning of the week, and the teacher wants her students to learn and then apply two ways to spell the long *i* sound: *igh* and *y* at the end of a one-syllable word. Rather than begin the lesson with a word-sort activity in which the students consider 12 word cards and sort them into piles that reflect patterns they discover, the teacher directly and explicitly teaches the students that the long *i* sound can be spelled *igh* and *y* at the end of a one-syllable word. She then models the concept, saying and spelling a number of words that use the patterns. Her instruction looks and sounds like this:

Teacher: Today, we are going to learn two ways to spell the long *i* sound. What are we going to do today, everyone?

Students: Learn three ways to spell the long *i* sound.

Teacher: The first way to spell the long *i* sound is *i-g-h*. Say that with me.

All: I-g-h.

Teacher: We use this spelling in the word *high*. Listen: /h/ /i/, *high, I jumped very high*. I spell the /h/ with an *h* and the /i/ with *i-g-h*. [Writes the spelling for all to see]

I also use it to spell the word *right*. Listen: /r/ /i/ /t/, *right, this is my right hand*. I spell the /r/ with an *r*, the /i/ with *i-g-h*, and the /t/ with a *t*. [Writes the spelling for all to see]

Here is one more. The word is *fight*. Listen: /f/ /i/ /t/, *fight, I saw the dogs fight*. I spell the /f/ with an *f*, the /i/ with *i-g-h*, and the /t/ with a *t*. [Writes the spelling for all to see]

Let's try one together. Get out your whiteboards. Let's spell the word *sigh*.

All: [The teacher and students segment and blend *sigh* and then spell it. The teacher spells the word out loud as she writes the letters.]

Teacher: Let's do a new word together. The word is *flight*.

Here's another scenario in which the teacher is introducing the strategy of using a book's cover as the starting point for comprehension. Her class is a group of kindergarten students.

Teacher: Today, we are going to learn about a book's cover. Say *book cover* with me, everyone.

All: Book cover.

Teacher: [Holds up the book] I notice three things on this book's cover: a picture, the name of the author at the bottom, and the book's title at the top.

A book cover has a title on it. [Pointing] This is the *book title*. What is this, everyone?

All: The book title!

Teacher: A book's title helps a reader understand what the book is about. Listen: [in a whisper voice] *A book's title helps us understand what the book is about!* What does a book's title help us understand, everyone?

Students: What the book is about!

Teacher: I will read you the book title: *The Little Red Hat*. What is the title of this book, everyone?

All: *The Little Red Hat*.

Teacher: The title tells me the book will be about a little red hat.

Next, I look at the picture. I see a boy and a girl playing with a doll. The doll has clothes on. It is not wearing a red hat. But I also see a little mouse down here. That little mouse has a little red hat on its head!

I want to stress that although I advocate direct and explicit instruction, I am *not* saying exploration, construction, and discovery should be tossed in the dumpster. Having students construct, explore, and discover text meaning, phonic patterns, and grammar rules are instructionally valuable things to do. And personally speaking, I love to watch kindergarten children create their own writing, second graders discover patterns during word-sort activities, and so on. The human mind is built for discovery and the construction of meaning. Nonetheless, I typically use direct and explicit instruction *first* for two reasons: (1) to be as efficient as possible, and (2) to minimize the possibility that incorrect learning will occur. Later, once my at-risk learners have developed some foundational knowledge, I bring in exploration and discovery activities.

Video example of direct and explicit instruction: https://www.youtube.com/watch?v=mINITRTxamA

Instantly Correct Errors

Practice makes perfect. It also makes permanent, and so it is important for learners to understand skills and information as accurately as possible the first time they learn them. Previously, we explored direct and explicit instruction, a teaching technique that minimizes errors during learning. If I want a student to understand the *ee* vowel digraph stands for the long *e* sound, I will not have him try to discover the association as I read a poem about seeds and trees, giving clues about letter–sound relationships and asking guiding questions like "What words make the long *e* sound and how are they spelled" or "How are the words *green* and *seeds* alike?" Rather, I will teach the spelling of the long *e* sound directly and explicitly, saying "The *ee* combination says /e/. What does *ee* say, everyone?" Next, I'll present a short list of *ee* words from the poem, read them with the *I Read, We Read, You Read* routine, and explicitly reinforce the *ee*–long *e* connection. This direct and explicit instruction will increase the chance that young readers will learn exactly what I want them to learn—that *ee* is a visual representation of the long *e* sound.

Like direct and explicit instruction, instant error correction increases the chance that correct learning will take root (Deci, 2014; Opitz et al., 2011; Samuels & Wu, 2003). Here's what it might look and sound like in a classroom:

Let's say that after reading a poem about seeds with the entire group, I bring that poem to a guided-reading group where students chorally read the poem with me. As students read, I hear two children stumble on the word *garden*. Rather than continuing on, I instantly stop, teach the decoding of the word, and give the correct pronunciation, saying something like this: "Stop. Let's accurately decode this word. Look at the letters from beginning to end. We can divide a word between the two middle consonants. Now, we see chunks we can decode. First is *g-a-r*. The *g* says /g/, the *a-r* says /ar/, and together they say /gar/. Then comes *d-e-n*. When we blend the sounds those letters make, we get *den*. Put *gar* and *den* together, and we get the word *garden*. What is the word, everyone? Does *garden* make sense in this sentence? Would we find seeds in a garden? Yes. The word *garden* makes sense."

By the way, you will notice that although I asked students to check for meaning, I did not ask them to use a meaning strategy first. Rather, the first strategy I modeled was reading the word the whole way through, noticing each letter, and employing letter–sound associations and chunking. This is in line with teaching students that the first line of attack for reading an unknown word is not a meaning-first three-cuing system, but a strategy with a much larger body of evidence behind it, namely letter-to-sound decoding (Adams, 1998; Paige, 2020).

Instant error correction can save time and diminish teacher headaches because it keeps incorrect learning from taking root. Once incorrectly performed skills and erroneous pieces of information are established in a brain, it takes a good deal of time and effort to uproot and then replace them with correct skills and content. I remember sitting with a kindergarten boy (we'll call him Max) for some one-on-one guided reading. Max picked a book titled *Mother Duck*. First, we discussed the cover art and title. "The title of this book is *Mother Duck*," I said, pointing to the words. "And look at the picture. That's Mother Duck. Who is it?"

"Mother Duck!" exclaimed Max. Then, we did a picture walk. As we turned the pages, we took turns describing what we were seeing. "I see Mother Duck sitting on her nest," I said. "Mother Duck with her babies," said Max. Finally, it came time to read. We turned to the first sentence on the first page.

"Get your tracking finger ready," I said. "Now, get your mouth ready to say the words. Read through each word. Go ahead."

"My duck . . . ," said Max.

"Stop," I said. "Look at the first word, Max." I pointed to *mother.* "I see an *m.* I know it says /m/. But the next letter is *o* and then comes *t-h. T-h* says /th/. Next, *is e*-r, and that says /er/. This long word is *mother.* What is the word?"

"Mother," said Max.

"The word *mother* matches the letters, and it makes sense. Try it again. Get your tracking finger ready. Read through each word. Go ahead."

"My duck . . . ," said Max.

In the end, it took multiple reteachings over the course of three or four minutes to get Max to unlearn a mistake he made in two seconds. That's the power of incorrect learning, and it's why you want to use teaching techniques that quickly correct it and minimize the possibility of it happening in the first place.

DOT AND CHECK SPELLING

One of my favorite instant error correction activities is *Dot and Check Spelling* from Dr. Richard Gentry. When combined with *Hear It, Say It, Write It, Read It* (also by Gentry), the activity incorporates direct and explicit instruction and activates the phonological, semantic, and orthographic processing systems of the brain. What a powerful combination!

Dot and Check Spelling can be used in lieu of a traditional spelling test, although you can certainly gather the student sample at the end and use it as a grade. The routines take slightly longer than a traditional spelling test, so if, for example, you give 15 words on a spelling quiz, you'll want to give only 10 words. Here's the sequence of the combined routines, *Hear It, Say It, Write It, Read It* and *Dot and Check Spelling*:

- The teacher says the word. (Students *hear* it.)
- The teacher defines the word directly and explicitly.
- Students *say* the word.
- Students *write* (spell) the word.
- The teacher gives the spelling, saying it and writing it out. Simultaneously, students check their spelled word by placing a dot under each letter as the teacher says it. If an error occurs, student circles the area where it occurred.

- The teacher then spells the word again. As she spells, students write the word next to their initially spelled word.
- Students *read* the word (the second spelling).
- If desired, students compare their two words, noticing what parts of the word they spelled correctly and what parts are spelled incorrectly.
- Teacher and students repeat the process for each subsequent word.

Figure 3.2 shows what the routine looks and sounds like in a second-grade classroom, using the word *subtract*:

And Figure 3.3, pulled from a student's 10-word list, shows a four-word sample of *Dot and Check Spelling* in action.

The beauties of *Dot and Check Spelling* are many. First, students instantly correct any spelling errors. Second, they are able to immediately process what they got right and what they got wrong.

Figure 3.2

Dot and Check Spelling Routine

Teacher Talk	Student's Verbal Response	Student's Written Response
The word is *subtract*. *Subtract* means "to take away." What's the word?	"Subtract."	
Write it.		subchack
Get ready for *Dot and Correct*: s-u-b-t-r-a-c-t		subchack . . . . .
Get ready to spell the word again: s-u-b-t-r-a-c-t		subchack subtract . . . . .
Notice where you made mistakes. Now, read the correctly spelled word.	"Subtract."	
Get ready for the next word!		

Figure 3.3

Dot and Check Spelling Student Sample

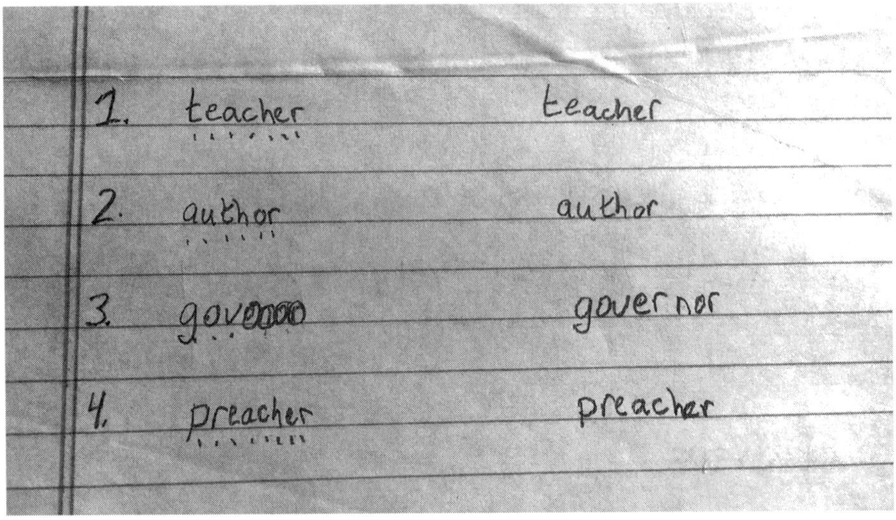

In other words, this activity is about learning, not testing. Third, when students work in pairs, *Dot and Check* can function as an *I Can List* activity (see Chapter 7) or as a literacy center. Once students know the routine, buddies can give each other a "spelling test," taking turns to give words (I suggest three to five words at a time), dotting, checking, and correcting each word, noticing what parts of the word caused trouble, and, after completing 8 to 12 words, turning in the final product to you. Finally, you can use information gleaned from this activity in a formative way, using it to guide future lessons, and, as mentioned earlier, as a summative grade. But the real purpose of this activity is to help students encode correct spelling sequences in their "brain dictionaries" through the act of spelling and the noticing of correct letter sequences and spelling patterns.

Video example of *Dot and Check Spelling*: https://www.youtube.com/watch?v=zdu-brfPiAY&t=36s

Give Wait Time

Wait time is an instructional technique that promotes language use (Hindman & Wasik, 2018). It also helps set the stage for learning, engages students, builds background knowledge, and increases comprehension (Rowe, 1986; Stahl, 1994). When you give students time to think, you allow their brains to more deeply and completely process questions and directions, recall facts and figures, and synthesize information. If you regularly fold wait time into your instruction, I guarantee you'll be amazed at how many more students engage in thinking and how their answers become richer and more sophisticated.

At its core, the technique involves asking a question or requesting an action and then requiring students to *think* silently for three to five seconds before raising their hands to answer or before turning to talk to a partner to share and/or discuss what they are thinking. For this reason, I use the terms *wait time* and *think time* interchangeably.

Before I say more, let me describe teaching that does *not* use the technique. While reading the book *Swimmy* by Leo Leonni to 20 kindergarteners, a teacher stops and asks the group, "What do you think will happen next?" Very quickly, three hands shoot into the air. Next, the teacher calls on one of the hand-raising students and listens to the answer. Perhaps the teacher picks one other student whose hand was raised and asks, "What do you think?" After hearing this student's answer, the teacher goes back to reading.

When using think time, however, the teacher asks the same question and then *requires* all students to think before raising their hands. The requirement is backed up when the teacher silently and slowly counts to three. As the teacher counts in her head, the children think. Perhaps the teacher scans the group, checking to see if the students are thinking. Maybe she prompts them with a scratch of her chin or a squint of mental exertion as she strikes a pose à la Rodin's *Thinker*. After three seconds go by, she signals it's time for students to raise their hands. This time, 15 or more hands whoosh into the air. Finally, she calls on a student, or even better, she gives a signal to the students that tells them to turn and tell their answer to a partner. As the children whisper their responses, she listens. Finally, she says, "I am going to read on and find out what happens next. Get ready!"

I suggest three seconds of think time for preK and kindergarten children because their attention span is very short (roughly that of a gnat or hamster). If you wait too long, you'll lose their attention. For first and second graders, you can increase think time to maybe five seconds. For older students, give up to six or seven seconds. Decide what amount of time works best for your students. The general behavior of different groups may demand more or less think time. Also, vary the amount of time depending upon the task.

Students will need more time when the question calls for a longer, more complex answer.

IMPORTANT POINT

Many teachers model *active listening*. Do the same for *active thinking*. But first model what *nonthinking* looks like: gazing around the room, fidgeting, playing with an eraser . . . the list here is endless! Next, model what *thinking* looks like: being totally quiet, having a furrowed brow and squinty eyes, and so forth. You can also do a think-aloud, saying something like, "I was just asked to name one color I see in the classroom. I looked around and saw yellow, blue, and red. Now, I am thinking that I will say blue. Blue is my answer!" In the end, constantly modeling how think time works, and consistently prompting students to use it, develops your good habit of using the technique and their good habit of thinking.

ADDING TURN AND TELL, TURN AND TALK

Take wait time to an advanced level by modeling "turn and tell" and "turn and talk." Use turn and tell to share an answer that only requires a word or short sentence. Turn and tell looks like a short burst of quiet talking in which one student turns to a partner and gives an answer. The youngest students, those in preK and early kindergarten, may not need more than 20 seconds to share an answer; if the answer involves only a few words, they may need only 5 to 10 seconds. You want to give them enough time to retrieve information and use language, but you also want to keep things moving so you don't lose their engagement. Turn and talk is a longer period of quiet talking where two or more students share and discuss their thoughts related to a question posed by the teacher. I think 45 seconds would be enough for first graders, maybe a bit less for preK and kindergarten students, and perhaps 60 to 90 seconds for second and third graders. But you be the judge. Try to listen in on the conversation. If you hear that it's generally focused, then let your students talk a bit longer. Conversely, if they've run out of steam or are off-topic, cut the conversation short.

One suggestion is using hand motions to signal the students for think (this is the wait time portion), turn and tell, and turn and talk. Hand signals keeps students focused on you, as well as ensure your instruction isn't broken up with too much teacher talk. Figure 3.4 shows some signal suggestions. If you have clever alternatives, feel free to substitute.

Figure 3.4

Wait Time Signal Suggestions

Action	Signal
Think	Point to and/or tap your temple with your index finger.
Answer	Point upward with your index finger, signaling "raise your hand." Alternately, simply raise your hand!
Turn and tell	Tap your index fingers together.
Turn and talk	Curve your index fingers and hook them.

Here are two examples of think time in action. They are labeled *first* and *second grade*, but depending upon the achievement levels of your students, the scenes could play out in other grade levels.

First-grade scene: Wait time then answer, followed by wait time then turn and tell

Setting: The teacher is teaching to the whole group. She has just compared the spelling of the short *a* sound /a/ with the long *a* sound. She lists pairs of words on the board and asks questions.

Teacher: Here are two words: *skate* and *cat*. Think. [She points to her temple.] Which word has the long *a* sound? [She silently counts to three. Then, she gives the "hands up" signal. Many children raise their hands. She calls on a student.] Ava?

Ava: Skate.

Teacher: Correct. Why do we read it as *skate*? How do we know to give the *a* in this word the long *a* sound?

Ava: There is a silent *e* at the end.

Teacher: Correct. Here are two more words: *mad* and *made*. Think. [She points to her temple.] Which word has the short *a* sound? [She silently counts to three. Then, she gives the "hands up" signal. Many children raise their hands.] Turn to your partner and whisper the word with the short *a* sound.

Students: [They turn and whisper.]

Teacher: The word with the short *a* sound is *mad*. When we see *m-a-d*, how do we know we read it as *mad*? How do we know the *a* in this word makes a short sound? Think. [She points to her temple, then silently counts to three.] Turn and tell your partner why *m-a-d* says *mad*.

Second-grade scene: Think time, then turn and talk

Setting: Small-group guided reading. The children have just finished reading Aliki's book, *Fossils Tell of Long Ago.*

Teacher: Using words and pictures, Aliki gives the reader the steps for making a fossil over time. Think. [She points to her temple.] How would you describe the process for making fossils? In your own words, how are fossils made? [She silently counts to five or six. Then, she interlocks her curved pointer fingers, signaling turn and talk.] Talk to your partner about how fossils are made. Number ones, talk to number twos.

Students: [The number one of the pair turns and begins to talk to the number two of the pair.]

Wait time quickly engages large numbers of students. Giving students time to think enables them to consider questions more broadly and deeply and to mentally rehearse appropriate answers. And when coupled with turn-and-tell sharing or turn-and-talk discussion, students have the following: social interaction time, occasions to practice speaking and listening, a chance to build background knowledge, and opportunities to use vocabulary and language.

Finally, wait time allows for what I call "self-differentiation." Self-differentiation occurs when students are given opportunities to reach their natural performance levels. If I ask my third graders "Who remember an event from the story?" and only give one second to think, students who have less memory ability or who have slower recall times may recall only the *last* event of the story (or no events at all). But if I give everyone five seconds to think, struggling thinkers will have a chance to recall at least some story information. Then, if I call on these students first, I give them an opportunity to share and enjoy success. After these students respond, I'll call on the students who typically remember many events. By inserting space for thinking into my questioning, I've enabled students to think at the level most natural for them. Also, providing think time and talk time helps prevent students from passively waiting for the teacher to provide the answer. They must actively think and do rather than sit and wait! For all these reasons, I believe think time is a must when teaching in special education classrooms and inclusionary settings.

FOR FURTHER STUDY ●●●

Research on the effectiveness of wait time began in the 1970s, hit its stride in the 1980s, and still regularly appears in journals. More than 40 years ago, Mary Rowe (1974) may have been the first to coin the term *wait time* and described its importance to the overall quality of student responses (and thus of learning). Later, Robert Stahl expanded on Rowe's concept and recommended three-second "waits" at various points during class periods. The research of Rowe, Stahl, and others shows that wait time is a powerful way to increase the length and quality of student responses, as well as boost student motivation. More recently, studies done by Barbara Wasik, Annemarie Hindman, and others have examined the effectiveness of wait time with students in first and second grade, kindergarten, and even preschool.

If you would like to read articles and studies authored by these specific researchers, see the reference section for a list of citations.

Activate the Senses With a Multisensory Component

Using multisensory teaching helps students learn by activating their senses. This means students not only learn through seeing and hearing but also by singing and chanting, moving their arms and legs, and manipulating objects with their hands. We don't need to have students do this hour after hour; short bursts of multisensory instruction distributed throughout the day is effective. And, of course, the more you use this technique, the more likely it is to become a good teaching habit.

There are many multisensory activities out there. In this section, I highlight four that efficiently help students to learn sounds, letters, and letter–sound associations.

TRACE MONTESSORI SANDPAPER LETTERS

An important part of preK, kindergarten, and beginning first-grade reading instruction is teaching children to identify the letters of the English alphabet and associate them with sounds. An especially effective routine for teaching letters is given in Chapter 6, as is a sequence for letter introduction. Once you are using the routine and sequence, you can supplement your instruction with letter tracing on Montessori sandpaper letters.

During short bursts of practice (just a few minutes) distributed across the days and weeks, students gently move their fingers over prewritten sandpaper letters, tracing the outlines of whatever letter or letters you want them to focus on. If you have enough materials, letter tracing can occur in whole groups. If materials are limited, do the tracing in small groups.

I like sandpaper letters because using them takes only a few minutes and they are easily managed and stored. In other words, they are efficient. I have heard of students tracing letters in boxes filled with sand or boards smeared with shaving cream, and I have observed students forming letters with modeling clay and wiki sticks, which are sections of waxed knitting yarn, bendable and slightly sticky. Although students enjoy working with these types of materials, using them for letter tracing strikes me as inefficient: It simply takes too much time for kids to form the letters and teachers to manage the materials.

An efficient follow-up activity to *Sky Writing* (see next activity) is "desk writing"—writing a word on a desk or tabletop using imaginary ink that flows from the tips of pointer fingers. The same idea can be applied to single letters. When students have practiced tracing sandpaper letters, they can trace their letters on the surface of the desk with their finger. First, though, have them imagine what color ink they are going to use—red, purple, yellow, blue, orange?

On special days, give them the option to mix in some make-believe glitter. Then, they can imagine they are writing their letters with "sparkle ink."

SKY WRITING

Intervention programs that incorporate multisensory learning can be especially helpful to students who have dyslexia, a neurobiological brain difference that leads to difficulties in learning how to read. And so *Sky Writing* is found in intervention programs such as Orton-Gillingham and Wilson reading programs (and probably other Tier 3 programs as well). But at heart, *Sky Writing* is nonprogrammatic: You can use it even when you haven't been formally trained in a specific intervention program. Like sandpaper letter tracing, *Sky Writing* is efficient. Use it to teach letters, irregular words, and frequently encountered words.

To start, model the Sky Write position: a straight, extended arm ending in two straight, extended fingers (pointer and middle). As I understand it, the reason for the straightness of the arm is to create more weight that must be supported. More weight demands more muscle use, more muscle use involves more nerve activation, and more nerve activation leads to more triggering of neural circuitry in the brain, thus increasing the chances that correct letter formations and letter sequences are stored in the orthographic processing system. The two fingers also have to do with increasing nerve activation.

Next, model the *Sky Writing* process. Because I want to show students how to Sky Write from left to right and because I am not good at mirror writing, I teach with my back turned to the group, keeping an eye on the action using the eyes in the back of my head (or craning my neck to look over my shoulder). If students are left-handed, they can use their left hand to Sky Write. Regardless of left- or right-handedness, students should start on the left side of their body and move in the air, across the midline, to the right side. The directionality of the letters, as well as the letter sequences in words, is learned through the physical motion of the arm (see Figure 3.5).

Once students can replicate the correct arm/finger position, I use *I Do, We Do, You Do* to write the letter, pattern, or word I want the students to learn. Students mimic the arm movement while they

Figure 3.5

Students Using *Sky Writing*

say the letter or letters (if you are writing a pattern or word). For the third repetition (*You Do*), I turn fully and observe the children as they model the letter or pattern. If I notice errors in learning the procedure, I directly and explicitly reteach the correct way of moving (instant error correction) and have the students practice again.

To learn a letter and its associated sound, students first swipe their arm in the air left to right and say the *sound* produced by the letter. Next, right above where they swiped, they form the letter and say the letter *name*. Finally, they swipe below again, left to right, and say the letter *sound*. Here's the sequence:

1. Swiping a line left to right, they say, "/m/."
2. They form the letter in the air and say its name: *m*.

3. Swiping a line left to right below where they wrote the letter, they say, "/m/."
4. Repeat the routine a total of three times.

The sequence for learning a word is very much the same: Swipe and say the word; Sky Write the letters, and as the letters are formed, say the letter names; swipe and say the word again. Here is the sequence for the word *one*:

1. Swiping a line left to right, they say, "/one/."
2. Above the swipe, they spell word in the air and say each letter as they spell it, starting on the left and moving across the midline to the right: "*o-n-e*."
3. They swipe in a line below the spelling, left to right (crossing the midline), and say the word: "One!"
4. Repeat the routine a total of three times.

After students become adept at *Sky Writing*, you may not need to do *I Do and We Do*. Three repetitions on the part of students are recommended: Every time they learn a letter, pattern, or word, they Sky Write the letter, pattern, or word three times in a row. Be aware that extended arms and fingers demand, a certain amount of classroom management because students need space to do movements.

FOR FURTHER STUDY ●●●

These short videos demonstrate *Sky Writing*. The first shows an older student using it to associate the vowel sound short *e* with the letter *e*. The writing sequence is repeated three times. The second shows a teacher and then a young student writing the sight word *once*. The student repeats the writing sequence three times.

Sky Writing demonstration: https://www.youtube.com/watch?v=yV-zCWRBTQs

Another *Sky Writing* demonstration: https://www.youtube.com/watch?v=Bdmm3U_iPOo

MANIPULATE MAGNETIC TILES

Manipulatives like magnetic letters and word families not only motivate and engage but also free students from the demands of letter formation, allowing them to make letter–sound connections, notice patterns in words, spell words, and read words. Some may associate magnetic letter manipulation with students in kindergarten and first grade, but manipulatives are useful for instruction in second grade, third grade, and beyond.

My favorite magnetic letter product is Wilson Reading's Magnetic Journal. The tiles are color coded and present not just single letters but also letter sequences in categories such as consonant digraphs (*ch, sh, th*), vowel digraphs (*ai, ay, ow, ee*), *r*-controlled combinations (*ar, or, ir, er*), final ending patterns (*tion, sion, ture*), and so on. Also, the magnetic journal presents letters and chunks on the left and has students cross the midline to spell (and then read) words on the right.

No matter what product you ultimately use, I suggest thinking beyond individual letters and digraphs to patterns, which we can also call chunks, word families, and phonograms. I find that providing magnetic tiles that show letter–sound combinations, such as *am, all, unk*, and *ing*, enable students to more quickly see how certain letter combinations cannot be broken apart (more on this in Chapter 6). Additionally, pattern tiles help both teachers and students make the connection that encoding and decoding (spelling and reading) are two sides of the same coin.

SING A *LETTER–SOUND SONG*

The "*Jeopardy* Alphabet Song"—or "Alphardy"—comes from Dr. Jean, a longtime provider of educational music and activities. When I say "longtime," I mean Dr. Jean has been around since the time of the cassettes tape, an ancient device made of plastic and spools of magnetic tape, once popular for storing music. Nowadays, you can find the music on YouTube and at Dr. Jean's website (www.drjean.org).

The "Alphardy" song is pretty easy: Just sing to the melody of the *Jeopardy* television game show theme, using an alphabet sound chart as your guide. The melody repeats after every four letters. Here are the "lyrics" to the first four letters. Start singing!

A for apple, /a/, /a/, /a/

B for bear, /b/, /b/-/b/-/b/-/b/-/b/

C for cat, /c/, /c/, /c/

D for dog, /d/, /d/, /d/!

As your students sing, make sure they point to and look at each letter. You want them to associate the sound with the visual and vice versa. Also, make sure that they (and you too) clip off any schwa sounds. For example, you want to voice the perfectly forced-air sound /f/ for the letter *f*, not say "fuh." By the way, if you need more guidance on how to sing the song or you want someone else to sing to your students, visit my YouTube channel and click on the *Alphardy* video.

Video example of MW singing "Alphardy": https://www.youtube.com/watch?v=rZm2sB6nZc4&t=12s

IMPORTANT POINT

Before you learn the "*Jeopardy* Alphabet Song" and sing it with your students, double-check your alphabet sound chart to make sure it is as effective as possible. Pay special attention to the pictures that produce the short vowel sounds.

In a Google image search, I looked at over 40 alphabet sound charts in various reading programs, Teacher Pay Teacher materials, and Pinterest pins. I even went to Dr. Jean's website and looked at the PDF chart that goes with her "Alphardy" song. Like many of the charts I perused, I cannot recommend it. Why? Some of its icons produce impure or hard-to-hear letter sounds.

Some charts use an *elbow*, *elephant*, or *egg* for the short sound of *e*. The word *egg* is one syllable, which is helpful, but the vowel tends toward the long *a* sound. As for *elbow* and *elephant*, it is harder for children to hear and then vocally produce a pure short /e/ when the sound is followed by an *l*. Also, if you say *elephant* and then ask a kindergarten child for the word's first sound, she may say /t/, the last and therefore easiest sound to remember in a very long word. A far superior choice is a picture of a man named Ed because *Ed* elicits a pure short *e* sound and contains only two phonemes. *Echo* is a good choice, too, but I like *Ed* even better.

Other less-than-stellar letter–sound charts include those with a picture of an *x-ray* for *x* (the initial sound is /e/), *ink* for short *i* (sorry, but yuck—the *i* sound is altered due to the *nk*), and an *orange* for short *o*. Say what? For young children, make letter associations easy to understand by presenting short vowel sounds that are as pure as possible. Wilson Language, Jolly Phonics, and other programs use key words such as these for their short vowel sounds: *apple, Ed, itch, octopus, up*. Also, to present the pure /ks/ sound of *x*, they often use *fox* to do the work. Putting the letter *x* in the final, not initial, position helps students hear the letter's two distinct sounds—/k/ and /s/.

You can find a full-page, printable effective letter–sound chart on the Mark Weakland Literacy.com website, like what's shown in Figure 3.6. The following QR code takes you to the site's File Cabinet tab. Next, look in the left-hand column toward the top. I suggest all grade-level teachers use same letter–sound chart. That way, when kids move up the grade levels or switch classrooms, they won't be confused by a different chart.

Scan for an effective letter–sound chart: https://www.markweaklandliteracy.com/file-cabinet.html

(Continued)

(Continued)

Figure 3.6

Alphabet Sound Chart

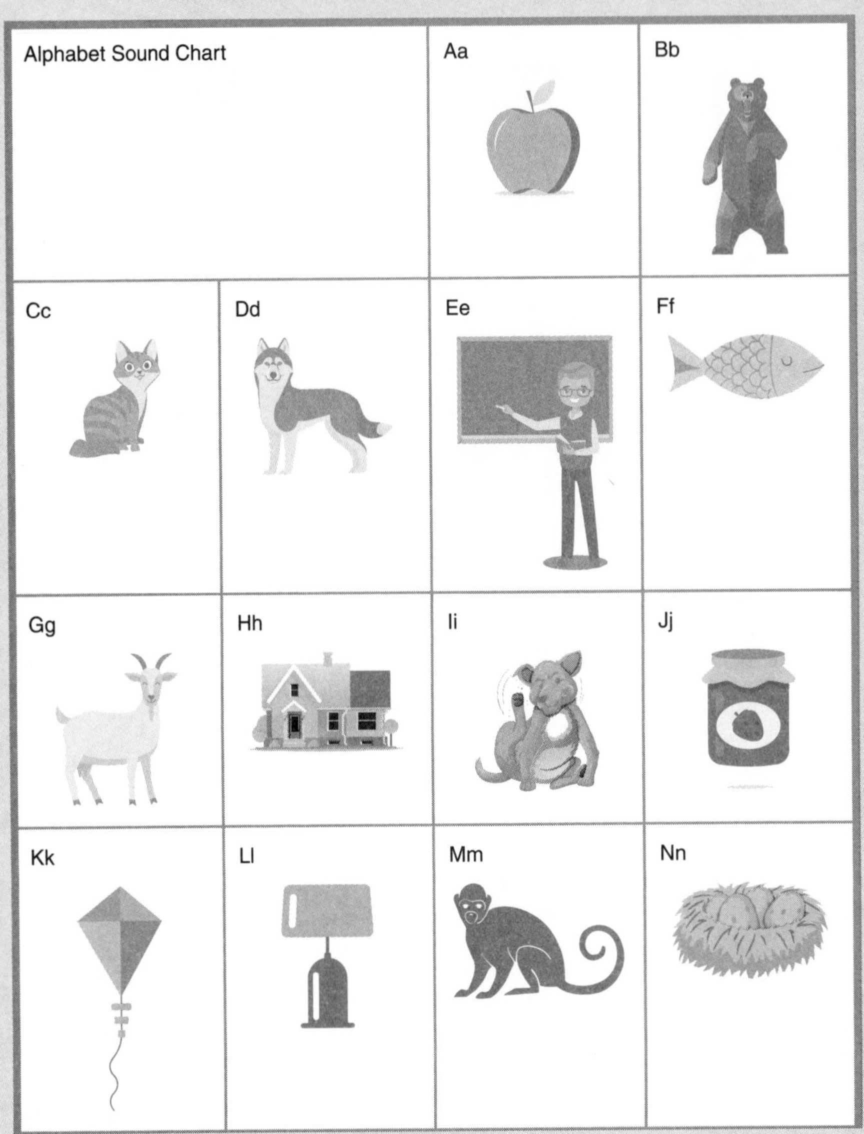

Images (from top left to bottom right): iStock.com/AntonioFrancois; istock.com/Oleksandr Chaban; istock.com/Volodymyr Kryshtal; istock.com/Nadzeya_Dzivakova; istock.com/MarinaMays; istock.com/SIlviaCV; istock.com/Bezvershenko; istock.com/Tera Vector; istock.com/blueringmedia; istock.com/FARBAI; istock.com/krugli; istock.com/ONYXprj; istock.com/Pirinal; istock.com/eduardrobert

Images (from top left to bottom right): istock.com/babushka_p90; istock.com/Sudowoodo; istock.com/Evgeniya_Mokeeva; istock.com/Tetkoren; istock.com/FARBAI; istock.com/terdpong pangwong; istock.com/Roman Bykhalets; istock.com/armckw; istock.com/NPavelN; istock.com/Alfadanz; istock.com/blueringmedia; istock.com/Sunny_nsk

FOR FURTHER STUDY •••

Ladders to Literacy (2005, 2nd ed.) by Angela Notari-Syverson: Full of engaging activities that include singing and moving, this book's focus is phonemic awareness, rhyming, letter sounds, oral language, and print awareness. I think it's an essential book for early childhood and kindergarten teachers.

Cursive writing: Cursive handwriting benefits all students, including those who have dyslexia (Berninger & Amtmann, 2003; Graham, 2010, 2019). Cursive's positive outcomes seem to flow from its connective nature, which leads to sensory feedback and helps integrate memory and fine-motor skills. To explore the pros and cons of cursive writing, start with this 2017 *Edutopia* article, "What We Lose With the Decline of Cursive" (www.edutopia.org/article/what-we-lose-with-decline-cursive-tom-berger).

CONNECTIONS

Other practices in this book incorporate activation of the senses through body movements, manipulating materials, or reading/singing out loud.

- *Hear It, Say It, Write It, Read It* (in this chapter)
- Chapter 5
  - *Feel the Chin Drop*
  - *Hands Together, Apart, and Away*
  - *Penny Push and Pull*
  - *Stretch the Word*
  - *Stretch It, Tap It, Zap It*
  - Unifix cubes and Lego blocks
- Chapter 6
  - *Letter-a-Day* routine
  - *Chunk Chants*
  - Building Words With Letter Tiles
  - Manipulating Morphemes
  - *Look, Touch, Say*
- Chapter 7
  - *Paintbrush Reading*

IMPORTANT POINT

The techniques mentioned in this chapter are appropriate for school children in preK programs. Wait time gives young students time to process their thoughts and come up with language; turn and talk gives them a chance to use that language, as well as practice the important social skills of speaking and listening. Multisensory activities that incorporate movement, chanting, tracing, and singing are engaging ways to present information to young children and move it permanently into their minds; repeating these activities in short bursts distributed over lengths of time also helps with engagement and information storage. Finally, although exploration and discovery activities are essential early childhood instructional practices, there are times when direct and explicit instruction is best, especially for imparting highly specific content such as letter names, letter sounds, and word definitions, as well as giving directions for routines and activities.

BUILDING LANGUAGE COMPREHENSION

CHAPTER 4

As a guest instructor in schools, I typically keep the pace of my lessons brisk. This helps me engage students, as well as cover everything I want to demonstrate to teachers. Not too long ago, I was teaching text annotations to second and third graders, using short nonfiction articles as the reading material. To keep my lesson moving, I kept my previews of the text brief. "Here's an article about a teenage scientist," I said. "And this one is about monkeys who hang out in hot springs. This one explains how to care for reptiles. And the last one is for sports fans—it's all about baseball."

When it came time for a boy named Sully to choose his article, he showed no sense of urgency. Rather, he mulled over each passage, verbalizing his thoughts along the way. "I don't like that one 'cause I don't like lizards. Especially bearded dragons. Hmm . . . the monkeys might be all right. But they look weird. Well . . . the science thing isn't very good. All right, I'm picking baseball. I know about it 'cause me and my dad watch it."

Although I found it nerve-wracking to wait as Sully moseyed up to his choice, it was worth it in the end because as he talked, I could see how personal preference and background knowledge played a part in his thinking. Later, when he translated his thoughts into annotation symbols, I saw a literal picture of his metacognition at work, especially how he used his knowledge of baseball to help him comprehend the text. Now, reflecting back on this scene, I realize that if Sully had been assigned a topic for which he lacked language comprehension (background knowledge, vocabulary, and so forth), he might have had real difficulties in reading and understanding the article.

We know from our study of the Simple View of Reading that language comprehension is fundamental to reading comprehension. Thus, it makes sense to help students build and strengthen it. There are many ways to do this. In this chapter, we will explore six classroom practices that build and strengthen language comprehension components, specifically background knowledge, vocabulary knowledge, topical knowledge, and metacognition strategies.

These practices can involve text. But they can use only oral language, aka classroom discussion and conversation, an especially effective medium when teaching children in preK and kindergarten.

Components of Language Comprehension

Through his thinking out loud and text annotations, Sully gave a glimpse into how he used knowledge and thinking strategies to understand an article about baseball. According to Kilpatrick (2015) and Scarborough (2001), metacognition, background knowledge, and topical knowledge are components of **language comprehension**, one of the Simple View of Reading's two variables (the other being word recognition). Other components of language comprehension include vocabulary knowledge, grammatical and syntactical knowledge, and self-monitoring. The more a student has of each, the more chance he has of understanding what he reads. Said another way, when the many parts of language comprehension are strong, reading difficulties are less likely to occur. Conversely, if the parts are weak, reading difficulties are more likely to occur.

The combination of language knowledge and the automatic recognition of words enables the reading process to unfold. In a 2018 overview of the process, researchers Anne Castles, Kathleen Rastle, and Kate Nation say this: "When children begin to learn to read, they usually already have relatively sophisticated spoken-language skills, including knowledge of the meaning of many spoken words." We know, however, that due to differences within families, languages, and social and economic environments, some children come to school with deficits in spoken-word knowledge. So to head off reading difficulties caused by a lack of language comprehension, we have to build language knowledge of all types, especially background knowledge, at all ages.

It's well-known that background knowledge is essential for reading comprehension (Coppola, 2014; Hattan, 2019; O'Reilly et al., 2019). This makes sense because to construct a mental model of what you are reading, it helps if you know something about the topic. This knowing can consist of specific information, general information, or both. Regardless, the more you know, the easier it is for you to read about it, understand it, and retain the text's information (Neuman et al., 2014). Professor Daniel Willingham (Sedita, 2018) puts it this way:

> Whether or not readers understand a text depends far more on how much background knowledge and vocabulary they have relating to the topic than on how much they've practiced comprehension skills. That's because writers leave out a lot of information that they assume readers will know . . . if readers can't supply the missing information, they will have a hard time making sense of the text. (para. 3)

Because background is crucial to text comprehension, many of the upcoming practices use classroom discussion, thematic teaching, a wide variety of books, vocabulary instruction (direct and explicit, as well as exploratory), and the use of high and low tech, all of which can be employed directly by teachers to help students in grades preK to third grade build background and topical knowledge.

Practices to Build and Strengthen Language Comprehension

SLIDESHOW

We all know the power of YouTube videos. In a matter of minutes, one clip can convey a lot of information. But my favorite activity for quickly communicating background and topical knowledge is a modern-day slideshow.

In the ancient days of my youth, slideshows were all about hardware. There were real slides (translucent film fitted inside a frame), a hard plastic carousel that stored them, and a slide projector that beamed light through the slides and onto a screen. Today's slideshows, however, are software-based, made from digital images culled from the internet and pasted into a slideshow app. Unlike video clips, slideshows have no animation or narration, meaning you can create space for contemplation, letting students ponder a particular slide, asking questions about it, and soliciting comments.

Set Up

To create a slideshow, you need an app like PowerPoint or Keynote, one that has a slideshow function. You also need a way to get the images into the eyeballs of kids. This could be a projector and screen, a smartboard, or even a laptop computer that kids can huddle around. Finally, you need a strong sense of what you want to teach. Examples include a science unit on erosion, a reading genre like fairy tales, or the setting for a story like *Nuts to You* (a power line cutting through oak and pine forests), *One Crazy Summer* (summer of 1968 in the city of Oakland, California), or *Owl Moon* (the woods on a cold, winter night under a full moon).

Once you have decided on what you want to teach, do a Google Image query and start sifting through pictures. Choose engaging ones that also tie into the words and concepts you will touch upon in your upcoming story, theme, or unit. The trick is to pick information-rich photographs that both pique the interest of kids and provide talking points for vocabulary and background knowledge. Next, import the pictures into your slideshow app and make some brief notes (mental or written) about the information you want to impart as you show each picture. Now, you're ready to go.

Modeling

It's always a good idea to model the behaviors you want your students to exhibit, so first model how to notice things on each slide. Using direct and explicit language, explain to the children what they are seeing in each picture and give definitions for vocabulary words. Here's an example: "The girl is wearing a kimono. A Japanese kimono is a traditional kind of clothing. In Japan, people wear kimonos for special occasions." Build in appropriately sophisticated language whenever possible and intersperse the noticing with questions such as "What do you notice in this picture?" and "What do you think this picture is showing us?"

The slideshow in Figure 4.1 could be used to build knowledge prior to reading books that reference Japan, such as *Wabi Sabi* by Mark Reibstein or *Grandfather's Journey* and *Kamishibai Man* by Japanese American author and illustrator Allen Say. Under each photo, I've included examples of what I might say to students as I show each slide. These comments are not part of the slides, and I don't show text to students. No matter the content, the big picture goal is to *orally* build language comprehension through showing pictures and verbally giving information.

Slideshows can be as long or as short as you want them to be. However, if you make them too short, they won't give enough information, and if you make them too long, you'll eat up too much

Figure 4.1

Slideshow for Building Background About Japan

"A girl wearing a kimono, a type of traditional clothing."

"A tori is a wooden gate that is often the entrance to a holy place. It is typically red."

"A bento box gives food for lunch. It is packed at home or made in a restaurant."

"A shopping district in a big city."

"A train operator. She runs a train that runs through a big city."

"Shoppers in a Japanese market. The flag with the circle is the national flag."

"Traditional Japanese architecture."

"A woman doing a Japanese dance to celebrate the blooming of cherry trees."

"Children often dress up when they visit shrines and sacred places."

Images (from top left to bottom right): iStock.com/Shoko Shimabukuro; iStock.com/olli0815; iStock.com/Ryzhkov; iStock.com/ke; iStock.com/coward_lion; iStock.com/Page Light Studios; iStock.com/Tanarch; iStock.com/Kirkikis; iStock.com/THEPALMER

time and your students may lose interest. Keep in mind the age and attention span of the children you teach. A show of 12 to 20 photos is a length to aim for, and total time for the activity is less than 15 minutes.

When to Use

I recommend showing a slideshow prior to reading a historical novel or any book with a setting unfamiliar to many students. Earlier, I mentioned *Nuts to You*, a fun book about the adventures of Jed, Chai, and TsTs, three squirrels who are the very best of friends. Before reading this book aloud to second or third graders, it would be a cinch to create and present a slideshow featuring red squirrels, gray squirrels, acorns and oak trees, pinecones and evergreens, animals that live alongside squirrels (including predators), and a high-voltage power line strung between tall metal pylons, the kind that plays a prominent role in the story. Not only would these pictures help students develop important background and topical knowledge, but they would also reinforce the book's regularly occurring line drawings.

The ultimate goal of a slideshow is to add words and associated meaning to a child's mental lexicon. Then, when it comes time to read, this knowledge is available to the reader. If a picture is worth a thousand words, then a slideshow with a dozen or more pictures really adds up!

Teaching Tip

Some photos generate more discussion and/or questions than others. If you notice that one of your slides is not engaging students or fostering discussion, take note of it so you can replace it with another picture at a later time. Also, team up with two or three other teachers, map out and list slideshows that would be useful in your grade level, and then divvy up the job of finding pictures and creating shows. If everyone swaps slideshows, you can create and store 10 or 12 of them without too much effort.

GOOGLE EXPEDITIONS

Personally, I am concerned about the amount of time kids spend in front of screens. And I'm often a late adopter when it comes to technology (the latest and supposedly greatest iPhone doesn't impress me). Still, I have to give a shout out to Google Expeditions, a virtual reality experience that can give students a blast of background and topical knowledge in a highly engaging way.

Google Expeditions is an immersive education app that allows anyone to explore the world through over 1,000 virtual-reality tours. Using the Expeditions app and smartphone-based viewers, students can swim with sharks, visit outer space, and hike among Aztec ruins, all without ever leaving the classroom or living room. Like a slideshow, an Expedition provides a digital "field trip" that builds and strengthens background before, during, and/or after reading a book or unit of study. So before tackling an earth science unit on erosion or reading *Grand Canyon* by Jason Chin, lead your students on an expedition to the Grand Canyon.

Set Up

To travel on an Expedition, you'll need the app on a Wi-Fi connected iPad, Chromebook, or other tablet-like device. You'll also need virtual-reality (VR) viewers for each student (other options are explored in a minute). Typically, a purchased Expeditions kit includes these items:

- A tablet preinstalled with the Expeditions app
- Smartphones preinstalled with the Expeditions app
- VR viewers (that hold the phones)
- A router that allows Expeditions to run over its own local Wi-Fi network
- A storage case with chargers

If your district has money for a kit like this, great. But if you are looking for a less expensive alternative, you can use an existing tablet for the teacher and cardboard viewers built from . . . wait for it . . . Google Cardboard . . . a low-cost, cardboard template (see Figure 4.2). Some schools are running BYOD (bring your own device) classrooms, which could cut the number of phones you need to purchase in half or more. But a virtual reality viewer isn't required. Another option is to forgo the 3D headsets and have students use a tablet for viewing, moving it up and down to look at the virtual environment around them. This is not as immersive or engaging, but it's still useful as a building background and topic knowledge tool. Also, the 360-degree videos can by shared by two students on one compatible device.

Figure 4.2

Smartphone With Google Cardboard Viewer for Google Expeditions

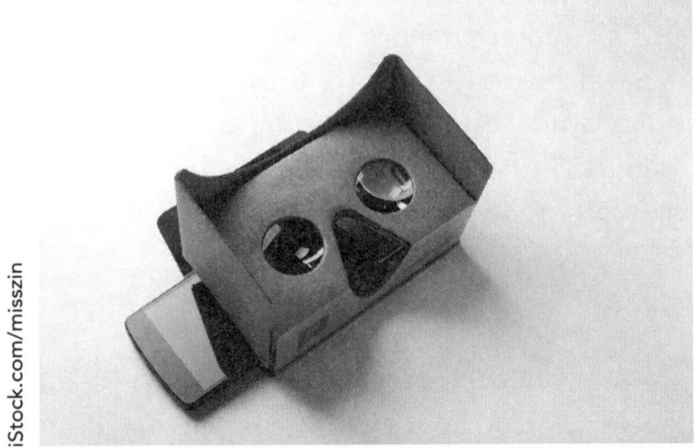

iStock.com/misszin

iStock.com/izusek

Modeling

Always preview the Expedition you want to take your students on—some are better than others. Each journey is made of scenes that combine 3D images and 360-degree panoramas gathered by Google Earth. The content also includes visual information provided by partners such as PBS, Houghton Mifflin Harcourt, and the American Museum of Natural History. There are literally hundreds of Expeditions to choose from, so you may want to get the Expeditions spreadsheet, peruse the options, and then gather with a number of tech-minded teacher friends over the summer to preview ones that supplement the social studies, science, or reading content you will be teaching.

Using the Expeditions app, you become the Guide. Meanwhile, your students use their viewers and become the Explorers. Looking up, they see objects in the sky. Looking around, they see scenery, from the halls inside the Taj Mahal to a panorama of the Rocky Mountains. During an Expedition, you control the content your students see on their devices. Best of all, by touching an image on your iPad or tablet, you can direct your students to look at a specific part of the scene that is supplemented with read-aloud information, such as fun facts, leveled questions, and additional pictures that provide points of interest. And if you are knowledgeable about the topic, you can bring your own comments and facts to the tour.

When to Use

The amount of time children spend looking at screens is a real concern, especially for younger children, so my suggestion is use this technology with students seven years old and up and then limit each expedition to 5 to 10 minutes. Also, if students are using headset viewers, it's best to have them sit, as this will keep them from losing their balance or bumping into a desk or a friend.

The downsides to Google Expeditions are cost, learning and managing technology, and controlling the chaos as two dozen or more learners interact with it. But if you can overcome these challenges, Google Expeditions is an amazing tool that brings the world to children who have little opportunity to travel beyond their own homes and schools.

CURIOSITY CORNER

An old-school, low-tech alternate to a slideshow or Google Expeditions is a Curiosity Corner (see Figure 4.3). It builds many types of knowledge, sets the stage for learning, promotes noticing details and asking questions, and engages learners of all ages, from preK kids to third graders. Like a slideshow, a Curiosity Corner presents objects in ways that promote noticing, thinking, talking, and even writing. But unlike the virtual objects of a slideshow or Google Expeditions, everything in a Curiosity Corner is real. Imagine that! Because objects in the Corner are real, they promote hands-on learning, a tried-and-true way to engage learners. And if you're a person who loves the physicality of objects and the feelings they evoke, then this is a classroom practice for you.

Set Up

Start by finding a place in your classroom large enough for a small table and two chairs. To make it a cozy Curiosity Corner, light it

Figure 4.3

Curiosity Corner Introducing the Book *A Seed Is Sleepy*

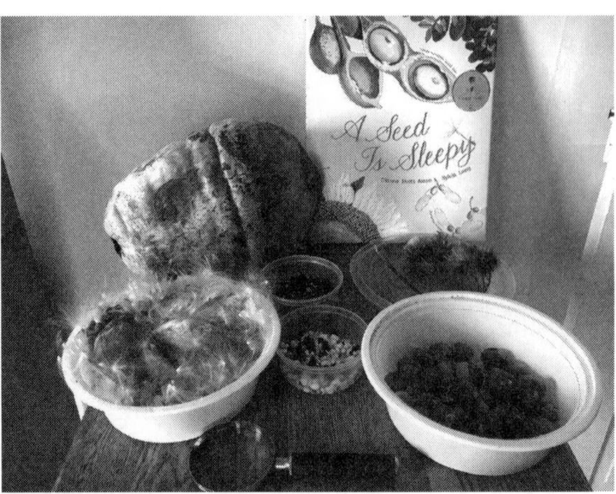

with a floor lamp and include some type of rug. If you are pressed for space, clear out part of a bookshelf (see Figure 4.4). If you have space and like alliteration, go for a Curiosity Cave, Club House, or Cubby formed inside a small tent, closet, or study carrel.

Once you've decided on a Corner, Cave, or Cubby, gather objects that spark discussion, questions, and exploration of the theme, unit, or story you will be teaching. Also, consider adding a few tools and materials, such as

- A magnifying glass
- Pencils, colored pencils, and slips of paper for recreating (illustrating) objects that are interesting
- For older students, slips of paper or index cards for writing, with sentence starters like these:
    - I saw . . .
    - I noticed . . .
    - I think . . .
    - I know . . .
    - I wonder . . .

Figure 4.4

Curiosity Shelf Introducing a Unit on Animal Homes

- One or two picture books that relate to the theme, unit, or topic
- An electronic tablet that children can use to take pictures and/or record audio (consider the SeeSaw app)

Modeling

To introduce your first Curiosity Corner, carve 20 minutes from your reading block on the day you start a new story or theme. You will need this time to go over the rules of how children use the Corner. After you've introduced your first one, you'll need less time to introduce subsequent Corners.

Start by having the kids gather round the Corner "fishbowl" style. Then, explain when the Corner will be open, model the correct handling of the objects, and describe any technology that you've included to capture thoughts and questions. This technology can range from a paper "thought journal" that sits on the table or index cards that are turned in for posting on a board to electronic tablets that can be used to snap photos and record spoken questions. Digital archiving is made easy through apps like SeeSaw. Personally, I like to include an old-school magnifying glass.

When to Use

Kids can visit the Curiosity Corner as part of the *I Can List* during guided-reading time (see Chapter 7), before classes officially start, or during homeroom time. To make learning richer and more permanent, include some time to debrief with the class on the Corner, engaging students in discussion about what was observed, what questions were asked, and what background knowledge kids have on the objects. If questions and thoughts were captured via index cards or journals, take some time to read and discuss those entries. Also, ponder (and possibly answer) the questions. The same holds true for thoughts and questions recorded via SeeSaw or a digital camera or voice recording device. Finally, encourage the children to bring in an object that would complement the Corner.

SEE, THINK, WONDER

See, Think, Wonder comes from Harvard University's Project Zero, which promotes visual thinking. I was introduced to it while working with the wonderful teachers of Nicholas County, West Virginia, where many of them enthusiastically endorsed the activity, saying it did wonders (pun intended) for building background, topical, and vocabulary knowledge; setting the stage for reading; and helping students develop the ability to ask and answer questions (metacognition). For preK and kindergarten children, it's an activity that builds oral language. For older students, it functions as both an activity and a reader-used strategy.

Set Up

As with a slideshow, you will need a strong sense of what you want to build background knowledge on. It could be a science theme like seeds and plants, a reading genre like biography, or a story setting like Mrs. Wade's bookstore in *Destiny's Gift*. Unlike with a whole slideshow, you'll only need one picture. It could be scanned from your text, copied from an internet source, or pulled from an existing slideshow. Or keep it super simple by opening up a book and sharing a big, bright picture with students gathered at your feet on the carpet. Regardless of the medium, pick your picture carefully. You'll want it to be closely aligned to your story or theme, as well as richly detailed enough to produce lots of language through discussion and questioning.

Modeling

To teach it, begin with a think-aloud. Show the picture to your students and tell them what you see. Be as concrete as possible and use "I see . . ." statements. Next, move to "I think . . ." statements. Finally, model "I wonder . . ." statements.

Figure 4.6 gives an example of teacher language that flows from the photo in Figure 4.5. This image could be used to kick off any first-grade science unit on the structure of plants. It's also appropriate for introducing a story like *A Seed Is Sleepy* by Sylvia Long or *Up in the Garden, Down in the Dirt* by Kate Messner.

Guided Practice

Once you have modeled the strategy, move to guided practice with the whole group. Show an appropriate picture, give your students 10 seconds to notice things in the picture (like a detective looking carefully for clues), and then randomly call on individuals to tell you **one thing** they see. Don't let them tell you everything they see, as some will try to do. Teach them to share one seen-item at a time.

After you have modeled this strategy with the students and then guided them through it as a whole group, put them into groups of two, three, or four and have them try it for themselves. I'd suggest

Figure 4.5

A *See, Think, Wonder* Image for Seeds

iStock.com/traveler1116

Figure 4.6

Possible *See, Think, Wonder* Language

I see . . .

Sand

Green water

Blue sky

The ocean

Small waves

A plant

A shadow

I think . . .

. . . the thing on the beach is a coconut.

. . . the plant growing from the seed is a coconut palm tree.

. . . there are roots growing out of the coconut.

. . . the beach is a tropical beach. That means it is warm there.

I wonder . . .

. . . if there are different kinds of coconut seeds.

. . . if the beach is part of an island.

. . . if it is Hawaii.

. . . if the coconut tree will grow in the sand.

. . . how the coconut got on the beach.

you just allow them to *talk* at first, rather than writing it down in three columns or completing some type of worksheet. Writing can come in later, when older students have a much firmer grip on using the strategy (see Figure 4.7). Also, writing everything down can be laborious for some students, while talking can be enjoyable, so why not give kids time to talk via an educational activity? Meander among the groups and listen to the talk, nudge into line any groups or individuals that are straying from the topic, and positively reinforce those groups and individuals who are exhibiting behaviors that are appropriate to the task. Later, spend a few minutes back in the whole group for a debriefing session. You can point out comments that were especially pertinent and provide praise for those who expended excellent effort.

Figure 4.7

A *See, Think, Wonder* Captured in Writing

When to Use It

See, Think, Wonder is both an activity and a strategy. As an activity, it builds language comprehension. Promoting *See, Think, Wonder* as something students do prior to independent reading turns it into a strategy that sets the stage for learning, activates prior knowledge, and generates questions that increase engagement. For example, this might take place in a guided-reading group; when you hand out books, talk about the title and then say, "Do a picture walk through this book and ask yourself, 'What do I see, what do I think, what do I wonder?'" Likewise, explicitly show a whole group how to use it prior to reading science or social studies text. Say things like, "Good readers take the time to see, think, and wonder about the pictures, maps, and diagrams in the books they read. We are practicing this strategy so that you can use it independently. When you use this strategy, you become a reader who understands more."

●●● FOR FURTHER STUDY

To learn about other practical and effective comprehension strategies, follow the QR code and visit the Visible Thinking website.

www.visiblethinkingpz.org/VisibleThinking_html_files/VisibleThinking1.html

Vocabulary Instruction That Builds Background Knowledge

Vocabulary knowledge is an important component of language comprehension, which is central to reading comprehension. Simply put, it helps to understand the meaning of most words in the sentences you are reading. This understanding is necessary for a child (or adult) to comprehend the meaning of any given sentence, paragraph, or story (Nation, 2008).

Teaching vocabulary is important to beginning readers because reading comprehension improves when vocabulary instruction is present (Adlof et al., 2011; Graves & Watts-Taffe, 2002). Vocabulary instruction and acquisition are especially important for students who may be at risk of reading difficulties due to social disadvantages. Why? When compared to the general school population, at-risk students are less likely to hear a wide variety of words used in their homes and more likely to have smaller vocabularies and read fewer words in context (Graves & Watts-Taffe, 2002; Hart & Risely, 1995). So for some children, the words you teach in your classroom may be a significant portion of the total number of words learned in any given year.

Word knowledge is complexly linked with real-world experiences and statistically intertwined with other words in text settings (Seidenberg, 2017). This means that effective vocabulary instruction in the classroom is not a simple matter of teaching a word and its definition, like a dictionary entry. If students are to truly master the definitions and usage of a new word, they need multiple exposures to it in a variety of instructional and text settings. Thus, effective vocabulary instruction incorporates synonyms, antonyms, grammatical knowledge, and pragmatic knowledge or the circumstances in which words are used (Shanahan, 2017a), as well as a variety of sentences that present the word in different ways. It is difficult to give the definitive number of repetitions it takes for a child to learn a word; estimates in the literature range from a low of one to four to a high of 7 to 15 (Kilpatrick, 2015; Webb, 2007). But repetition is not enough. Effective vocabulary instruction gives students opportunities to understand how their target vocabulary word relates to other words. This improves the "Lexile quality" or nuances of understanding of each word they encounter (Castle et al., 2018).

FIVE-DAY VOCABULARY CARD ROUTINE

A *Five-Day Vocabulary Card* routine incorporates a number of instructional best practices, including giving multiple opportunities to (1) see, say, and use words in multiple ways; (2) use language and acquire background and topical knowledge around words, and (3) build relationships and associations between other words that are in addition to the 6 to 10 words typically taught with a primary grade story.

Ways to help children process meaning and build associations include calling attention to the morphemes of words (see Chapter 6), pointing out other words that use those same morphemes, and bringing in associated synonyms and antonyms. Additionally, the card method engages students through multiple modalities that include writing, physically manipulating cards, and oral storytelling. Finally, each vocabulary session takes little more than 10 minutes a day, and additional learning can take place through activities done during independent work time.

Day 1: Direct and Explicit Instruction, Definitions, and a Slideshow

To begin, you'll need a zip-top bag for each student with the student's name written on it with a permanent marker and 6 to 10 carefully chosen words written on a cardstock sheet. By "carefully chosen," I mean don't simply give the list from your basal reading program. One well-known way to choose vocabulary words is to use the three-tiered model, made famous by. In the three-tiered model, teachers avoid words that are too familiar (Tier 1) and too esoteric (Tier 3), going with words that can be found across content areas and have a high degree of academic usefulness (Tier 2).

Another word selection model to use is based on the following: (1) how a word is distributed across texts, (2) the likelihood the word is already known by students in various grade levels, (3) the ease with which the word can be explained at any given grade level, and (4) how many other words are morphologically related to the word. Regarding this model, I refer you to the work of Elfrieda Heibert referenced in the For Further Study box at the end of this section.

No matter how you ultimately choose your words, you will need a kid-friendly definition for each word (no more than six words long). Regarding the definitions, I prefer to have them written on the back of the card. This allows students who need support to simply flip the card over and review the basic definition. If your students are not capable of writing down definitions or if writing takes too long, then print the definitions on the back via two-sided printing.

One final note: You can also provide two or three pictures of each word gathered into a slideshow (see the Slideshow section). This takes time and effort, but it provides a burst of context and meaning for each word that can be invaluable to young learners.

Figure 4.8 shows an example of eight words from a second-grade Reading Streets' story, "Cowboys." On the flip side of the word cards are kid-friendly definitions given in six words or fewer.

Figure 4.8

Vocabulary Word Cards and Definitions

cowboy	Man on horseback who tends cattle
herd	Group of large animals
campfire	Small fire at a campsite
cattle	Cows, bulls, calves

gallop	Run, like a fast horse
trail	Narrow, winding dirt path
bellow	Loud, low-pitched calling or yelling
climate	Types of weather in an area

After students cut out their eight cards, present the first word and give its definition using this direct and explicit instruction routine:

Teacher: Here's a new word: _____. Say it.

Students: [They say the word.]

Teacher: "_____" means _____. [Teacher provides kid-friendly definition that is six words or fewer.] What does _____ mean?

Students: [They orally repeat the definition.]

Teacher: [Shows slides from the vocabulary slideshow, quickly describing each picture using the vocabulary word and its definition]

[Gives kid-friendly definition (six-word maximum) once more, and students write it on the back of card.]

Using one of the "Cowboys" story words mentioned in Figure 4.8, the routine looks like this:

Teacher: Here's a new word: *cattle.* Say it.

Students: Cattle!

Teacher: Cattle are cows, bulls, or calves. What are *cattle*?

Students: Cows, bulls, or calves.

Teacher: Here are three pictures of cattle. The first is dairy cows. This one shows cows and bulls raised for beef, which is cow meat. And this picture shows baby cows, or calves. They are also called cattle.

Write this definition on the back of your card: cows, bulls, calves.

The direct and explicit routine is short, sweet, and powerful. Remember: Keep your pace of instruction brisk. Once you get good at remembering the script, you'll be able to effectively introduce 8 to 10 new words in 12 to 15 minutes.

Video example of direct and explicit vocabulary instruction: https://www.youtube.com/watch?v=mINITRTxamA

At the end of the direct instruction, slideshow, and definition writing, the vocabulary cards go into the ziplock bag with the student's name on it. Then, the bag is placed into the student's reading folder, a common bin, or in some other easily accessible place.

Day 2: Alphabetical Order and Look, Touch, Say

To begin, have the students put their words in **alphabetical order**. Some students need practice in alphabetizing—a skill that involves memory, sequence, organization—and putting the cards in order gives them the chance to practice all these skills in a kinesthetic, non-pencil-and-paper way. Also, having everyone's words in order makes it easier to monitor student responses during subsequent activities.

Next, do three or four minutes of *Look, Touch, Say* (more on this Chapter 6). This simple routine allows children to practice reading the words, take notice of patterns, and have additional exposures to the meaning of the word. At its most basic, the routine is this:

Teacher: Look for the word *cattle*. Touch it.

Students: [They look for the word and touch it. Teacher meanders, waiting until all children have found the word and are touching it. Teacher guides students that need guidance.]

Teacher: Say it.

Students: Cattle!

Teacher: [Repeat the routine for other words.]

At a more advanced level, the routine involves meaning, which would sound something like this:

Teacher: Look for the word that means a group of large animals. Touch it.

Students: [Students touch *herd*. Teacher meanders, waiting until all children have found the word and are touching it. Teacher guides students that need guidance.]

Teacher: Say it.

Students: Herd!

Teacher: Look for the word that means a narrow, winding dirt path. Touch it.

Students: [Students touch *trail*. Teacher meanders, waiting until all children have found the word and are touching it. Teacher guides students who need guidance.]

Teacher: Say it.

Students: Trail!

Day 3: Pick Up the Word; *Inflectional Endings; Closed-Word Sorts*

Pick Up the Word is a simple two-minute routine in which children pick up a single word card at a time, keeping each card in their hand until only one is left in the pile. In the end, everyone should have the same word on their table or desk. Once again, you may want to start by having the students put their cards in ABC order.

Like *Look, Touch, Say, Pick Up the Word* can be used to draw attention to the correct letter sequence of the word as well as word meanings. Here's an example of language using the eight words from "Cowboys." The first two commands are for word recognition; the last five give practice in word definitions.

Teacher: Pick up the word *bellow.*

Teacher: Pick up the word *trail.*

Teacher: Pick up the word that means a man who herds cows. [Wait] What is the word, everyone?

Students: Cowboy!

Teacher: Pick up the word that means a fire at camp. [Wait] What is the word, everyone?

Students: Campfire!

Teacher: Pick up the word that means a large group of animals [*herd*].

Teacher: Pick up the word that means to run fast like a horse [*gallop*].

Teacher: Pick up the word that means cows, bulls, or calves [*cattle*].

Teacher: What word is left, everyone?

Students: Climate!

By Day 3, you can begin to broaden vocabulary study beyond the original word list with **inflectional endings**. Do this by bringing in morphemes, specifically the use of inflectional endings (such as *-ing, -ed, -s,-es, -y)* that change a base word's tense, number, or grammatical category. For example, first ask students to pick up all the verbs. This instantly provides a point of discussion and instruction because *gallop, bellow, trail,* and *herd* all function as both a noun and a verb. Informing students that words often have multiple meanings and then regularly teaching those multiple meanings is an important part of rich vocabulary instruction (Heibert et al., 2018). Once the verb is discussed and contrasted with the noun, ask students to orally create tense versions of the target words, such as *gallop/galloping/galloped* and *trail/trailing/trailed*, or noun plurals, such as *cowboys, herds, trails,* and so on. You can spend time on spelling conventions if you want (when to drop a silent *e*, when to double a consonant, etc.). In all cases, write out words so students have a visual representation.

After doing *Pick Up the Word*, segue into a **closed-word sort**. Word sorts help students recognize linguistic or semantic relationships among words. In a word sort activity, no paper or pencil is used. Kids read, think, and then physically move cards to show relationships for any given category, such as verbs and nouns or spelling patterns.

In a closed sort, children categorize their words in defined, often binary ways. Examples of this are a sort for compound words (words are either a compound word or not) and a sort for syllables (words have a definite number of syllables). Here is an example of teacher talk for a closed-compound word sort using the "Cowboys" words from Figure 4.8:

Teacher: You are going to sort your words into two piles. How many piles, everyone?

Students: Two!

Teacher: One pile is for words that are compound words. What's the first pile, everyone?

Students: Compound words.

Teacher: The second pile is for words that are not compound words. Two piles: compound words and not compound words. Begin.

Students: [Students sort their words into two piles. Pile #1: *cowboy, campfire*; Pile #2: *herd, trail, gallop, bellow, cattle, climate*]

Teacher: Find your elbow buddy. Number-one buddy, read your compound words. Number-two buddy, read the words that are not compound words.

Students: [Students pair up and read their words to each other.]

Day 4: Open and "Clopen" Sorts; Introducing Synonyms

Open sorts foster relational and associative thinking. In an open sort, students create their own semantic constructions. To begin an open sort, say to your class, "I want you to think about the meaning of your words and how they relate to each other. Then, sort your words into two, three, or four groups. When you are done, you will tell me or a partner why you sorted your words into your particular piles."

Because you have taught your students how to perform closed sorts, some will automatically default to this way of thinking for their open sort. For example, some children might sort *cowboy* and *campfire* together because they are both compound words or start with the letter *c*. To help students sort words in ways that foster relational thinking, try narrowing the openness of the sort. I call this a "clopen" sort (see Figure 4.9).

Somewhat closed and somewhat open, a **clopen sort** moves students toward thinking about the relationships between word meanings. It provides more support than an open request but is less dictatorial than a closed one. For example, if I were to say, "Sort your words into two piles—one for words that have to do with cowboys and one for words that have to do with cattle," students could sort *gallop* into the cowboy pile (a cowboy's horse gallops) or into the cattle pile (the cows gallop to get away). The same holds true for *herd* because one child might think of a cowboy managing a herd while another might think of cattle moving in a herd.

At this point, work in synonyms to some of the original vocabulary words. You can **introduce synonyms** through oral discussion only, by writing them on the board and discussing them, by introducing additional cards, or through some combination. Like the study of multiple-meaning words and inflectional endings, the regular study of synonyms leads to richer vocabulary instruction, which in turn can lead to more fluent reading and greater reading comprehension (Heibert, 2020). No matter how you present the words, first directly and explicitly define the synonyms. Also, ask your students into what category the word would fall. For example, if you introduce the words *path* and *track* as synonyms for *trail*, ask your students, "Would you sort these words into the 'cowboy' category or the 'cattle' category?" and then "Why would did you put them in the ____ category?"

Finally, ask your students to come up with additional words that fall into the clopen categories. With the examples *cowboy* and

Figure 4.9

Open- and Clopen-Word Sorts

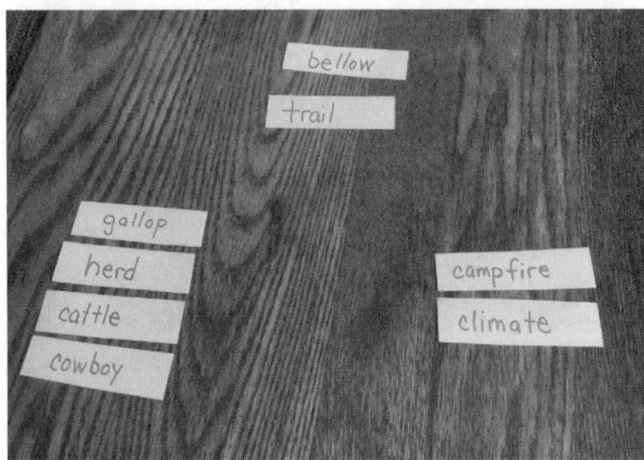

cattle, ask, "What words could you add to the cowboy pile?" "What words could you add to the cattle pile?" and most importantly, "Why would you add these/those words to the category?" Students might come up with words that are not synonyms but are still topically related. For example, a student might say, "Hats" for the cowboys category. Always ask, "Why did you put ____ in this category?" In this case, the student might say, "Because cowboys wear those big hats." Every student answer is an opportunity to build language and vocabulary; in this case, add a little more by saying something like, "Those hats are called Stetsons. Sometimes, they are called 10-gallon hats. Those hats are related to the Mexican sombrero. Say the words with me, everyone—*Stetson, 10-gallon, sombrero*." Talk about rich vocabulary instruction!

Day 5: Bull's-Eye Brainstorming; *Make a* Six-Word Story

Bull's-Eye Brainstorming is a whole-class exercise in generating words strongly or weakly related to a target word, which is presented in the middle of three concentric circles. This activity directly ties to synonym study, the study of words with multiple meanings, and even antonyms.

First, write the target word in the center of the concentric circles. Then, let the brainstorming begin. Start with a prompt, something like, "What words relate to this word?" "What other words do you think of when you see this word?" and "What words are like this word?" Better yet, provide a model first: "When I think of *gallop*, I think of horses trotting. So I am going to write down *trot*. But I am going to place it out here on the second ring because trot is not vigorous like a gallop. It's slower and gentler."

As students come up with words, graph each word onto (or within) a circle and explain why you are placing it close to or far away from the target word. The stronger the positive relationship to the target word (the more it is like a synonym), the closer to the bull's-eye you graph it. Conversely, the weaker the relationship (the more it is like an antonym), the farther out it goes. Figure 4.10 shows a *Bull's-Eye Brainstorm* for the word *gallop*. You may disagree with how I've placed some of the words, and this is fine. Use your professional judgement on how you want to present and discuss words that are increasingly unrelated to the target word.

A *Six-Word Story* is students picking six of their vocabulary words and stringing them together to tell a coherent story. Many kids will want to use all their words. I say, let them! To keep your

Figure 4.10

Bull's-Eye Brainstorming

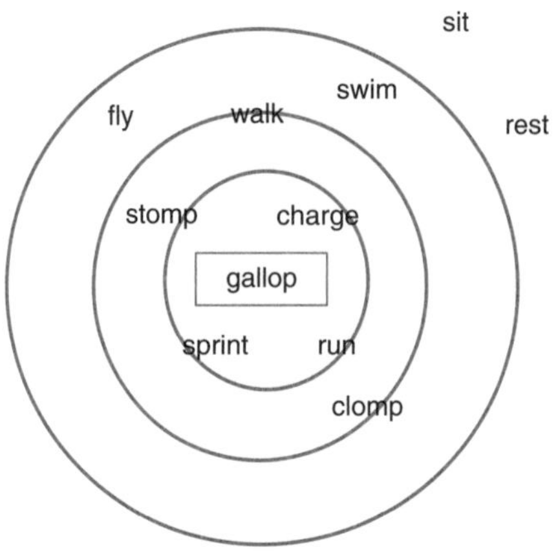

instruction focused on the original words but also allow for enrichment and the building of vocabulary through word families, allow your students to use inflectional endings. You can also let them bring in synonyms and antonyms. For example, here is a story that uses unaltered words, base words with inflectional endings, and synonyms and antonyms:

> It was a dark and quiet night. A group of *cowboys* were sitting next to a *campfire*, *whispering* ghost stories to each other. Then one of them said, "Listen!" They could hear *bellowing* in the distance. The bellowing grew louder. It was coming from a *trail* on their right. Suddenly, a *herd* of frightened *cattle galloped* down the *path* and into the clearing. But it wasn't the cattle bellowing. It was a giant ogre, chasing the *cows* and *yelling* at the top of his lungs!

If you want, you can have your students write their stories as a culminating activity. But I find it is more efficient (and fun) to simply have kids create a story in their head, repeat it twice under their breath (to rehearse it and practice its flow), and then orally share it with a partner. Volunteers can then share with the class or draw numbers for random sharing.

Combining Cards; Using the Card Routine Independently

Consider putting the words from the following week's story on different-colored paper. On Days 1 through 4, introduce and work with only these new words. Then on Day 5, ask your students to combine all 16 (or however many they have) and do any activity of your choice, such as *Pick Up the Word*; *Look, Touch, Say*; open or closed sorts, and a 10-word or even 16-word story! Also, after your guided-reading groups are up and running and you have thoroughly taught the vocabulary card routines, allow students to buddy up and practice their words during independent work time. All you have to do is put "study vocabulary words" on your *I Can List* and provide them with a list of the activities they can do (see Figure 4.11).

Figure 4.11

Vocabulary Activities List

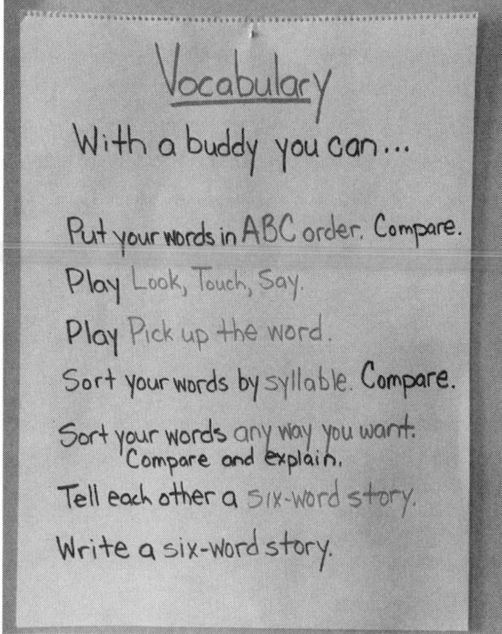

IMPORTANT POINT

In addition to direct teaching, vocabulary acquisition occurs naturally as children actively process the words they hear (listening), say (speaking), and see (reading). In reading, most vocabulary is gained during periods of extended reading in connected text (Graves & Watts-Taffe, 2002). Typically, this interaction with vocabulary words occurs during independent and guided-reading time. However, most basal reading programs don't include long periods of time for students to read from a variety of books on their instructional and independent reading levels, and some families don't promote reading at home. Therefore, programming more guided reading and independent reading routines into all primary grades gives students greater opportunities to build vocabulary.

To take vocabulary instruction to an even higher level, program topically-related text. This means bring stories and articles into guided reading (and independent reading) that are thematically related. Using thematic text increases the chance that a student will encounter an unknown word multiple times, and as we learned in Chapter 3, repetition and distributed practice help make learning perfect and permanent. For example, a week of reading multiple guided-reading books that all relate to a common topic like gardens can increase by 50 percent the number of words (like *vine*, *harvest*, and *flower*) a student encounters three or more times (Heibert, 2020).

••• FOR FURTHER STUDY

https://www.prel.org/wp-content/uploads/2014/06/vocabulary_lo_res.pdf

- "Engaging Vocabulary Units: A Flexible Instructional Model" by Patrick Manyak and Michelle Latka in *The Reading Teacher*, August 2019. This article directly connects primary grade readers with vocabulary instruction, thematic teaching, explicit instruction, read-alouds, and other topics mentioned in this book.
- "The Core Vocabulary: The Foundations of Proficient Comprehension" by Elfrieda Hiebert in *The Reading Teacher*, February 2020. This article condenses and clarifies ideas present in a 2018 study (*Reading Research Quarterly*) and points the way to a new and possibly more effective way of choosing vocabulary words (other than Beck et al.'s three-tier model).
- *Teaching Vocabulary Explicitly* by Susan Hanson and Jennifer F. M. Padua, 2011. A short but informative book, it is available as a free PDF from Pacific Resources for Education and Learning.
- *Bringing Words to Life, Second Edition: Robust Vocabulary Instruction* by Isabel L. Beck, Margaret G. McKeown, and Linda Kucan, 2013. Written by

renowned vocabulary researchers Beck and McKeown, in collaboration with fellow University of Pittsburgh professor Linda Kucan, this book is a great read for understanding vocabulary theory. Combining it with the following book gives a balance of theoretical understanding and practical classroom activities and strategies.

- *Creating Robust Vocabulary: Frequently Asked Questions and Extended Examples* by Isabel L. Beck, Margaret G. McKeown, and Linda Kucan, 2008.

Bringing It All Together: The Interactive Read-Aloud

Reading out loud to children is a simple pleasure. Kids universally love listening to a good story or a fascinating set of facts. Adults enjoy reading out loud, too, channeling their inner actor with dramatic monologues and wacky character voices. And there are many educationally valid reasons to read aloud: promoting reading, supporting young writers, celebrating the written word, and building a classroom literacy community, among others (Walther, 2019). But elevating a read-aloud to the point where it becomes a tool that helps prevent reading difficulties demands adding components to the basic practice.

In this section, we look at adding purposefully picked books, previewed routines, modeled strategies, and carefully chosen questions to the simple practice of reading out loud, effectively transforming it into the more instructionally powerful interactive read-aloud. This practice typically takes place during "shared reading time," can be done with any age student, from preK to third grade, and is essential for a number of reasons. First, it builds language comprehension, including background and vocabulary knowledge, genre understanding, and the use of metacognition strategies (such as predicting or visualizing). Also, for students who cannot read the book on their own it provides access to text and information. Conversely, it piques interest in a story that some can read independently at a later time. Finally, an interactive read-aloud not only strengthens components of reading comprehension in a general way but also provides an opportunity for teachers to model specific reading skills, such as fluent reading, rereading, and defining vocabulary from context (Walther, 2019). Let's take a look at how to set it up for classroom success.

Set Up

At the start, you will need a carefully chosen children's book, one that is engaging, of any genre, and full of rich vocabulary and concepts. You'll also need a strong sense of what language comprehension components you want to focus on and an understanding of how to teach them. Let's tackle this last element first.

A series of purposeful activities makes up a typical interactive read-aloud. These activities can include any or all of the following, done for a variety of purposes.

1. Title talk, picture walk, and/or book walk
   - Each of these is a method of previewing a book, which, in turn, sets the stage for learning and allows kids to activate prior knowledge. The activities also provide a chance to build background knowledge when children don't have it. For example, if a child doesn't know anything about glaciers, she or he will pick up information about glaciers when you discuss the book's title, *Glaciers of the Mountains*, when you read the book blurb on the back, and when other children talk about what they see in the pictures on the book's pages.
2. Teacher think-alouds given between bouts of oral reading
   - Think-alouds can focus on vocabulary meaning, as well as metacognition strategies that assist comprehension, such as making a connection, engaging in a prediction, or asking and then trying to answer a question. As with all think-alouds, directly and explicitly describe your thinking to students as you proceed through pages in the book.
3. Rich, complex, and purposeful questions posed by the teacher and explored and/or answered by the students
   - Teacher-generated questions, which are sometimes also answered, engage learners as you move through the book. They also build vocabulary, give opportunities for processing, and provide a model for asking questions while reading, an important meaning-making act that all accomplished readers engage in.
4. Summarizing the story at the end
   - Summarizing is essential to solidifying comprehension of a text. At first, you can provide summaries to your students. Then, gradually release that responsibility. There are

numerous strategies and routines for summarizing, from graphic organizers to the five-fingered *Somebody, Wanted, But, So, Then.*

5. Sharing that includes how the students related to the story
   - Sharing thoughts and feelings about a book increases motivation and engagement. It also provides yet another opportunity for students to hear, speak, and internalize English-language words.

Choosing the right book for the class is important. First and foremost, you'll want one that lends itself to whatever literacy element you are focusing on, be it genre, grammar element, or comprehension strategy. For example, *What Do You Do With a Tail Like This* is perfect for predictions (it's a fun nonfiction read, too), while *Exclamation Mark* is my favorite picture book for teaching—you guessed it—the exclamation mark. But the book you choose for an effective interactive read-aloud must also engage readers for an extended period of time. The following book selection tips help hold the attention of young students, as well as provide opportunities for building language comprehension (Burkins & Yaris, 2018; Walther, 2019). Please consider them as you choose a book for your interactive read-aloud.

Does the book have . . .

1. An engaging plot or sequence of events?
2. Rich language?
3. A unique perspective and/or original premise?
4. Diverse characters?
5. A thought-provoking theme?

Modeling

Here's an example of an interactive read-aloud with first graders using one of my children's books, *Bubbles Float, Bubbles Pop* (2011; see Figure 4.12). In this example, my three main goals are to (1) build general language comprehension through the reading of text and discussion, (2) model fluent and expressive reading, and (3) draw attention to asking and answering questions, a strategy that readers often use.

Figure 4.12

Author Presenting Book Cover

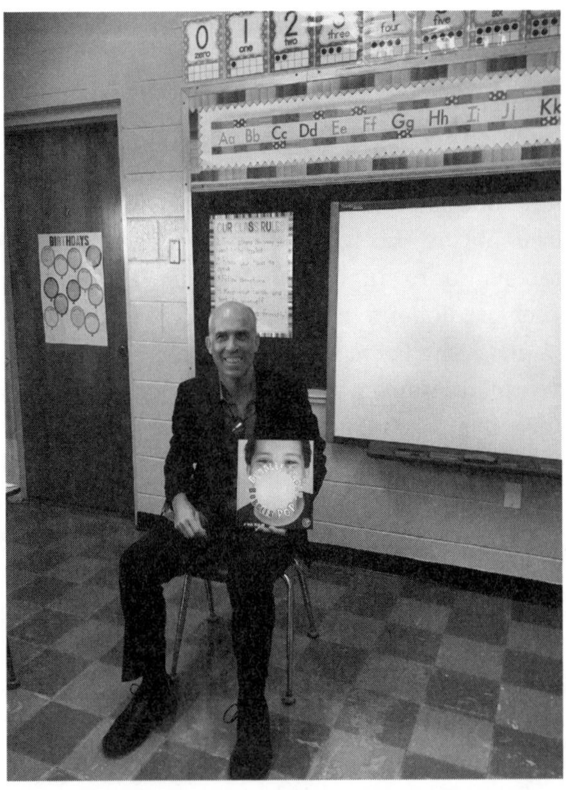

MW: Today, I am going to read an informational book to you. What kind of book am I going to read to you, everyone?

Students: Informational.

MW: An informational book gives the reader information on a subject. Look at the cover of this book. The title of this book is *Bubbles Float, Bubbles Pop*. Think: What do you think this book will be giving us information about? [I give three seconds of wait time.] Use your quiet voice to tell the person next to you your thoughts.

Students: [They give a variety of answers.]

MW: In this informational book on bubbles, you will hear lots of facts about bubbles. Think in your head: What do you know about bubbles?

Students: [They think.]

MW: Tell your elbow buddy something you know about bubbles.

Students: [They talk.]

MW: I'm wondering what this book will say about bubbles floating and popping. Listen to these questions from the back of the book. [I flip the book over and read the back.] "What makes a bubble float? Are the bubbles in your soda the same as the bubbles in your tub? What makes a bubble pop?"

Before I read, let's take a picture walk through the book and look at some pictures. [I show select pictures from the book. I comment on some of them briefly and ask questions about others, such as "What do you think this is? What do you see here?"]

When readers read a book, questions pop into their heads, questions like "Why do bubbles float?" "Why do bubbles pop?" and "I wonder if a bubble gum bubble is like a soap bubble." Your brain will be asking questions as I read this book. So if a question floats into your head, raise your hand and ask your question so that the entire class knows it!"

[I read from the book, pointing out some of the questions that the text asks and allowing children to ask questions as I read. I also draw attention to vocabulary, such as the words *sphere* and *solution*. At the end of the book, I summarize the information.]

Turn to your elbow buddy and tell him or her one thing that you learned about bubbles.

Students: [They turn and talk.]

MW: [I pull names from the popsicle-stick name jar and ask if the named student would like to share one thing he or she learned.]

●●● FOR FURTHER STUDY

Rich and complex practices like the interactive read-aloud demand rich and complex study, more than what this book can provide. Perhaps you'll want to check out one of these resources, as it might take your instruction to a higher level:

- *The Ramped-Up Read Aloud* by Maria Walther, 2017
- Interactive read-aloud books authored by Linda Hoyt
- *Reader, Come Home: The Reading Brain in a Digital World* by Maryann Wolf, 2018; Chapters 5, 6, and 7 are especially relevant to topics discussed in this chapter (and generally in this book).
- *The Fountas & Pinnell Classroom™ Interactive Read-Aloud Collection*
- "Interactive Read-Aloud Strategies—23 Lessons to Use at Home" by Erin Lynch (https://www.sadlier.com/school/ela-blog/interactive-read-aloud-strategies-23-printable-read-aloud-lessons-to-get-you-started)

Why Language Comprehension Is So Important

Because the Simple View of Reading equation is multiplicative, not additive, each variable plays a powerful role in determining the ultimate outcome or reading comprehension. To illustrate the point, let's consider an extreme scenario: a child who fluently reads every word in a sentence such as this—"The sound of fifteen hounds baying in their kennels was deafening"—but does not understand the meaning of even one word. In this example, we have a student with 100 percent word recognition (WR) but 0 percent language comprehension. In numbers, the Simple View equation then looks like this: $1 \times 0 = 0$. So although the student outwardly presents as a "perfect" reader (he fluently reads each and every word), his reading comprehension is zero, and all he is really doing is word calling, not reading.

Of course, no reader would ever demonstrate a profile as extreme as this. But consider the child who reads very accurately, with a word recognition score of .90 but due to deficits in vocabulary and background knowledge, understands text at a diminished level (say at a score of 0.45 as determined by some measure of language comprehension). After multiplying the variables, this student's reading comprehension is below 50 percent.

The Simple View of Reading helps us more fully understand just how important language comprehension is to the process of reading. It also reminds us of why it's critical to build background, topical, and vocabulary knowledge prior to teaching a story, as well as teach metacognition skills and strategies that students can use before, during, and after their reading of text.

CONNECTIONS

The following activities in Chapters 6 and 7 build vocabulary knowledge, topical and background knowledge, understanding of genre, and/or knowledge of grammar and sentence structure.

- *I'm Thinking of a Word*
- Meaning-based word ladders
- Meaning-based *Look, Touch, Say* routines
- *Kid Writing*
- Extended reading of all types, including independent reading, guided reading, and poetry reading

BUILDING PHONOLOGICAL SKILLS

CHAPTER 5

Only reading teachers have stories about phonemes. Here's one of my favorites. I was working with a team of kindergarten teachers shortly after the National Reading Panel came out with Five Big Ideas of Reading: phonemic awareness, phonics, fluency, vocabulary, and comprehension. Recognizing they weren't doing enough to teach phonology, the teachers created a phonological awareness program that taught kindergarteners to analyze and manipulate the sounds of spoken words, including syllables, onset-rimes, and phonemes. Children who failed to progress through the program at an appropriate pace were placed in an intervention group where they received regular and intensive instruction on sounds within words, letter identification, and letter–sound association. I taught some of these kindergarten intervention groups.

One day, I was helping a group of four children learn to hear the /sh/ phoneme and spell its associated digraph *sh*. First, we practiced identifying the sound in words. Then, we brainstormed words that started with the /sh/ sound. The kids came up with *shirt*, *shell*, and a few others. When they could go no further, I gave them a clue. "Look down," I said. "On your feet are two things that begin with /sh/."

"Socks!" said a little boy.

"Socks begins with the /s/ sound," I replied. "Let's find a word that starts with the /sh/ sound. Look at your feet again."

A little girl bent down her head then looked up and grinned. "Sh-flipflops!" she exclaimed.

The incident made me laugh out loud. But it also made feel good in a teacherly way, for there was no denying the little girl was phonemically aware. She identified the target sound /sh/ and then added it to a known word, correctly placing it in the initial position to create a brand-new word—*shflipflops*!

Phonological, Phonemic, and Phonics

Before we discuss why being phonemically aware is so important to young readers, let's define three words that are sometimes confused with one another: phonological, phonemic, and phonics.

The terms *phonological* and *phonemic* refer to sound only. To discriminate between sounds and produce them, you don't need to see anything and so phonological and phonemic activities can be done in in the dark. In a purely phonological activity, no text is involved.

Phonological and phonemic activities, however, are not synonymous. Rather, phonological is the more encompassing term. Think of it as a big bookshelf labeled "general awareness of the sound structures of speech." This long shelf is divided into sections that include, moving from the largest units of speech to the smallest, whole words (*sunset*), syllables (*sun* and *set*), onsets and rimes (*s-un* and *s-et*), and phonemes (*s-u-n-s-e-t*). If children are phonologically aware, they can hear and count the number of words in a sentence, as well as the number of syllables in a word. They can also understand and produce rhymes and alliterations, such as Henny Penny and Peter Piper, and segment words into their onsets and rimes.

Phonemic awareness is a subset of phonological awareness; it occupies a small but very important space on the big bookshelf of phonology. If children are advanced in their phonological awareness, they are phonemically aware. This means they not only understand that words are an amalgamation of discrete sounds, but they can hear the individual sounds within words, segment them from a whole word, blend them together to create a spoken word, and even create a new word by manipulating, subtracting, or adding sounds, as the little girl did when she said "shflipflops." The term *phonemic* refers to phonemes, the smallest sound units of words. Some languages are made up of over 100 discrete phonemes. Others, like Hawaiian, have fewer than 15. The English language has 44.

While phonological and phonemic refer to sound, *phonics* refers to print. Upon seeing an unfamiliar printed word, a beginning reader applies letter–sound associations to decode the word. From the stimulus of printed letters, sound arises. Knowing the meaning of the word is not strictly necessary.

You could say phonics grows out phonemic awareness because the skill of phonic decoding begins when a child learns letter–sound relationships, such as the /m/ sound is represented by the letter *m*. Young children apply rudimentary knowledge of phonics when they see the word *pit*, saying the sound associated with each letter, /p/-/i/-/t/, and then blending the sounds together to make a single, coarticulated word—*pit*! Later, chunks or phonic patterns (phonograms) are recognized and decoded (*pit-y* and *pul-pit*), and all types of meaning knowledge, from topical to background to vocabulary, are activated. In time, long sequences of letters are instantly recognized and known (*pitfall, piteous, pittance*), resulting in hundreds of whole words being read out loud on sight. At this point, the spelling-meaning-sound triangle is completely engaged, resulting in fluent reading.

As a wrap-up, let's connect all of this to the Simple View of Reading, as well as reading difficulties, which we now understand as problems caused by specific skill deficits. In terms of the Simple View, phonic reading develops from a synthesis of phonemic awareness, letter identification, letter–sound associations, pattern and word recognition, and decoding. As for reading difficulties defined as skill deficits, if through observation and assessment we know a student cannot hear that the words *lake* and *rake* rhyme, cannot strip the syllable *car-* off the spoken word *carnation* to come up with *nation*, and cannot accurately segment the word *flap* into /f/, /l/, /a/, and /p/, then we know this student lacks phonological and phonemic awareness skills. If, on the other hand, we know a student can do these sound tasks but cannot accurately read simple words—saying *bake* for *lake* and *rack* for *rake*—or accurately sound out word patterns—such as *car-*, *-na*, and *-tion*—then we know this student lacks phonic skills.

Advanced Phonological Awareness Is Important

The educational community has known for decades how important phonemic awareness is. Although many researchers had pointed it out prior to 2000 (Bradley & Bryant, 1983; Ehri, 1998;

Stanovich & Siegel, 1994), it really moved front and center when the National Reading Panel report named it as one of the Five Big Ideas of Reading, along with phonics, fluency, vocabulary, and comprehension. The Panel (part of the National Institute of Child Health and Human Development [NIH]) said that teaching phonemic awareness not only helped preschoolers, kindergartners, and first graders learn to read, but it also helped older readers with reading problems (NIH, 2000).

Since that time, the National Early Literacy Panel (2008) and reading researchers like Sally Shaywitz (2003), Maryanne Wolf (2008), David Share (2011), Louisa Moats (Moats et al., 2012), and Mark Seidenberg (2017) have all highlighted the importance of both phonological and phonemic awareness to beginning reading. As Moats says, "Phonemic awareness instruction, when linked to systematic decoding and spelling instruction, is a key to preventing reading failure in children who come to school without these prerequisite skills" (2020, p. 20). And here's Seidenberg talking about it in his book, *Language at the Speed of Sight*: "For reading scientists the evidence that the phonological pathway is used in reading and especially important in beginning reading is about as close to conclusive as research on complex human behavior can get" (2017, p. 124).

David Kilpatrick (2015) highlighted the importance of phonological and phonemic awareness within intervention programs, saying that the ones that are especially effective "aggressively address and correct students' phonological awareness difficulties and teach phonological awareness to an advanced level" and mentioned a study that showed how "training in phonological awareness and letter-sound skills reduced the number of struggling readers by 75%" [Shapiro & Solity, 2008].

IMPORTANT POINT

Even when using direct, explicit, multisensory teaching, moving students with reading difficulties to advanced levels of phonemic awareness may take many repetitions of skill practice over many months (Kilpatrick, 2015).

But why wait until students are struggling to teach phonological awareness to an advanced level? To prevent reading difficulties, let's teach sound skills in Tier 1. In the following sections, we discuss classroom activities that move children of many ages toward advanced phonological and phonemic awareness. We will start with large chunks of sound (single-syllable words, the rime of those words, and multiple syllables in longer words) and then progress to phonemes. As you consider each, I encourage you to make connections to the general teaching techniques we discussed in Chapter 3. We can help students become phonologically and phonemically aware if we teach directly and explicitly, model everything we want students to do, give lots of repetition, distribute that repetition across days and weeks, and keep students engaged (and promote more robust brain wiring) with multisensory instruction and materials.

IMPORTANT POINT

Second- and third-grade students who exhibit reading difficulties may lack advanced phonemic awareness. If you have assessment data that shows certain students are unable to analyze and manipulate phonemes (hear, segment, blend, subtract, add), it pays to work phonemic awareness activities into their guided-reading group, as well as quickly tie this sound-based practice to encoding and decoding practice (spelling and phonics).

Activities That Teach Large Chunks of Sound: Phonological Awareness

HOPPY KANGAROO

Hoppy Kangaroo helps preK and kindergarten students hear and count the number of words in a sentence. Hoppy jumps each time a word is said. If a sentence has four words—"The cake is tasty"—Hoppy jumps four times. Notice we are not talking about syllables (*tasty* has two). Rather, the emphasis is on recognizing words, the largest blobs of sounds in language.

Modeling

If you happen to have a kangaroo hand puppet, great. But my Hoppy is simply clip art attached to a ruler. Student kangaroos are the same art, scaled smaller and taped to popsicle sticks. Figure 5.1 shows teacher- and student-made examples.

Figure 5.1

Hoppy Kangaroo, for Teacher and Students

To teach, directly and explicitly tell students that sentences are made of words. Then, introduce Hoppy in whatever way you like. Tell the children Hoppy is here to help them count the number of words in a sentence. He only jumps when whole words are spoken. Next, say a sentence, such as "I like grapes." I think it's best to start with sentences that have only single-syllable words. Have students say the sentence with you and maybe even on their own (*I Say, We Say, You Say*). As you hold Hoppy, repeat the sentence once more, and this time, make her hop each time a word is said: "I (hop) like (hop) grapes (hop)." Repeat the sentence once more and have your students count the number of times Hoppy hops. Tell your students there are three words in the sentence. Model a few more three-word sentences. Finally, ask students to think of a sentence that has three words. Give them some wait time and then have them share their sentences with each other. If you hear a student sharing an interesting three-word sentence, ask her if she would share it with the whole group. Give Hoppy to the student and let her make Hoppy move for each word in the sentence.

Take the activity to the next level by saying sentences with more words, first four and then five. Bring in some two-syllable words, but remember, Hoppy hops on words, not syllables. For preschool and early kindergarten children, six to seven words might be a lot to count but see how far you can go. An even more advanced form of Hoppy Kangaroo is to not use Hoppy at all! Tell the kids that Hoppy is away, perhaps having breakfast at the IHOP (that's International House of Pancakes). Then, say a sentence at a slow to medium tempo and allow students to count the words without the kangaroo.

Segue to Written Text

To connect oral language to writing (and reading), represent each spoken word as one short line. After saying a sentence ("The dog is hungry"), making Hoppy hop, and counting the number of words, draw four short lines on the whiteboard. Then, put a period at the end (see Figure 5.2). Tell the students the lines and the period make a sentence, with each line representing one word and the period telling the reader where the end is. Count the lines and tell the students the sentence has four words. Make Hoppy hop across the lines on the board, "reading" the sentence and stopping at the period. Make up another four-word sentence ("The cat is thirsty") and have Hoppy hop across the lines again, stopping at the period. Call a student to the board and ask him to make Hoppy hop for each word. Model one or two more sentences and then ask students to think (use wait time) of a sentence that has four words. Have students quietly share with each other. If you hear a student sharing a four-word sentence, ask that student to share it with the whole group. Have Hoppy hop across the lines that represent that student's sentence.

Here are other sentences to say as you make Hoppy Kangaroo hop once for each word.

- *I like cake. Please don't run. I can jump. Airplanes can fly.*
- *My dog is big. Please eat your snack. My bike is yellow. Grandma likes to read.*
- *Where is the big cat? The lion runs and leaps. My sister is very tall.*

By the way, using lines to represent words is not strictly phonological (you can't do it in the dark). Rather, it serves as a connection to writing words in sentences and directly relates to the Magic Line students use in programs like Kid Writing (see Chapter 6).

Figure 5.2

Kindergarten Student Writing With Magic Lines

HANDS TOGETHER, APART, AND AWAY

Advanced phonemic skills include adding, subtracting, and substituting phonemes to make new words out of existing words. Set the stage for this skill by teaching children to add and subtract larger sound chunks such as syllables. Deleting one word of a compound word eases them into this concept; replacing the deleted word with a different word, thus forming a new compound word, takes the skill to the next level. To help children better understand how deletions and additions work, use the *Hands Together, Apart, and Away* activity.

Modeling

You'll need to turn your back to your students and present the back of your hands to preserve "reading left to right." With your hands together, thumb touching thumb, say, "Daylight." Pull your hands apart and say the compound words as separate words: "Day, light." Next, put your hands back together and say, "Daylight." Then, ask your students to say *daylight* without *day*. Model taking away your left hand and gently shaking your right. If they don't know the remaining word, say, "Light." Ask your students to say *daylight* without *light*, taking away your right hand and gently shaking your left. If they don't know the word, say, "Day." Figures 5.3 and 5.4 give examples of what this looks like.

Figure 5.3

First grader practicing *Hands Together, Apart, and Away*

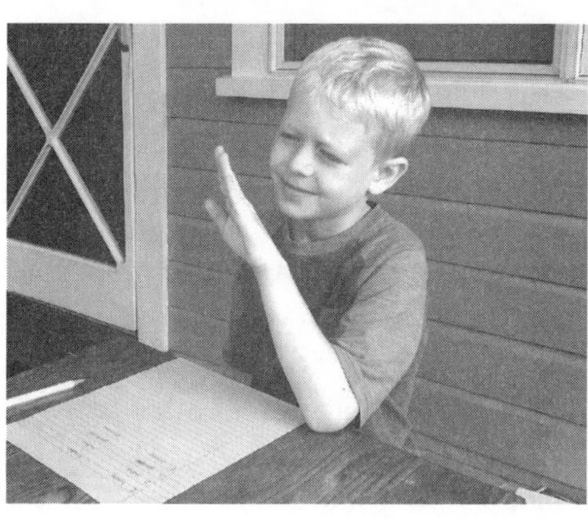

Figure 5.4

Hands Together, Apart, and Away Using the Word *Daylight*

Say daylight. Now, move your hands apart. Say each word.

Daylight Day light

Say daylight. Now, say it without *light.*

Daylight Say daylight without "light"

Say daylight. Now, say it without *day.*

Daylight Say it without "day."

Images from iStock.com/IconicBestiary

Here are other words and language to use for syllable deletion and addition:

- Say *moonlight.* Now, say it without *moon.* Say *moonlight.* Now, say it without *light.*
- Say *daydream.* Now, say it without *day.* Say *daydream* without *dream.* Keep *day* and add *break* to the end.
- Say *increase.* Say *increase* without *crease.* Now, say it without *in.* Keep *crease* and put *de-* in front. What word?

Remember that the goal of teaching phonological activities is getting children to an advanced level. An advanced form of *Hands Together, Apart, and Away* is to do the activity without using hands at all. Once kids can accomplish this with a two-syllable compound word, go to three-syllable words. At this point, unless you are an octopus, you cannot use your hands to segment syllables. Have students say a three-syllable word like *December*. Then, ask them to say the word with a syllable deleted. For example, "Say *December* without the *De*." (*Cember*) Or say, "Say *December* without the last syllable." (*Decem*) Or ask them, "What is the first syllable? What is the last syllable?"

Video example of *Hands Together, Apart, and Away*: https://www.youtube.com/watch?v=KJEftNEinbo

FEEL THE CHIN DROP

Connecting sound chunks to physical actions can support students learning to identify syllables within words. But clapping can be inaccurate. A more accurate way to count syllables within a word is to feel your chin move downward when you speak a word and then count the number of times your chin drops—hence, *Feel the Chin Drop*.

Set Up

In English, every syllable contains a vowel, and without fail, our chins drop every time a vowel is uttered. Thus, each vowel spoken equals one syllable. Sometimes, the movement of our chin is large and easily discernible, as when we say *pass* or *gumdrop*, and sometimes, it's subtle, as in *pool* or *teacher*. But a downward motion caused by the vowel is always there. If kids can feel and then count the number of times their chin drops while saying a word, they can accurately count the number of syllables in that word.

Modeling

To model *Feel the Chin Drop*, put your hand, with your palm facing down, under your chin. The fingertips can be pointing directly toward your throat or placed parallel to your chest. Either hand will do.

Say a one-syllable word slowly but naturally. Start with long vowel words that cause a deep drop in your chin, such as *stop, place, phone,* and *flat*. Tell your students how many times your hand moved and tell them why it moved: Every syllable has a vowel, and vowels make our chins drop. Next, have the children say the word or words with you as they place their hands under their chins. Once you have practiced one-syllable words, move to two-syllable words.

Video example of *Feel the Chin Drop* for syllables: https://www.youtube.com/watch?v=fQRptl4AeuU&t=7s

Choose your two-syllable words carefully. Compound words with short *a* and *o* sounds are good places to start—*backpack, hotshot, jackpot,* and so on. Have your students repeat the words with you, feel their chins, and count the syllables. Next, say three- and four-syllable words, such as *volcano, condensation*. Finally, mix up the words and after each pronunciation ask your students how many syllables they felt.

Video example of *Feel the Beat*: https://www.youtube.com/watch?v=B8lwnc3UnTc

Teaching Tip

We can think of syllables as beats or pulses within words. A fun, multisensory activity that helps preK and early kindergarten children understand the concept of a beat is *Feel the Beat*, in which a slow and steady chant has students feel a regular pulse over many parts of their body. Start by steadily tapping the top of your head with both hands (see Figure 5.5), gently and not too fast. The kids will soon follow along. Then, chant the following questions as you tap, changing up the body part after every four or eight beats. When you get to your ears, one hand goes to each ear. When you get to your nose, both hands tap at the tip. In the following chant, the words in all caps land on the beat—1, 2, 3, and 4. Each beat gets one tap.

> "Can you FEEL the BEAT ON your HEAD?
>
> Can you FEEL the BEAT ON your EARS?
>
> Can you FEEL the BEAT ON your SHOULDERS?
>
> Can you FEEL the BEAT ON your NOSE?
>
> Can you FEEL the BEAT ON your BELLY?"

Keep moving around, from "ON your SEAT," which kids love, to "ON your FEET." I like to end with "Can you FEEL the BEAT IN your HEART," repeating this phrase multiple times and quietly fading to a whisper.

Figure 5.5

Feel the Beat

Activities That Teach the Smallest Chunks of Sound: Phonemic Awareness

In a 2015 article on early literacy research, D. Ray Reutzel identifies phonemic segmentation as an activity that gives a lot of bang for buck. To be clear, he still encourages the teaching of onset-rime, rhyming, and alliteration. But he does give segmenting more emphasis.

Phonemic segmentation, however, is not enough. Remember: To increase the chances that students will develop strong word recognition ability, help them develop *advanced* phonological skills. This means going beyond segmentation to identifying phoneme positions, as well as adding, deleting, and moving phonemes from one place in a word to another.

The following activities run from basic phoneme segmentation to advanced phoneme manipulation. You can do these activities with a whole group or in small groups. Also, there is no reason to confine phonological activities to just kindergarten and first grade; they work with older students who have deficits in phonemic awareness, too, although I would add that for older students you'll want to quickly segue from phonemic activities to phonics and spelling activities. Finally, work to integrate the effective teaching techniques mentioned earlier. Direct and explicit is best, as is repetition, distributed practice, and multisensory.

STRETCH THE WORD

Sound stretching (*Stretch the Word*) helps students hear the individual sounds of a word. Later, they can segment the phonemes more discretely through activities like *Penny Push and Pull*, Unifix cubes, and *Stretch It, Tap It, Zap It* (more on these in a minute).

As with all activities, model them first. Use the *I Do, We Do, You Do* sequence described in Chapter 3. To stretch a word, tell your students to pretend the word is a big rubber band. Or if you live in western Pennsylvania, ask them to imagine a "gum band." They'll know what you mean. Grab hold of either end of the word (make two fists and hold them close to each other in front of you). Then, slowly pull your hands away from each other, stretching the word out, holding out the vocalization of each phoneme as you stretch (see Figure 5.6).

After the rubber band is stretched as far as it can go and all of the phonemes have been drawn out, snap the band back together

Figure 5.6

Stretch the Word and Blend It Back Together

with a handclap. When students clap, they say the word. In this way, phonemes are blended back together to make a word. For example, *flip* would be modeled *ffff-llll-iiii-p,* (clap) *flip*!

Some teachers teach this technique as "bubble gum words," stretching the word out from the mouth as they were stretching a wad of chewed bubble gum. Is this disgusting? Perhaps. But if kids are engaged, do it. We do whatever it takes to get our students to learn, right?

IMPORTANT POINT

To build vocabulary for students, use sophisticated words as well as common ones. For example, when having students phonemically segment closed-syllable words, use *vast* as well as *big* and *dash* as well as *run*. Quickly and effectively, define these words for children through direct and explicit instruction.

SOUND BOXES AND THE *PENNY PUSH* (AND *PULL*)

Sound boxes are the precursors of letter boxes or spelling grids (found in the next chapter). Their use is often associated with children in kindergarten and first grade. But you can use them with older students who have not yet mastered the ability to segment, identify, and manipulate the phonemes of a word.

Each box represents one phoneme (see Figure 5.7). Students listen to a word, say the word, and then segment the word into individual

Figure 5.7

Sound Boxes With Pennies for Pushing

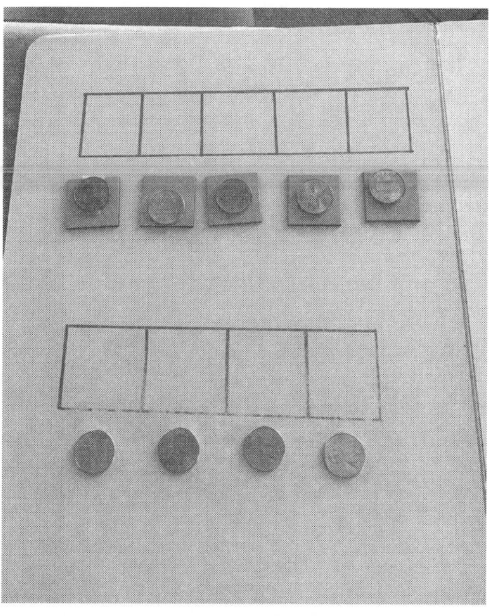

phonemes by pushing pennies (or other tokens) into each box as each segmented sound is spoken. To be clear, there are no letters involved in this activity or any other pure phonological activity. Because it so important for young students to develop the ability to hear, segment and blend, and manipulate the individual sounds within words, it pays to spend time on activities that are strictly sound-based.

When teaching the *Penny Push* routine, start with simple three-sound words that have consonants or consonant digraphs that are continuants, meaning they can be "held out," such as *m, l, f,* and *sh. Mash, map,* and *fill* fit the bill. Then, add four-phoneme words. Words such as *shame, fine, home, slam, list,* and *float* are three- and four-phoneme words that work well for initial teaching.

Typically, sound boxes come as whiteboards (for later writing on with erasable markers or for organizing letter tiles) or magnetic boards (for later using magnetic letter tiles). You can make your own write-and-erase boxes by printing grids on cardstock and laminating them. When introducing sound boxes, tell your students up front how many boxes will be filled by pennies (or other tokens).

Using the target word *lap*, here is one possibility for a routine:

1. Say the target word.
2. Say the first sound of the word, /l/, pushing a penny into the first box as you say it.
3. Say the second sound of the word, /a/, as you push a penny into the second box.
4. Do the same for the third sound of the word, /p/.
5. Run your hand under the space below the penny-filled boxes and say the word *lap*. This blends the phonemes (an artificial construct) back together, creating a real spoken word.

Move from modeling to guided practice, monitoring and correcting errors as necessary. You can also add *Stretch the Word* prior to the *Penny Push* routine. In this case, the routine is as follows:

- Teacher says the word.
- Students repeat the word.
- Students and teacher stretch the word and then blend it.

- Students push up pennies to segment the word's phonemes and then blend them back together.

Once students have mastered segmenting the sounds, move to a more advanced level by having your students practice identifying the position of each phoneme in a word (see Figure 5.8). Point to a specific sound box and ask, "What is this sound?" Point to another block and ask, "What is this sound?" Or ask, "What is the first sound? What is the last sound? What is the middle sound?" Medial position vowel sounds are often the hardest ones for children to identify, and identification becomes more difficult when a word contains four and five phonemes.

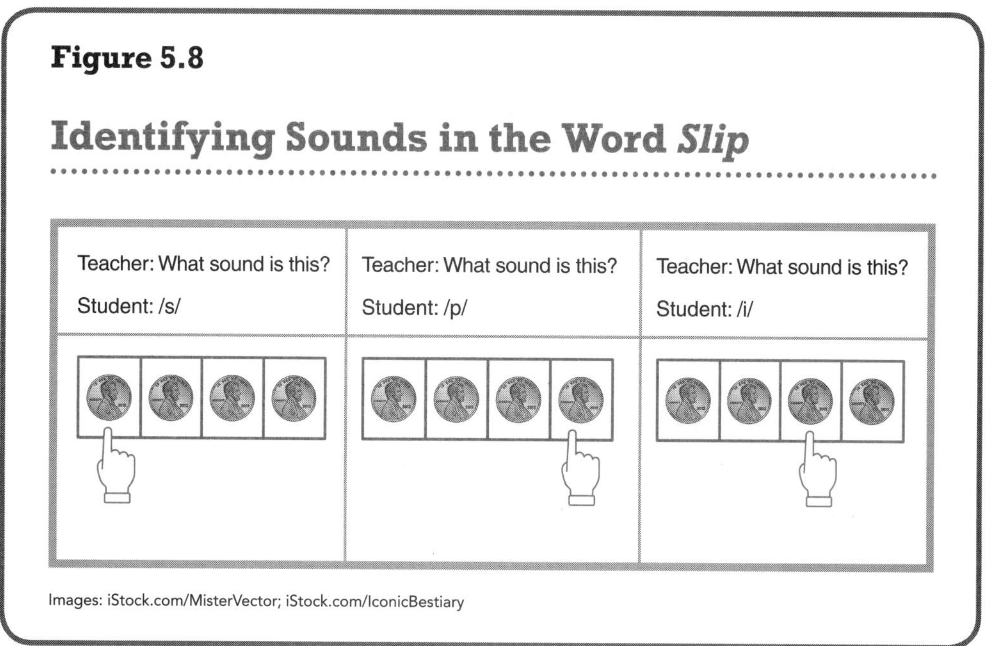

Another advanced variation is the *Penny Pull*. Here, you pull down a penny from the front or end position and ask the student to say the new word (see Figure 5.9). Pulling a penny out of its box represents a sound deletion. If you like to keep instruction focused on real words, start with a word that will remain a real spoken word even if a sound is removed; Figure 5.10 provides a starter list of words. For example, take the /s/ sound off the word *lips* and you have *lip*, or take the /t/ sound off *float* and you have /flo/, which, if we were using letters, we would spell *flow*. If you are fine with "nonsense" or pseudo-words, any word that easily segments will do.

Video example of *Penny Push* and *Pull*: https://www.youtube.com/watch?v=8_qj-uPXKOw

Figure 5.9

Penny Pull

Images: iStock.com/MisterVector

Figure 5.10

Three- and Four-Sound Words for *Penny Pulling*

Word	Take Away the First Sound	Take Away the Last Sound
hat	at	
bad	ad	
stab	tab	
trip	rip	
teen		tee
moon		moo
tent		ten
date	ate	da- (like *day*)
goat	oat	goa- (like *go*)
flight	light	fligh (like *fly*)
brain	rain	brai (like *bray*)

STRETCH IT, TAP IT, ZAP IT: USING FINGERS TO SEGMENT SOUNDS

Many physical actions can represent phoneme segmentation. We have already explored pushing and pulling pennies in and out of sound boxes. If we take away boxes and pennies, we are left with just fingers. The Wilson Reading Program teaches students to tap out sounds using fingers and thumb. But the kindergarten teachers I worked with taught a different action, which they called zapping.

To model zapping, say the target word as you make a fist. Next, segment the word into the sounds you hear, pumping your hand and throwing out a finger for each sound you say. For example, the word *it* gets two pumps. The index finger comes out when you say /i/. The middle finger comes out when you say /t/. Finally, draw your fingers back into a fist, blending the sounds together and saying the word.

When giving words, it is important for you to say the word and have your students repeat it with you (*I Say, We Say*) before the zapping begins. *I Say, We Say* gives a model of the correct pronunciation of the word prior to sound segmentation and an opportunity to repeat that correct pronunciation. After all, one cannot segment phonemes correctly if the word isn't pronounced correctly.

Here is an example of a teaching routine I still run in classrooms. If I use six or seven words, it takes about five minutes. In this routine, keep your instruction direct and explicit, use modeling, and proceed at a brisk pace. The point is to work in lots of practice so the kids can master the technique. Once mastered, children can use zapping as an independent strategy for spelling and reading many unknown monosyllabic words. In this lesson, we'll imagine the teacher is working with a group of second graders on the *r*-controlled syllable.

Teacher: This lesson is about hearing *r*-controlled sounds. What is this lesson about, everyone?

Students: Hearing *r*-controlled sounds!

Teacher: The /ar/ sound is spelled *a-r*. The /or/ sound is spelled *o-r*. But right now, we are going to simply use our voices to practice segmenting the /ar/ and /or/ sounds from other sounds in a word.

Watch me as I zap out the word *stork*. Stork! [Say the word and make a fist.] /s/ /t/ /or/ /k/ [Pump hand, putting out a finger for each phoneme.] *Stork*! [Pull fingers back into a fist.]

Watch! I'll do it one more time. [Repeat the process.]

Now, you try it. Your first word is *card*. Say it.

Students: Card! [They make a fist.]

Teacher: Zap it.

Students: /c/ /ar/ /d/. [They pump their hand and throw out a finger for each sound, ending with index, middle, and ring fingers out. Then, they draw their fingers back into a fist and say the word again.] Card!

With short bursts of repeated practice distributed over time, students can master the art of stretching, zapping, and chin drops in just a few weeks. Combine stretching and zapping, stretching and tapping, or all three into short routines (see Figures 5.11 and 5.12 and the QR code for a video example). Next, when students are ready, show them how to combine physical cues to segment the sounds in multisyllable words. For example, it's difficult to

Figure 5.11

Stretch It, Zap It, Tap It Chart

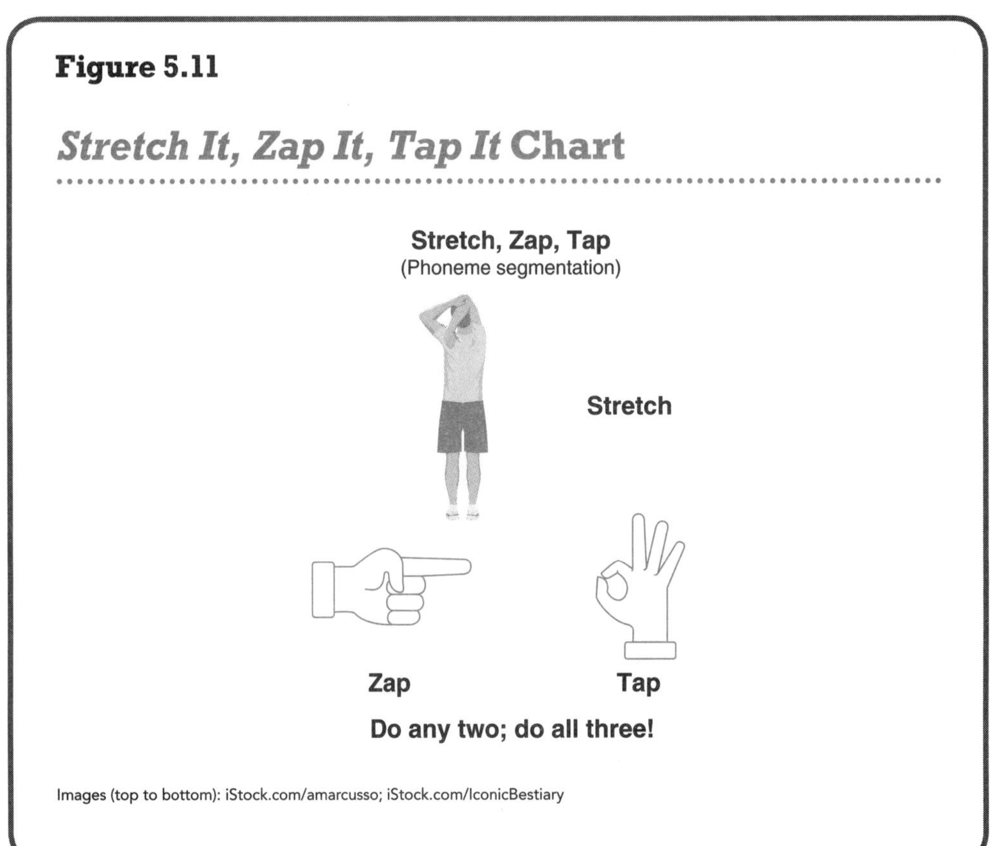

Images (top to bottom): iStock.com/amarcusso; iStock.com/IconicBestiary

Figure 5.12

Stretch It, Tap It, Zap It in Action

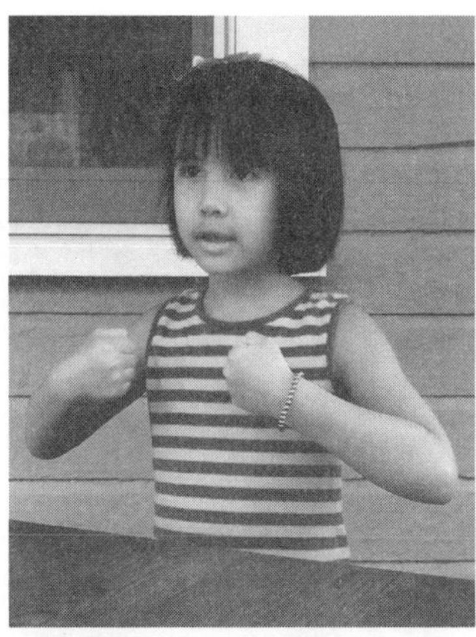

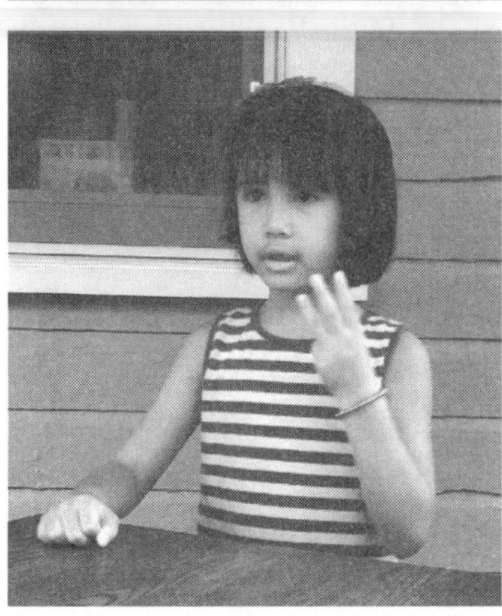

Video example of *Stretch, Tap, Zap* routine: https://www.youtube.com/watch?v=Wp8lfGhcmXw

phonemically segment the word *segmentation*. But by placing their hand under their chins and saying the word, students can break the word into four syllables. From there, they can zap out the phonemes of each syllable, /s-e-g/ /m-e-n/ /t-ay/ /sh-u-n/.

You may have noticed that zapping and tapping reaches only the basic level of phonemic awareness—segmentation. To move students to more advanced levels, let's consider building words with cubes and blocks.

●●● FOR FUTHER STUDY

If you prefer to use ready-made materials and programs, here are four effective, low-cost resources:

1. *Equipped for Reading Success: A Comprehensive, Step-By-Step Program for Developing Phonemic Awareness and Fluent Word Recognition* by David Kilpatrick, 2016
2. *Heggerty Phonemic Awareness Curriculum* published by Literacy Resources, Inc.
3. *Kindergarten and First Grade Student Center Activities and Teacher Manuals* published through the Florida Center for Reading Research (downloadable for free at their website)
4. *Phonemic Awareness in Young Children: A Classroom Curriculum* by Marilyn Jager Adams, Barbara Foorman, Ingvar Lundberg, and Terri Beeler, 1997

BUILDING WORDS WITH BLOCKS, LEGOS, OR UNIFIX CUBES

To build words from individual sounds, place foam blocks next to each other or snap Unifix cubes or Lego blocks together to form rods. Each block or cube represents a sound. Each contiguous length of blocks or cubes represents a word. Figure 5.13 shows a configuration for the words *fat* and *baby*.

The colors of Unifix cubes and Lego blocks make phonemes easy to see. Thus, they are great aids when teaching children basic, midlevel, and advanced phonemic awareness. Model how to snap apart (segment) a four-block word into four phonemes. As you segment the sounds, say each phoneme and hold it up or point to its associated block. Then, snap the blocks back together (blend) and say the whole word. Point out the patterns the rods

Figure 5.13

Block and Lego Sequences Can Represent Words

are showing. Associating repeated colors with repeated sounds might help children hear how sounds and word "chunks" are the same.

Video example of sound segmentation and manipulation with blocks and Legos: https://www.youtube.com/watch?v=V3gJudl8N1Y&t=30s

In subsequent lessons, work on phoneme identification by pointing to a specific block and asking, "What is this sound?" Move to another block and ask the same question, as in Figure 5.14.

Advanced activities include making new words by snapping off sounds, adding sounds, or moving sounds around, as in Figure 5.15.

Figure 5.14

Sound ID With Cubes

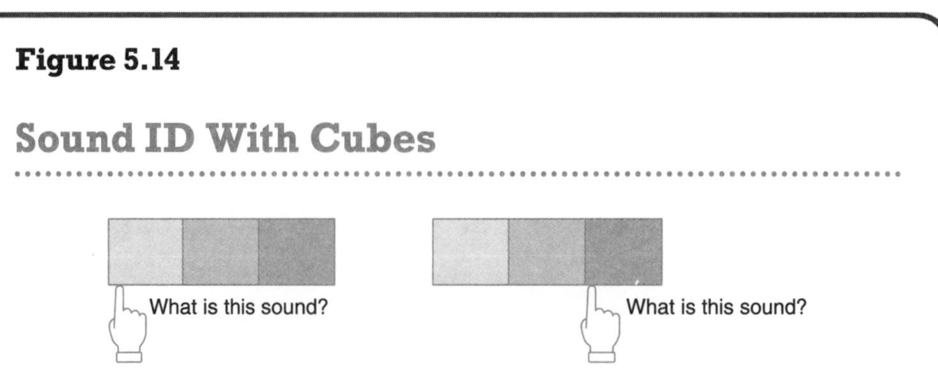
What is this sound?
What is this sound?

iStock.com/IconicBestiary

Figure 5.15

Advanced Phonemic Manipulation

Start with *slip*.	Take off the /s/.	Put /s/ on the end.	Change /i/ to /a/.	Put /c/ in the beginning.
slip	lip	lips	laps	claps

IMPORTANT POINT

Many of the phonemic analysis and manipulation activities presented in this chapter are multisensory in nature—that is, they make use of hand movements, pennies that can be pushed and pulled, and color-coded blocks that can be manipulated. All of these provide support to young learners. But because the goal is to move students to the most advanced state of phonemic awareness possible, remember to gradually fade these supports. When students can accurately, consistently, and repeatedly do tasks such as "segment the sounds in the word *blind*" and "say *farm* without the /f/" without moving their hands or manipulating objects, then these students have achieved advanced phonemic awareness.

JUST FOR FUN: PIG LATIN

With third-grade children, try speaking some Pig Latin. If children can move the onset sound of a word to the final position and then add /ay/ after that, they definitely have advanced phonemic awareness ability.

Start simply. Pig Latin-ize CVC words, turning *cat* into *atcay* and *dog* into *ogday*. Use manipulative activities such as *Penny Push* and Legos to add a visual and kinesthetic element to your teaching. Then, move to more complex one-syllable words, such as *flake* and *strike*, then to two-syllable words. Maybe some of your students will eventually speak in Pig Latin sentences. Avehay unfay ithway igpay atinlay!

TOGGLING BETWEEN SOUNDS AND LETTERS

Because the sounds of speech are coarticulated, it is hard to pick apart certain sound combinations, and some children will find it difficult to master more advanced phonemic awareness tasks, such as segmenting initial blends. As part of phoneme instruction for students who know their letters, don't be afraid to occasionally attach letters to the sounds. Directly and explicitly showing letters helps students "see" the individual phonemes in sound combinations such as /fl/, /tr/, /aps/, and /ump/. Once you've shown letters, toggle back to just phonemes. Toggling back and forth gives additional support to the students who need it and can help prevent further difficulties.

While working on phoneme segmentation with groups of end-of-the-year kindergarten children, I noticed one of the students, Emma, was experiencing difficulty with *l*-blends (*fl*, *gl*, *sl*). This wasn't surprising; *l*-blends are often problematic for five- and six-year-olds. Emma was a whiz at phonemically segmenting three-phoneme CVC words, but her parsing of *flat* and *slip* came out just like *fat* and *sip*. To support her efforts and make the learning easier, I used a four-box sound grid with this routine:

- I said the word *flat* slowly, stretching out the sounds and using my hands.
- Using the four-box sound grid, I pointed to each box as I segmented the phonemes once more.
- I wrote *f* and *l* in the first and second boxes. Then, I pointed to each box as I said the phonemes.
- I erased the *f* and *l*, pointed to each box as I said each phoneme, and then ran my finger under the sound boxes and said the word *flat*.
- I said to Emma, "You try it. The word is *flat*."

Emma and I repeated the procedure for three more words (*slid, glad, flame*). By the end of our seven-minute session, when I gave Emma a word to do on her own (*slip*), she was able to segment the *sl* blend. Bingo!

Toggling also works with Unifix cubes and Legos. Check out Figure 5.16 to see how this works.

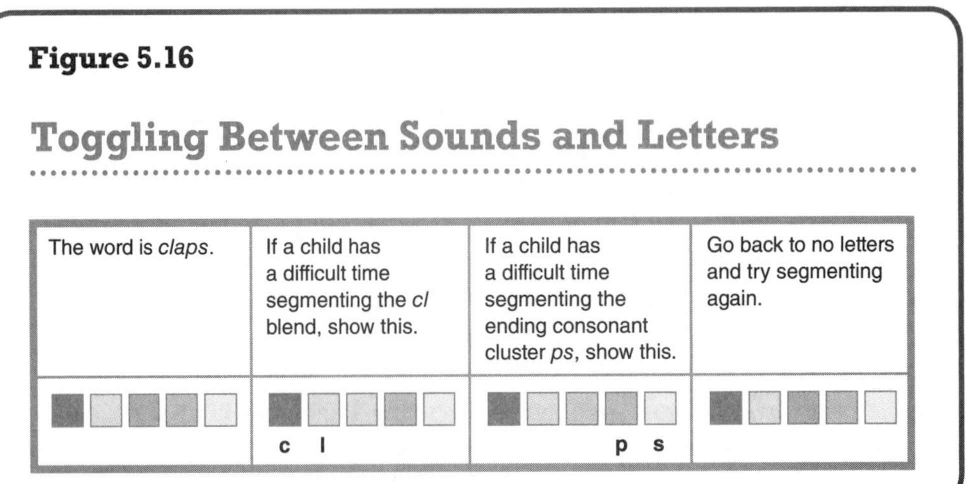

Figure 5.16

Toggling Between Sounds and Letters

The word is *claps*.	If a child has a difficult time segmenting the *cl* blend, show this.	If a child has a difficult time segmenting the ending consonant cluster *ps*, show this.	Go back to no letters and try segmenting again.
	c l	p s	

IMPORTANT POINT

Students may have phonological and phonemic awareness deficits due to lack of instruction, poor instruction, difficulties in attending to the task, or some combination thereof. But deficits can also be caused by differences in brain wiring that lead to difficulties with phonological processing (International Dyslexia Association, 2015). Phonemic deletion tasks can uncover problems with phonological processing. Some children who have dyslexia struggle to delete the phonemes of words, and this is why diagnosticians often use phonemic deletion tasks as a way (one of many) to identify students who have dyslexia.

Phonological Foundations

To move students to an advanced level of phonological and phonemic awareness, aim for completely fading manipulatives like pennies, blocks, and fingers. Also, keep in mind the goal is to go beyond segmenting and sound position identification. You want your students to add, delete, and move phonemes around. Why the emphasis on advanced phonemic awareness?

Advanced phonological awareness is important because it acts as an anchor for orthographic mapping (Ehri, 1998; Phillips & Piasta, 2013), the mental process our brain uses to learn and store the correct letter sequences of words. At its most basic, orthographic mapping occurs when teachers help young readers to associate a letter with a sound: the symbol *s* stands for the sound /s/, the symbols *o-i* stand for the sound /oy/, and so forth. Later, strings of individual sounds (for example, /ch/, /o/, /m/, /p/) associated with strings of single letters and letter combinations (*ch-o-m-p*) come together to make words (Kilpatrick, 2015). By mapping letter and letter combinations onto sounds, we come to store the letter sequence and sound of *chomp* in our brain dictionary. Equally important, these stored words, which are also attached to meanings, become available for immediate and effortless retrieval during reading. At its most advanced level, orthographic mapping happens on its own as fluent readers interact with more and more text while reading. This is the principal (or hypothesis) of self-teaching. But without phonemic awareness, the brain lacks an anchor for written-word learning. And without written-word learning and subsequent instant word recognition, there is no reading.

Lack of word recognition ability (word-level reading) is the number-one skill deficit for most children experiencing reading difficulties (Kilpatrick, 2015). One reason that students may lack word recognition (especially children with developmental dyslexia) is they lack a solid foundation of phonemic awareness and/or their phonological processing is compromised in some way (Ozernov-Palchik et al., 2017; Wolf, 2018). Deficits in phonemic awareness make encoding words in brain dictionaries more difficult. And if a brain dictionary is poorly stocked, fluent word reading is less likely to happen.

Creating that solid foundation of phonology (to a level of advanced phonemic awareness) is paramount for teachers of young children because it is a way to head off reading difficulties before they arise (Kilpatrick, 2015; Moats, 2020; Moats et al., 2012; Muter et al., 2004). It is also a part of helping some struggling readers overcome their already developed problems. In 2014 when I was teaching low-achieving third graders in a corrective reading classroom, I wish I would have known how important it was for my students to have advanced phonemic awareness. I bet that if I had assessed the two or three lowest-performing kids in my class of 16 children, I would have found that these students had underdeveloped phoneme analysis skills (possibly due to the condition of dyslexia).

And perhaps if I had taught advanced phonemic tasks (addition, deletion, and substitution) to mastery levels within the first 12 weeks of school, these same students would have made swifter progress in "cracking the code" and gaining reading fluency and spelling ability. But alas, my coteacher and I didn't assess our students' phonemic analysis ability at a nuanced level, and I only taught phonemic analysis informally through spelling and writing instruction—and then only to the basic level of segmentation.

According to reading disabilities expert and assessment guru David Kilpatrick, intervention approaches that lead to highly successful reading outcomes "aggressively address and correct students' phonological awareness difficulties and teach phonological awareness to an advanced level" (2015, p. 290). Reading researchers Barbara Foorman and Joe Torgesen take it a step further, saying, "The components of effective reading instruction are the same whether the focus is prevention or intervention" (2001, p. 203). So when it comes to phonemic awareness, teach it aggressively in Tier 1 settings, as well as in intervention settings for those children who need it.

CONNECTIONS

Other practices in this book that connect to phonological concepts and activities are listed here:

- Repetition and distributed practice, direct and explicit instruction, and activating the senses with multisensory activities (Chapter 3)
- Letter–sound chart (Chapter 3)
- Sky Writing letters and saying their associated sounds (Chapter 3)
- Sound boxes turned into letter boxes (Chapter 6)
- Connecting phonemic segmentation routines to *Segment to Spell* activity (Chapter 6)
- Sound-based spelling strategy in *Kid Writing*, word ladders, and *Look, Touch, Say* (Chapter 6)
- *Chunk Chants* (Chapter 6)

BUILDING ORTHOGRAPHIC SKILLS

CHAPTER 6

While modeling *Kid Writing* lessons for a cohort of primary grade teachers, I arrived at one first-grade classroom a few minutes early. The teacher, Mrs. W, was at the back of the room setting up an easel for my lesson, and the first graders were in their seats, practicing their reading and writing. I strolled to the front, said hello, and asked the kids what they were working on. "Reading and writing the short *e*," said one little boy.

"Wow," I said, looking over their word list. "Look at all of the words with the short *e* sound: *sled, then, red, stem* . . . and oh, my favorite, *Beth*! My wife's name is Beth."

Mentioning this opened the first-grade flood gates. Suddenly, a dozen children were waving a raised hand, eager to tell me about the Beth in their lives. "My aunt's name is Beth," said a little boy. "My grandma's name is Beth" and "My sister's name is Beth," said two more. "My dog's name is Beth!" exclaimed another. Then, a little girl piped up from the back, "My mom's lawyer's name is Beth!"

Fortunately, Mrs. Wilson was already hurrying to the group. "1-2-3, eyes on me! No more Beths, children. Let's get ready for *Kid Writing*!"

The Beth story makes me chuckle. But its real import is its reference to elements of early reading development. In first grade, students solidify their identification of letters and letter combinations (*b-e-th*), associate them with discrete sounds (the letter *b* says /b/), blend the sounds of the decoded letters into words (*Beth*), encode the sounds into writing, and connect words to meanings (Beth is a person, a woman, an aunt, a grandma, a dog, and a lawyer). This chapter is about these skills and more. But before we get to activities that teach the skills, let's review *orthography*, a term fundamental to how reading occurs in the brain.

Review of Orthography and the Brain Dictionary

Orthography, or the conventional spelling system of a language, can be thought of as the recordings of correct letter sequences. These sequences, stored in our brain as chunks and whole words, are used for spelling and reading.

As we learned earlier, both the lexical and sublexical reading pathways rely on orthography. When using the first pathway, readers automatically recognize entire words, fluently reading them with no need for bit-by-bit decoding. Using the second route, sometimes called the "sounding out" pathway, sequences of known letters are turned into sounds and then blended together to make words. The words could turn out to be ones you know, such as *turnip* and *trumpet*, words you might not know, such as *palimpsest* and *persiflage*, and nonsense words that have no true meaning, such as *mimsy* and *borogoves*. Regardless of whether an unknown printed word means something to you or not, you read it by translating its letter sequence into sounds.

Orthography works in the opposite direction too. Upon analyzing the individual sounds of an orally produced or internally audiated word, you encode the sounds into a known sequence of letters. For common words like *trumpet* and *turnip*, which are stored as whole sight words in your brain, you simply hear the words and spell them in their entirety without much thought. Spelling unknown or nonsensical words is more problematic, but because you know specific letters and patterns that represent specific English language sounds, you can spell words such as *persiflage* and *borogove* even if don't know the word's meaning or it has no meaning. You also bring to bear knowledge of spelling conventions or rules. For example, most proficient readers and writers of English would not spell *borogove* as *borogov* because in English the letter *v* does not end a word. Rather, a silent *e* is added after a final *v*, as in *have*, *give*, *love*, *dove*, and *borogove*.

I use one term—*orthography*—to discuss phonics and spelling because I want to drive home the idea that phonics and spelling are best understood when presented together. Linnea Ehri (2000) famously pointed out that decoding and encoding (phonics and spelling) are "two sides of the same coin." Vocabulary, which has to do with meaning and may involve the analysis of morphemes (word parts that have meaning), enters the picture, too, and so I often think in terms as one hyphenated concept: *phonics-spelling-morphology.*

With its roots firmly in phonological awareness and its branching parts intertwined with language comprehension, phonics-spelling-morphology becomes much *less* than itself when disassembled into parts and taught in isolation. One of the fascinating aspects of the reading process is how holistic and emergent it is. Although breaking it apart helps us understand how it works, it is only when we consider reading as a whole that we see its true nature. In my worldview, everything from climate to culture arises from the interdependent nature of things. Why should the reading process be any different?

Reading disabilities expert David Kilpatrick references the interconnectedness of reading components in his 2015 book, *The Essentials of Assessing, Preventing, and Overcoming Reading Difficulties*, where he points out how all intervention approaches that lead to highly successful reading outcomes (i.e., weak readers gaining word reading skills at accelerated rates) have three things in common:

1. They aggressively address and correct students' phonological awareness difficulties and teach phonological awareness to an advanced level.
2. They provide phonic decoding instruction and/or reinforcement.
3. They provide students with ample opportunities to apply these developing skills to reading connected text.

If Kilpatrick's trio is capable of accelerating low-achieving readers to the point where they can catch their typically achieving peers, it stands to reason the trio is also capable of preventing reading difficulties from occurring in the first place. Reading researchers Barbara Foorman and Joe Torgesen say this very thing: "The components of effective reading instruction are the same whether the focus is prevention or intervention" (2001, p. 203).

In service to this chapter, I have restated and slightly expanded Kilpatrick's list into three general instructional practices. For me, they are guideposts for teaching reading in any primary grade classroom:

1. Teach phonological awareness to an advanced level. Teach it to all students in the earliest grades; teach it to those who need it in the upper grades but here quickly connect it to phonics and spelling.
2. Directly, explicitly, and systematically teach phonic and spelling patterns to a point of mastery, kindergarten through fifth grade, and possibly beyond.
3. Provide many opportunities for all students in all grades to read extended text for extended amounts of time. This gives them chances to practice phonic, semantic, and phonological skills in real reading situations and helps build the elements of language comprehension, such as background, topical, and vocabulary knowledge, metacognition, and more.

IMPORTANT POINT

If young students are to become readers, explicit and direct phonics–spelling instruction must be a daily occurrence. The same is true for opportunities to read connected text for extended amounts of time. But some students may require different content, type of instruction, and/or amount of teaching in each area. One effective way to accomplish this is to differentiate phonics–spelling instruction, book browsing bins, and guided-reading groups, activities, and schedules. This differentiation, however, should never reach the point where phonics–spelling instruction supplants guided and independent reading, leading to a situation where a group of struggling readers receives 50 minutes of phonics a day, minimal guided reading, and no time to independently read! For all students, and especially for those who struggle, phonics–spelling, guided reading, and independent reading should reside together.

While the previous chapter addressed phonology, number-one on Kilpatrick's list, this chapter focuses on orthography, specifically the direct, explicit, and systematic teaching of phonics and spelling. The ultimate goal is to help students store entire words, instantly recognizable by sight, in their brain dictionaries. Amazingly, many children need only one to four reading repetitions to store a word in memory (Kilpatrick, 2015). Some children, however, need more. So to help students develop well-stocked brain dictionaries, let's provide multiple opportunities to build and store words, using a multitude of effective practices in our daily reading instruction.

I leave it to you to decide how and when to incorporate any or all of these practices into your teaching day. But I will offer two suggestions. If you use a basal series, such as McGraw-Hill's *Reading Wonders* or Houghton Mifflin Harcourt's *Journeys*, deemphasize or even remove less-than-effective practices such as workbook pages, letter-a-week pacing, and overly broad spelling lists, replacing them with more effective practices like spelling grids and word ladders, *Letter-a-Day* pacing, and spelling master lists narrow in scope but rich in words. If your teaching model is workshop-based, such as Lucy Calkin's *Units of Study*, beef up the phonics component for those children who need it, using any number of activities and routines given in this chapter or similar ones pulled from other sources.

As a segue to phonic–spelling activities, I offer this Oscar Hammerstein lyric from *The Sound of Music*: "Let's start at the very beginning. A very good place to start. When you read, you begin with *a-b-c*. . . ."

Building Letter–Sound Associations

In her 2018 book *Reader Come Home: The Reading Brain in a Digital World*, Maryann Wolf expounds upon the deep reading circuit of the brain, at one point mentioning a decade of reading research that says "when the major components in the reading circuit are explicitly emphasized—the earlier the better—children become more proficient readers, even when they begin with significant challenges like dyslexia" (p. 162). One major reading circuit component is recalling letter–sound associations, an ability that depends upon phonemic awareness and letter identification. Chapter 3 presented three practices that help young students learn letters and develop the ability to accurately and rapidly recall letter–sound associations: Montessori sandpaper letters, *Sky Writing*, and singing the letter–sound chart. This chapter gives additional ones, namely *Letter-a-Day* instruction, an effective sequence for letter introduction, and *Segment to Spell* spelling grids, all taught with effective teaching techniques such as repetition, distributed practice, instant error correction, and multisensory learning.

LETTER-A-DAY INSTRUCTION

Learning the name, sound, and print formation of every letter in the English alphabet is foundational to learning to read. Kindergarten and first-grade core-reading curriculums certainly teach these skills, often rolling out the letters at the rate of one per week. There is strong evidence, however, that a letter-a-week pace is too slow (Jones & Reutzel, 2012; MacKay & Teale, 2015). A more effective instructional practice is to begin the year by introducing one letter every day. That's right—a letter-a-day! Jacklyn Klein, a talented kindergarten teacher I recently worked with, does this very thing during her monthlong kindergarten Alphabet Boot Camp, which she runs in September of every school year.

Introducing one letter every day is a powerful practice, especially when the introductory sequence takes into account each letter's frequency in the English language, as well as the letter's contribution to basic words (more on this in a moment). Using *Letter-a-Day* instruction is potent because it gives young students the chance to experience five or more cycles of distributed practice in a school year, much greater than the one or one-and-a-half cycles they would receive with a letter-a-week pace. Additionally, introducing small groups of letters in quick succession gives children the chance to begin blending and segmenting words sooner rather than later.

How To

In his excellent 2015 *Reading Teacher* article, reading researcher D. Ray Reutzel suggests a lesson routine for using *Letter-a-Day* instruction. Twelve minutes is dedicated for each lesson, although I think 15 might be more practical. Every day, a teacher teaches using the same routine but with a different letter. Figure 6.1 shows a synopsis of the routine, adapted from Reutzel's article.

For teaching, you will need a mixture of lowercase and uppercase letters. For my example, I've chosen the letter *m/M*. After reading through the routine, reflect on how many times in this 12-to-15-minute lesson young students see the letter *m*, hear its name, hear the sound it makes, identify it, and form it in writing.

Effective Sequence

The sequence in which you introduce letters can also influence how easily and thoroughly letters are learned. Here are evidence-based guidelines for a powerful letter introduction sequence (adapted from Reutzel, 2015). Consider them as you think about the introduction sequence you use. Doing so will help you determine if it is effective.

Figure 6.1

Letter-a-Day Teaching Routine

Explanation	**Direct and explicit explanation of the objective.** For example, say "Letters allow us to read and write words. Today, we will learn to name, say the sound, and write the upper and lowercase letter *M/m*."
Letter name identification	**Direct and explicit teaching of the letter and its name.** For example, point to the uppercase *M* and say, "This is the uppercase *M*. Let's name this letter. What letter is this, everyone?" Repeat explanation for lowercase. Next, randomly point three times to either of the two letters, asking children to name them.
Letter–sound identification	**Direct and explicit teaching of the letter and its sound.** For example, point to the uppercase *M* and say, "This letter says /m/. Listen, /m/. Say the sound with me." [Students say the sound with the teacher.] Point to the lowercase *m* and say, "This letter says /m/. Listen, /m/. Say the sound with me." [Students say the sound with the teacher.] Teacher randomly points to one letter or the other, three times in a row, asking children for the sound. "What sound does this letter make?"
Sort the letters	**Teacher and students sort uppercase and lowercase letters.** Teacher shows a handful of letters (foam, plastic, or letter tiles) pulled from a bag or presented on a smartboard. Letters should include three to four uppercase letters (*M*) and three to four lowercase letters (*m*). Teacher says, "These are uppercase and lowercase *M*s. We will sort them." She places all the letters in the bag. "We will put all the uppercase *M*s together and all the lowercase *m*s together. I will start." She pulls out a letter and names it: "This is lowercase *m*." She pulls out an uppercase *M* and names it. Then she says, "I will pull more *M*s from my bag. If it is an uppercase *M*, quietly say 'uppercase *M*.' If it is a lowercase *m*, quietly say, 'lowercase *m*.'" [She pulls letters, has students name, and sorts into categories until all of the letters are done.]
Find the letters	**Students find the lesson's uppercase and lowercase letter in text.** In this example, it is uppercase and lowercase *m*. The text is a sentence, written on the board or smartboard or found on the page of a big book—for example, "On Monday I saw the moon" or "Are you my mother?" Teacher models the procedure first, scanning through the text and pointing to the target letter. Next, the students scan and identify. When found, letters can be highlighted, circled, underlined, or the like. Pacing is brisk.
Write the letters	**Teacher models and students practice.** The teacher names the lesson's letter (for example, uppercase *M*), names its component parts (straight lines, angled lines, arcs, etc.), and describes and models how the parts are formed to make the letter. This is followed by student practice using any one of a variety of media: on paper with a pencil; in the air using *Sky Writing*; tracing a sandpaper letter and then writing the letter using a dry erase marker and a personal whiteboard. The cycle is repeated for the lowercase version.

1. The first letters of the sequence are some of the most frequently occurring letters of English, such as *a, i, s, t,* and *l.* Additionally, many of these letters make continuant sounds (sound that can be held out), such as those made by vowels as well as consonants like *m, l, s,* and *f.*
2. The sequence quickly introduces letters that can be combined to form a large number of easily decodable words.
3. The sequence avoids the back-to-back introduction of letters that can be easily confused, such as *b* and *d* or *m* and *n.*

Figure 6.2 shows an effective letter introduction sequence based on the work of Ed Kameenui and his colleagues (1997; also Carnine et al., 1997); it tacks closely to the sequence provided in most (but not all) core-reading programs and would be a good place to start if you are building your own reading curriculum. Note that although the sequence looks as if it includes only some of the uppercase letters, they are all there; these researchers recommend introducing dissimilar lowercase letters first (e.g., *t/T,* l/*L, f/F*) and similar uppercase and lowercase letters simultaneously (e.g., *s*/S, *o/O, u/U*).

Figure 6.2

An Effective Letter Introduction Sequence

a s t p i m f d o r g l h u c b w n e k j v y M L A T F I D N E R H G B x qu z J E Q

Source: Adapted from Carnine et al., 1997.

Teaching Tip

The *Jolly Phonics* program, developed in the United Kingdom, teaches children ages four to five the letters and letter combinations that represent 42 English language sounds. The program's letter introduction sequence is *s, a, t, i, p, n, c, k, e, h, r, m, d, g, o, u, l, f, b, ai, j, oa, ie, ee, or, z, w, ng, v, oo, y, x, ch, sh, th, qu, ou, oi, ue, er, ar.* With this sequence, developmentally ready students can quickly move to reading and writing words such as *sat, sip, pat, tin, snap,* and *snip.* How exciting and motivating for young children to realize they can read and write! Also notice that high-frequency, highly usable vowel digraphs like *ai, oa,* and *ee* are taught before low-frequency consonants like x and z.

SEGMENT TO SPELL SPELLING GRIDS

Previously, we learned that pushing and pulling pennies in and out of sound boxes is an activity for teaching students phonemic segmentation, blending, and manipulation. We can repurpose these sound boxes to hold the written letters and letter combinations that represent phonemes. In this way, we can teach students this alphabetic principle: Sounds can be represented by letters; letters represent sounds.

Letter boxes (or spelling grids) help students segment the sounds of words and then spell each discrete sound with an appropriate letter or letter combination. Grid activities like *Segment to Spell* are typically used with the youngest readers and writers, but they are also appropriate for older students who haven't mastered the alphabetic principle, especially regarding vowels. I used letter boxes frequently when teaching general education classrooms of third graders who were reading below grade level.

Materials

Outside of specific programs, spelling grids can be purchased as whiteboards (for writing) or magnetic boards (for manipulating magnetic letter tiles). You can also make your own write-and-erase spelling grids by printing grids on cardstock and laminating them or drawing them on whiteboards with permanent marker; Figure 6.3 shows examples. If you have magnetic letter tiles, you can use steel cookie sheets. Finally, you can even go the paper route, giving students a printed sheet with three to four spelling grids on each side and then having them pencil in their letters. When finished, please recycle! A sheet of spelling grids can be found in Appendix D.

How To

Each box in a spelling grid represents one phoneme. Students listen to a word, segment the word into individual phonemes, and then fill in the boxes of the grid with the letter or letters that spell each sound (see Figure 6.4).

Students in various stages of spelling and reading development can use spelling grids. Young ones might use three-box spelling grids to spell CVC and CVCC words such as *sip, bat, rich,* and *lock.* Older students with more advanced vocabulary and knowledge of

Figure 6.3

Example of Spelling Grids

Figure 6.4

Spelling Grids With Box Numbers That Match Word Phonemes

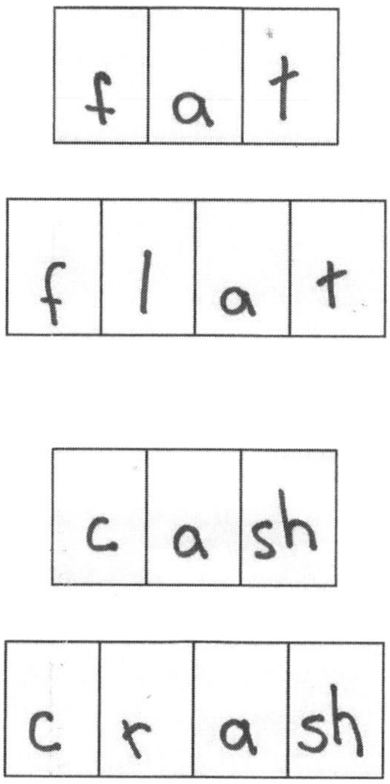

f	a	t

f	l	a	t

c	a	sh

c	r	a	sh

spelling patterns might use the same three-box grid to spell *gaff*, *church*, and *thought*.

When leading a group of students through this activity, support them by telling them up front how many boxes will be filled. For young children, use grids with a prescribed number of boxes. For example, give only three box grids when presenting three phoneme words (like *pen*, *fit*, and *porch*). For children who have advanced to the next level of understanding, use a single grid with five or six boxes. Allow these students to decide how many boxes they will fill to spell any given word. Reinforce that the first sound goes in the first left-hand box and that not all boxes on the grid may be filled. For example, in a five-box grid, the word *chin* fills just three boxes, *freight* uses four, and *stretch* uses all five (see Figure 6.5). Some teachers don't like to see empty boxes at the end of a spelling grid. Others, like myself, don't mind.

Figure 6.5

Five-Box Spelling Grids With Unused Boxes

ch	i	n		

f	r	eigh	t	

s	t	r	e	tch

Here's a suggestion for a teaching routine:

- Say the target word. Have the students repeat that word.
- Have the students stretch the word, zap out the sounds of the word, and then spell the word, filling each box of the grid with a spelling for the phoneme (see Figure 6.6). This can be done via writing letters or by manipulating tiles. If they need to, students can subvocalize the sounds as they fill in each box. Monitor them as they spell and guide them if they are stuck or incorrectly spelling a sound.
- If necessary, remind students that each box holds one phoneme, but the grapheme representing the phoneme may be made of more than one letter. For example, the /ch/ sound in *witch* has three letters (*tch*), and the long *a* sound in *eight* has four (*eigh*).
- Provide a written model for the correct spelling. When the students all have the correct spelling, have them read the word.

Video example of *Segment to Spell*: https://www.youtube.com/watch?v=iAWEucRajfk

Another option is for students to stretch the word and then segment by pushing up individual sounds one at a time (as if they were pushing invisible pennies). Each time a sound is pushed into the box, the student immediately writes the letter or letters representing the sound (see Figure 6.7).

Figure 6.6

Stretch, Zap, Spell

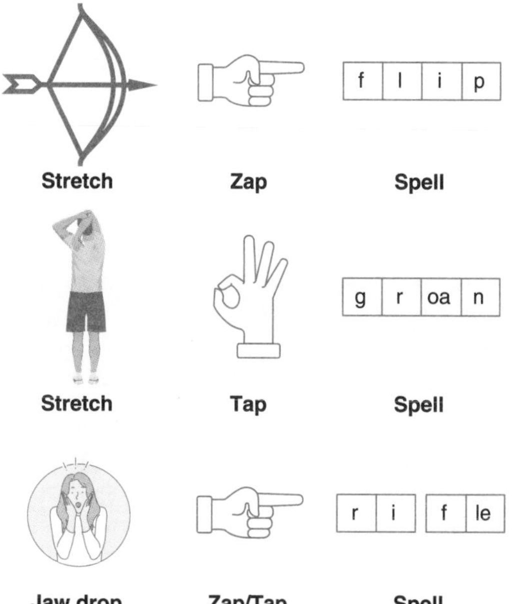

Images (left to right, top to bottom): iStock.com/Visual Generation; iStock.com/amarcusso; iStock.com/Aleksei Morozov; iStock.com/IconicBestiary

Figure 6.7

Push Up and Spell

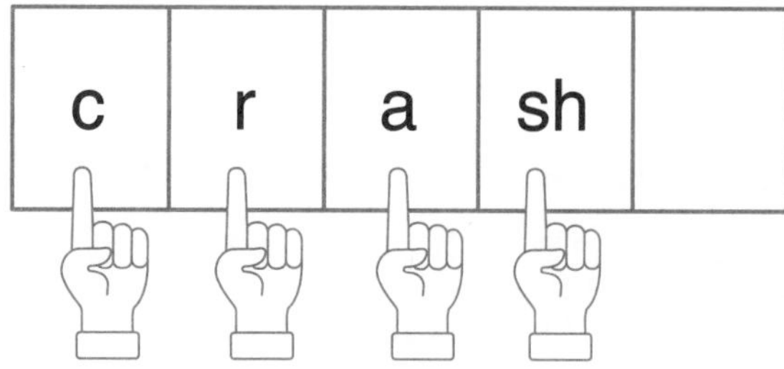

Image: iStock.com/IconicBestiary

CONNECTIONS

Other practices in this book connected to learning one letter a day and spelling grids:

Chapter 3

- Repetition and distributed practice
- Montessori letters
- Letter–sound chart
- Sky Writing letters and words

Chapter 5

- Chunking words
- Phonemic segmentation
- Sound boxes

●●● FOR FURTHER STUDY

If you are a preK teacher wanting to learn more about how to connect letter–sound associations to writing, consider the article "Help Me Where I Am: Scaffolding Writing in Preschool Classrooms" by Margaret Quinn, Hope Gerde, and Gary Bingham in *The Reading Teacher*, July 2016. And if you teach kindergarten or first grade, I suggest *Kid Writing in the 21st Century: A Systematic Approach to Phonics, Spelling, and Writing Workshop* by Eileen Feldgus, Isabel Cardonick, and Richard Gentry (1999). More than a book, *Kid Writing* is a primary grade program that marries the best parts of writing workshop and systematic phonics and spelling instruction. I recommend this program because it teaches and reinforces critical components of the foundational reading circuit, including letter–sound association, spelling patterns, background knowledge, and phonic decoding. For beginning readers, phonics and spelling develop hand in hand, growing and deepening when embedded within authentic reading and writing experiences and contributing to reading and writing growth in general (Ehri, 2000; Foorman et al., 2006; Moats, 2005; Wright & Ehri, 2007). *Kid Writing* neatly captures spelling and phonics but also expands to encompass grammar, genre, story elements, and more. I've seen it work in dozens of primary grade classrooms, helping kindergarten and first-grade students simultaneously learn to read, write, and spell.

Noticing and Using Patterns for Reading, Spelling, and Vocabulary Meaning

When I first started to present workshops and trainings, I often told teachers my two classroom mantras were "read, read, read" and "write, write, write." Reflecting on my instruction at the end of a teaching day, if I felt I had given my students many opportunities to read and write, then I knew my instruction was on the right track. After deeply diving into brain-based reading, however, I've added a third teaching mantra: "Patterns, patterns, patterns!" What follow are classroom activities, routines, and materials that can help you build pattern study into your literacy instruction.

STUDYING PATTERNS AND BUILDING WORDS

Once students have mastered letter–sound associations—such as the sound /sh/ represented by the *s-h* digraph—they are ready to begin exploring larger patterns. These patterns have many names (phonograms, word chunks, rimes, word families), and from this point on, I will use the terms interchangeably. Typically, word families are presented at the rime level, which is the part of a one-syllable word that stretches from the first vowel to the end of the word. For example, the rimes of *bake, ink, home,* and *clump* are *ake, ink, ome,* and *ump.*

Patterns are terrifically important because they move children toward whole-word reading and spelling. Teachers who teach pattern recognition hijack the brain's natural ability to recognize patterns. But don't worry, this hijacking is a good thing. When we teach students to notice patterns, we help them see how words are made up of predictable chunks and understand that words relate to one another via these chunks. Keeping one chunk the same (the rime) but changing its initial letter or letters (the onset) produces a list of words that rhyme. Also, when students engage in activities that focus on letter patterns and their associated sounds, they may be more likely to recognize the chunk in other written words (which helps them to decode), as well as hear the sound chunk in words they want to write (which helps them to encode).

Researchers Wylie and Durrel (1970) famously showed that some word families are more common than others. They referred to these families as *phonograms.* Figure 6.8 gives a list of the 37 phonograms they identified as most common. The list is an excellent starting point for phonics–spelling instruction in the primary grades.

Activities that show how words work at the pattern level take many forms. My favorites involve manipulating materials that are easy to store, transport, and clean up afterward. All the following activities can be easily made; many can be purchased.

Figure 6.8

The 37 Most Common Phonograms

ack, ain, ake, ale, all, ame, an, ank, ap, ash, at, ate, aw, ay	eat, ell, est,	ice, ick, ide, ight, ill, in, ine, ing, ink, ip, it,	ock, oke, op, ore, ot,	uck,ug, ump, unk

When you first introduce an activity, model its use. Then, model it again! If you don't have enough materials to run the activity for a whole group, consider pairing the kids (with each pair getting a whiteboard, egg carton, magnetic journal, etc.) or using the materials only in small-group settings or in a word work center.

Foam Blocks

You will need two sets of foam blocks: one set with phonograms or families such as *ack*, *ain*, *ill*, and *ot*, and one set with consonant and consonant blends, like *d*, *g*, *br*, and *fl*. Students work in pairs. One student tosses each block and puts the blocks together to form a word. It might be a real word; it might be a nonsense word. The other student reads the words. Next, the students reverse roles. You can buy blank blocks as well as blocks printed with onsets and rimes from online vendors such as Oriental Trading or your local craft store (see Figure 6.9a).

Flip Books

Flip books have two sections: the first flap is the onset (consonants and consonant blends), and the second flap is the rime (see Figure 6.9b). Students create words by flipping the pages and reading each combination. Sometimes, the words are real (*bake, cake, flake, stake*) and sometimes not (*dake, glake, prake*). Onset-rime flip books can be purchased, but it's easy to make them; all you need is a spiral-bound book of index cards. Cut the cards down the middle and write in the onsets and rimes with a marker. Card books in colors (yellow, green, blue, pink) let you categorize the rimes: yellow for vowel-consonant-*e* (*ake, ame, ine*) or pink for vowel teams (*ain, eat, ay*). Students can work and read on their own or in pairs (one flipping and one reading).

Ping Pong Balls in Egg Cartons

The balls can be purchased in bulk for under $15 and are available in various colors. Buying two or more colors gives you options: blue for consonant onsets (like *t, s, p*), green for blend onsets (like *gr, sh, fl*), pink for vowel-consonant-e (VCe) rimes (like *ame, ine, ode*), and so forth (see Figure 6.9c). You'll also need a Sharpie and an empty egg carton. Organize the onsets and rimes in ways that are most beneficial to your students. Students pick one onset (*t*) and one rime (*ame*) and then pair them to make a word (*tame*). Next, they read the word. Then, they either swap in a new onset (*sh* to make *shame*), bring in a new rime (*est* to make *test*), or put both balls back and build a completely new word.

Wheels and Sliders

Students turn the wheel or slide the slider to form new words and then read them. Wheels and sliders can be purchased, but you can also make your own with colored cardstock (see Figures 6.9d and 6.9e).

Personal Whiteboards

On their board, students write down the target rime and then spell and read words by swapping beginning letters in and out. If you want to make your own board, go to Lowe's or Home Depot and buy a 4 × 8-foot sheet of white panelboard, from which you can get twenty-four 12 × 16-inch rectangles. If you ask nicely, it's a good bet someone at the store will cut the pieces for you right then and there. Take the pieces home, sand the edges with fine sandpaper, and boom, you have 24 whiteboards for less than a buck a piece.

Letters and Tiles, Magnetic or Cut From Paper

There are many possibilities for tile sets, both self-made and purchased. Do-it-yourself options include sets of onsets and rimes printed on cardstock, cut out, and then placed in clasped envelopes. You may want to include a blank 8½ × 11-inch sheet of stock (for a sorting mat). Steel cookie sheets are useful when using magnetic letters and word families. Magnetic whiteboards (see Figure 6.10) cover a lot of ground, from magnetic letter manipulation to word and sentence writing. Some magnetic letter sets come with steel letter trays that can be adapted for onset-rime practice If you have money to spend, I highly recommend the Wilson Language Training *Magnetic Journal*, which features a clever system of color coding and an emphasis on the six syllable types.

Figure 6.9

Activities for Pattern Manipulation and Reading

a

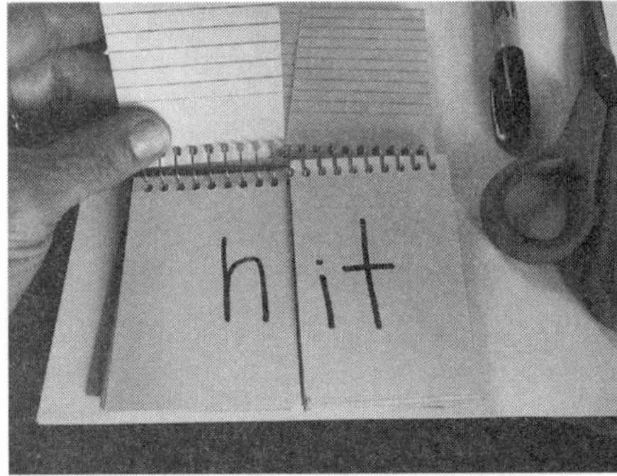

b

c

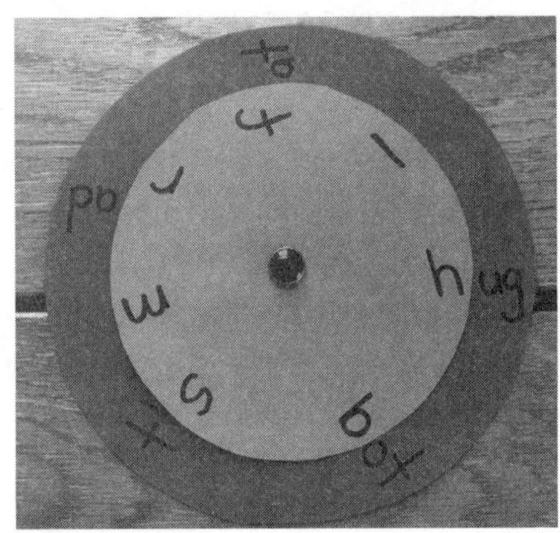

d

e

Figure 6.10

Magnetic Whiteboard

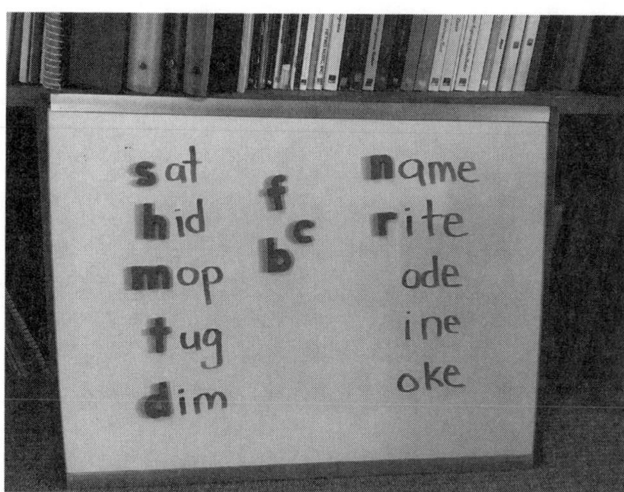

Pattern-Based Word Ladders Using Word Families

Word ladders show letter–sound associations within words, the prevalence of word families, and how words relate to each other through patterns. A basic word ladder for first graders might show how one word transforms into another, one letter change at a time. Starting with a bottom word, it may take a speller four, five, or more words to reach the target word at the top. Each change creates a new word, and each new word is a rung on the ladder (see Figure 6.11).

To change one word into another, students must listen to sounds (phonology) and decide on letters (orthography). A basic word ladder helps students notice sounds, especially inner vowels, which can be particularly difficult for some children.

A more advanced pattern-based word ladder explicitly shows how the same pattern can be found in multiple words. Pattern word ladders are also helpful for practicing spelling rules, such as the vowel digraphs *ow* and *ay*—typically end words, but *oa* and *ai* are always closed in by a consonant on the right. Words in pattern-based word ladders often transform groups of letters at a time (see Figure 6.12).

Figure 6.11

A Basic Word Ladder

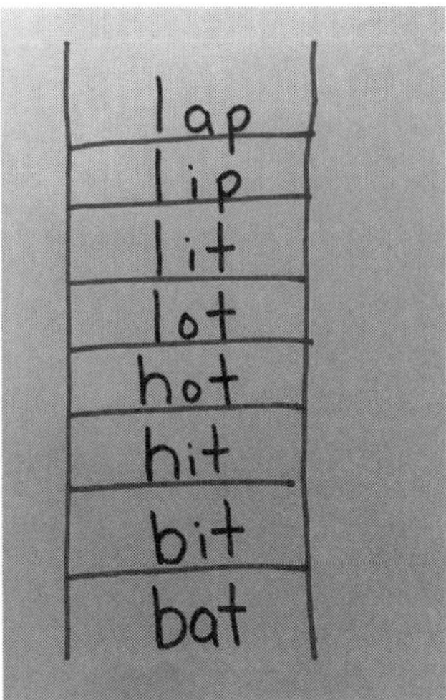

Figure 6.12

Pattern-Based Word Ladder: ai, ay, oa, ow

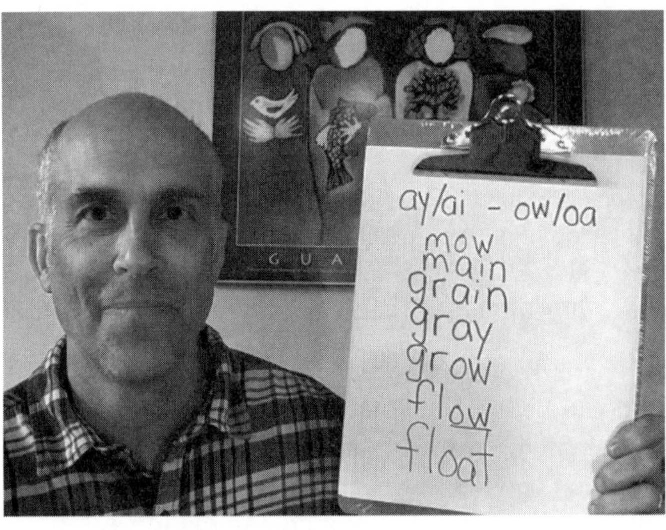

You can provide different levels of support by giving different types of directions. Consider this word ladder sequence: *pray-ray-rain-grain-brain-bray-gray*. For higher-achieving students with a wide vocabulary and a lot of background knowledge, you might use meaning-first prompts as you lead them. For example, you might say this:

- Change the word *pray* into a three-letter word that is a beam of light (*ray*).
- Change *ray* into a kind of precipitation (*rain*).
- Add a letter to turn *rain* into kind of seed, like oats or rice (*grain*).

But for students struggling to master spelling and reading, I suggest lots of concrete support. This means you directly tell them the word you want them to spell, provide an explicit definition, and point out how and why the patterns differ between the words. Here is what this type of instruction might look and sound like as students complete the same word ladder *pray-ray-rain-grain-brain-bray-gray*:

- Take one letter off *pray* and turn it into *ray*, which is a beam of light.
- Turn the word *ray* into *rain*. Remember, when the long *a* sound is in the middle of a word, it is often spelled *a-i*.
- Add one letter to the beginning and turn *rain* into *grain*, a seed like oats or wheat.
- Change one letter and turn *grain* into *brain*.
- Turn *brain* into *bray*, the sound a donkey makes. Remember, when the long *a* sound is at the end of a word, it is often spelled *a-y*.
- Change one letter and turn *bray* into the color *gray*.

To wrap up this type of word ladder, you might say, "Look for all the words that use the *ay* pattern. Touch each *ay* word and whisper read it. Now, look for all the words that use the *ai* pattern. Touch each *ai* word and whisper read it."

Video example of pattern-based word ladder: https://www.youtube.com/watch?v=vqgKPLK4N8w

IMPORTANT POINT

Align your phonics scope and sequence with your spelling scope and sequence. Spelling and phonics should march arm in arm, lockstep. One great way to align phonics and spelling is by using the six syllable types. Consider learning the syllable types and then incorporating them into your reading, writing, and spelling instruction.

Chunk Chants

When first using spelling grids for *Segment to Spell* and when constructing basic word ladders, I would steer clear of using words that use the phonograms *am*, *an*, and *all*, as well as words built with *vowel-ng* and *vowel-nk*. You will notice the list of 37 most common phonograms includes these: *all*, *an*, *ing*, *ank*, *ink*, and *unk*. These letter combinations can be troublesome for young decoders because they cannot be segmented and correctly sounded out at the individual letter level. For example, the chunk *am* does have two distinct sounds. But the *m* influences the vowel sound, causing the *a* to have a nasal quality rather than a pure short sound, as in *at* and *ash*. To test the nasal quality of the *a* in *am*, pinch your nose shut and say the word *ham* and *sham*. Then, say *cat* and *cash* as you continue to pinch your nose.

Because the two letters of the phonogram *am* cannot be decoded individually, it makes sense to present them as an inseparable chunk, sometimes called a *glued* or *welded* sound combination. We can help students encode the spelling of these glued sound combinations into their long-term memory by presenting them with rhythm and repetition—*Chunk Chants*!

How To

The *Chunk Chant* routine is this: (1) Spell the letters of the glued chunk; (2) point to a picture of a key word that uses the chunk; (3) say the word; and (4) say the chunk. When multiple chunks are presented in a row and the routine is set to a rhythm, a chant is born. It sounds like this: *a-n-g, fang, ang! i-n-g, ring, ing! o-n-g, song, ong! u-n-g, lung, ung*!

Students construct their own hand-drawn sheet to make a visual aid for the chant. But before they do this, know what chunks and key words you'll give them. For example, for the chunk *ing* you could use the key word *ring, sing,* or *wing*. Or just use my key words, which are based on ones used in the Wilson Language System: *ham* (am), *man* (an), *ball* (all), *fang* (ang), *ring* (ing), *song* (ong), *lung* (ung), *bank* (ank), *sink* (ink), *honk* (onk), and *junk* (unk).

Next, have students write and illustrate their word glued chunks on an 8½ × 11-inch sheet of oaktag, which is more durable than paper. I suggest that students draw their own picture rather than that you provide it for them. Sheets with spellings, key word pictures, and blank spaces for pointing and saying the chunk sound are shown in Figure 6.13. The sheet is similar to the letter–sound chart presented in Chapter 3, but here there is a maximum of four pictures per sheet and now students are working at the pattern

Figure 6.13

Student Sheets With *Chunk Chants*

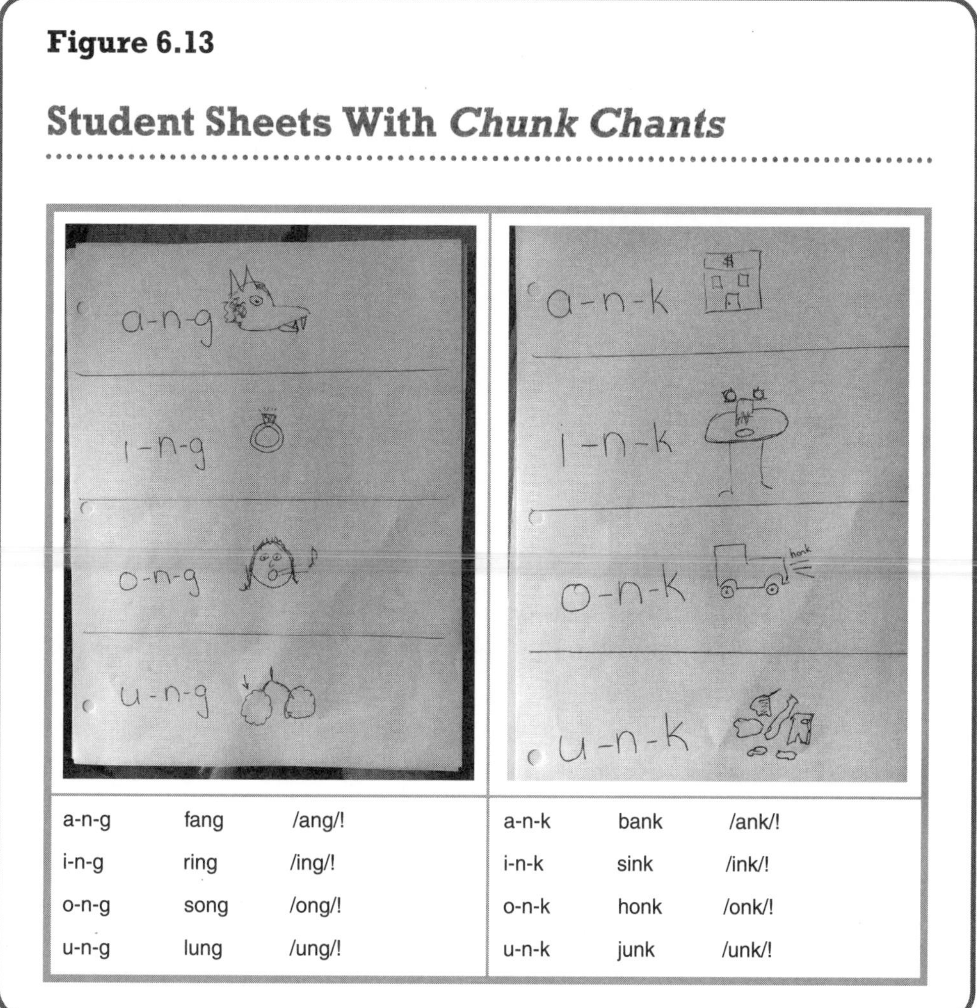

a-n-g	fang	/ang/!	a-n-k	bank	/ank/!
i-n-g	ring	/ing/!	i-n-k	sink	/ink/!
o-n-g	song	/ong/!	o-n-k	honk	/onk/!
u-n-g	lung	/ung/!	u-n-k	junk	/unk/!

Video example of *Chunk Chant*: https://www.youtube.com/watch?v=wz3Piz-aY1A

level, not the individual letter level. The instructional routine is similar, too: Students point to the spelling, say the spelling, point to the picture, say the picture, and point to the blank space and say the chunk sound. To make it a chant, do it in rhythm.

Chanting can be done as a warm-up or cooldown to any writing, spelling, or guided-reading group. As more glued chunks are accumulated, chant through a number of the sequences. Remember: repetition and distributed practice. Also, additional phonograms in Wylie and Durell's (1970) list can be presented as spelling patterns with an associated key word and illustration. Many of these phonograms, however, are totally separable and feature predictable features, such as vowel-consonant-*e*, doubled *ll* in final position, and so on. If so desired, you can group the phonograms on a chart according to their beginning vowel. Figure 6.14 shows my take on phonograms beginning with *i*. You and your students can make up your own versions.

Figure 6.14

Chant for Common Phonograms

i-c-e	mice	/ice/!	i-c-k	lick	/ick/!
i-l-l	Jill	/ill/!	i-n-e	pine	/ine/!
i-d-e	ride	/ide/!	i-n-k	sink	/ink/!

EFFECTIVE SPELLING LISTS

To help students master spelling patterns, give them spelling lists that include many words that use only a few patterns rather than lists that present many patterns, each seen in only a few words. For example, consider the second-grade spelling list shown in Figure 6.15, meant to give practice in spelling the "soft" *c* and *g* sounds at the end of a word, with four review words at the end.

In this list, the VCe rime pattern (here, *ace* and *ice)* is easily discernible. But the rimes of words ending in *ge* are all over the map. There is vowel-*ge* in *huge*, vowel-*r*-*ge* in *barge*, the glued-together /ul/ sound in *bulge*, the *long a* sound of *range*, and the *dge*

Figure 6.15

Spelling Word List, Second Grade

ice	place
mice	huge
barge	trace
cage	Review
space	tune
range	out
bulge	watch
badge	been

chunk, which has a silent *d*, as in *badge*. Unfortunately for young spellers, each of these *ge* rimes is presented in only one word.

The list in Figure 6.15 is not effective for teaching because it is broad in patterns and shallow in word examples, leading to exposure but not mastery and promoting a "memorize and move on" mentality. To create an effective list, one that helps students see, practice, and master patterns used for reading and spelling, focus on just a few patterns and give numerous words built from each. The end result is what I call a master list.

How To

To create a master list, first select a limited number of patterns to focus on, perhaps one to two for first graders and two to four for second and third graders. Then, generate many examples of words that feature these patterns. These words will be useful in a variety of activities, from word ladders and the *I'm Thinking of a Word* game to *Look, Touch, Say* (all discussed later in the chapter) and decodable sentences. They will also be useful for creating differentiated take-home spelling lists.

Figure 6.16 shows the earlier spelling list pared down to three patterns I want students to learn thoroughly. I've placed words with matching rimes next to each other and grouped them into these categories: vowel-*ce*, vowel-*ge*, and vowel-*dge*.

Figure 6.16

Pared-Down Word List

place, trace, ice, mice

cage, huge

badge

Finally, Figure 6.17 is my master list, with many word examples in each of the three categories. Words from the original list are in bold.

Figure 6.17

Master Word List

ace, **place**, race, **trace**, brace, grace, space, face, lace, replace, retrace

ice, mice, dice, rice, price, twice

age, **cage**, rage, page, stage, upstage, outrage/**huge**

badge, edge, hedge, ledge, pledge, bridge, porridge, drawbridge, lodge, dodge, budge, fudge, judge, Mudge, smudge, trudge

This focused spelling list, rich with words, enables repetition and distributed practice, giving students multiple exposures to just a few patterns and thereby helping them commit those patterns to their brain dictionaries. Additionally, a list like this gives more vocabulary opportunities, which contribute to language comprehension. Finally, if you choose to give "take-home" spelling words, there are now enough words to create differentiated take-home lists, even as you teach the same concepts and patterns. For example, one group of students might take home a list with *race, space, ice, mice, age, cage, huge, badge, edge, bridge,* and *lodge.* Another group might take home *place, trace, replace, price, twice, pledge, drawbridge, lodge,* and *smudge.* The second list, with many words starting with consonant blends and a few two-syllable words, is a more complex list than the first.

Teaching Tip

If you feel your spelling program is less than effective, want to create a spelling program from the ground up, or are simply looking for a few new spelling ideas, check out my *Super Spellers: Seven Steps to Transforming Your Spelling Instruction* (2017). One chapter is devoted to effective master spelling lists like the ones just described, as well as ideas for primary grade spelling activities, assessment, and word study centers. Also, the book has a companion resource, the lesson-based *Super Speller Starter Sets* (2019).

MORPHEME STUDY: WHEN CHUNKS HAVE MEANING

Morphemes are the elements of words that carry meaning. *Skunk* is a morpheme because it means something, as opposed to *unk*, which is a pattern with no meaning. Adding an *s* to *skunk* creates *skunks*, a word with two morphemes: *skunk* + *s*, with *s* denoting the plural. A complex word like *autobiographic* has four morphemes: *auto*, *bio*, *graph*, and *ic*.

Learning morphemes, mastering their meanings, and using them to spell and read words are important parts of learning how to read (Rastle, 2018). As teachers, we know it's important to teach students that words have meaning and that "thinking about meaning" is an important strategy to use while reading. The study of morphemes, however, goes deeper than this, down to the point where you directly and explicitly teach students specific word parts that have meaning (such as inflected endings, suffixes, and prefixes) and then give them practice in decoding, encoding, manipulating, and deciphering these parts during phonics and spelling work. But what morphemes should we teach? Consider these research-based tips to maximize your time and effectiveness (Manyak et al., 2018):

- Teach the most common affixes and roots.
- Teach them in related or thematic groups.
- Present words in ways that give many exposures to each morpheme and enable differentiation.

The research of Patrick and Ann-Margaret Manyak identifies the most common affixes and roots, saving teachers a lot of guessing and sleuthing. Figure 6.18 shows a snippet of their work (Manyak et al., 2018), listing common second-grade prefixes and suffixes, as well as words that incorporate them. I have listed the affixes in related or thematic groups (e.g., *un-* and *dis-* both mean "not" or "opposite"), added words, and arranged the base words so they range from simple closed syllables (CVC, CVCC, CCVC) to more complex VCe, vowel teams (*ea, oi, oo*), and *r*-controlled spellings. This arrangement allows you to differentiate for two groups of children: a group that still needs to master short vowel spellings and a group that is ready for vowel teams. For example, if I were teaching the prefixes *un-* and *dis-*, I might give the first group these words: *unlock, uncap, unclip, unzip, distrust, disband.* Every syllable in these words is a closed syllable with a short vowel sound. My second group of students might get these words: *unseal, uncoil, unhook, disown, discard.* These words use closed syllables, vowel team syllables, and *r*-controlled syllables, making the words more complex.

Figure 6.18

Common Second-Grade Prefixes/Suffixes

Affix	Meaning	Words
un-	Not or opposite	unlock, uncap, unclip, unzip, unsafe, unlace, unseal, unseat, uncoil, unhook
dis-	Not or opposite	distrust, disband, dispatch, dislike, distaste, disprove, disown, disarm, discard, discover, disorder
-er	Person	batter, sitter, planner, robber, shopper, writer, baker, maker, driver, teacher, preacher, eater, farmer, worker
-or	Person	actor, doctor, victor, jailor, author, sailor, editor, visitor, emperor
-er	Comparison	older, bolder, colder, bigger, madder, sadder, neater, moister, sooner, smoother
-est	Superlative	oldest, boldest, coldest, biggest, maddest, saddest, neatest, soonest, smoothest

FOR FURTHER STUDY ●●●

The following are resources for exploring common prefixes, suffixes, and roots:

- Patrick C. Manyak, James F. Baumann, and Ann-Margaret Manyak. 2018. "Morphological Analysis Instruction in the Elementary Grades: Which Morphemes to Teach and How to Teach Them" in the April 2018 issue of *The Reading Teacher*, pp. 289–300.
- Mark Weakland Literacy blogs on spelling, September of 2019 and December of 2018, found at www.MarkWeaklandLiteracy.com.

IMPORTANT POINT

Word work, pattern work, and *word study* are terms often used in schools. I collectively define all three as instruction and activities that give students practice with phonics-spelling-morphology. I use hyphens to make one term because I want to promote holistic teaching (as opposed to isolated skill work). For example, consider this little spelling list: *actor, doctor, jailor, sailor, teacher, preacher, baker, maker, farmer, worker.* Using these words, what spelling concepts would you teach? How would you use the same words to teach strategies for word attack/phonic decoding? Finally, what would you teach regarding morphemes and vocabulary?

MORPHEME WORD LADDERS

Now that we know about master lists containing words built from morphemes, we can run classroom activities that promote noticing and manipulating these chunks of meaning, as well as reading and spelling words that incorporate them. One option is a morpheme-based word ladder. In this activity, one word is transformed into another—not a letter at a time, but chunks at a time. By adding and subtracting affixes, root words, and bound roots, students morph one word into another, with each new word being a rung on the ladder.

How To

To change one word into another, students listen to sounds and syllables, think in terms of patterns, and access meaning. Figure 6.19 shows three-word ladders that focus on present and

Figure 6.19

Morpheme-Based Word Ladders

lock	smoke
locking	broke
locked	bike
rocked	biked
rocking	liked
stocking	liking
stacking	like
stacked	bake
stack	raked
stock	raking
	rake

past tense endings in combination with closed and VCe syllable words. Read these ladders from the bottom up.

As mentioned in the basic word ladders section, you can provide different levels of support (differentiation) by giving various kinds of directions. If students are ready for meaning-first prompts, say things like "Turn *stock* into a pile made by carefully placing one object on top of another." The answer is *stack*. For students who need more support, directly say the word you want them to spell, provide a definition as needed, and point out how and why the patterns differ between the words. Here's an example: "Turn *stock* into *stack*, a pile built by carefully placing one object on top of another. You only need to change one letter. Listen: *stock*, *stack*."

Video example of morpheme-based word ladder: https://www.youtube.com/watch?v=vCunK7xSp4I&t=7s

See Appendix C for more morpheme-based word ladders.

I'M THINKING OF A WORD

This three- to four-minute activity gives students an opportunity to notice letter–sound relationships and spelling patterns. You can use it to review past patterns or to reinforce what students are currently learning. As with other activities in this chapter, it connects to vocabulary meaning and morphemes.

How To

If you are a kindergarten or first-grade teacher, you can use your word wall for this activity. If you teach older students, perhaps you have a vocabulary wall or bulletin board that presents reading, science, or social studies words. Any type of word list—be it math, science, or phonics—will also work.

The big idea in this practice is to cue students to look at the visual aspects of a word first. Thus, a teacher gives two letter- or pattern-based prompts (visual) and then a meaning prompt at the end. Here are two examples of the activity in action; Figure 6.20 shows first using words that might be found on a first-grade word wall, and Figure 6.21 uses science-based weather words that first or second graders might study.

Figure 6.20

I'm Thinking of a Word Using Word Wall

Words from a first-grade word wall	**know** **like** **my** **not** **keep** **look** **make** **new** **kite** **little** **mine** **nice** **kick** **late** **mother**
Teacher (visual cue)	I'm thinking of a word that ends with a silent *e*. [Teacher gives wait time as students scan the word wall.]
Teacher (another visual cue)	I'm thinking of a word that ends with a silent *e* and begins with an *l*. [Teacher gives wait time as students scan the word wall.]
Teacher (a meaning cue)	I'm thinking of a word that ends with a silent *e*, begins with an *l*, and is the opposite of early. [Teacher gives wait time.] Whisper your answer to your elbow partner.
Teacher	That's right, I'm thinking of *late*!

Giving the most broadly applicable visual cue first helps keep everyone engaged. For example, if you were using the words in the previous weather word list and you wanted to lead students to *cloudy*, don't say, "Look for a word that ends with *y*." Rather, say, "Look for a word spelled with a vowel team." Your next visual cue might then be, "Look for a word that has a vowel team and is two syllables in length."

Figure 6.21

I'm Thinking of a Word Using Science Unit Words

Words from first- or second-grade weather word list	**tornado** **rain** **cold** **wind** **thunder** **cloudy** **storm** **darkness** **sun** **hail** **hurricane** **rainbow** **snow** **snowstorm**
Teacher (give visual cue)	I'm thinking of a word spelled with the *ai* vowel team.
Teacher (add visual cue)	I'm thinking of a word spelled with the *ai* vowel team and beginning with *r*.
Teacher (add meaning cue)	I'm thinking of a word that is spelled with the *ai* vowel pair, begins with *r*, and is a colorful arc in the sky.
Student	Rainbow!

Times to play *I'm Thinking of a Word* include these:

- When students are in line, waiting to transition somewhere
- A start-the-day activity
- While cooling down after recess or physical education
- As a warm-up to a spelling or reading instruction; also as a warm-up to social studies or science

LOOK, TOUCH, SAY

Recognizing and reading words, solidifying letter–sound relationships, noticing patterns, reviewing word meaning and morphemes—all of these can be practiced through a quick and easy routine called *Look, Touch, Say*. Done with a large group or in a small group as a warm-up or cooldown to a spelling or phonics lesson, *Look, Touch, Say* takes only four or five minutes. Because the routine incorporates wait time, it gives all students an opportunity to feel successful and provides support for students who struggle. Also, it's kinesthetic and doesn't involve writing, a plus for many children. Finally, because it's such a simple routine, you can teach aspects of it to even the youngest students, who can then buddy up and do it themselves.

How To

Start with a phonics or spelling word list, varying the list's number of words based on the age and abilities of your students. Younger students might have five or six words on a list while older students could have 12 or 15. The upcoming examples use a second-grade phonics list of *oy* and *oi* words.

There are many ways to finesse *Look, Touch, Say* to give students word-reading practice, opportunities to find patterns, and a chance to review vocabulary meaning. The easiest version covers word recognition and word-reading practice. What follow in Figure 6.22 are four variations of the routine. The first gives practice in word reading, the second in rime recognition, the third in pattern recognition, and the fourth in meaning.

Video example of *Look, Touch, Say* routine: https://www.youtube.com/watch?v=qu7u7EHK7fc&t=6s

Figure 6.22

Look, Touch, Say Variations

Word List **soil** **toys** **oyster** **join** **joy** **moist** **enjoy** **spoil** **cowboy** **tinfoil**	
1. Look for the word. . . . Touch it (wait). . . . Say it!	2. Look for a word that ends with . . . . Touch it (wait). . . . Say it!
T. Look for the word *moist*. [Students scan.] T. Touch it. [Teacher waits, monitoring until she sees all students touching it.] T. Say it. S. Moist! T. Look for the word *cowboy*. [Students scan.] T. Touch it. [Teacher waits, monitoring until she sees all students touching it.] T. Say it. S. Cowboy!	T. Look for a word that ends with *oin, o-i-n*. [Students scan.] T. Touch it. [Teacher waits, monitoring until she sees all students touching it.] T. Say it. S. Coin! T. Look for the words that end in *oil, o-i-l*. [Students scan.] T. Touch them all. [Teacher waits, monitoring until she sees all students touching them.] T. Share your favorite one at your table. S. Soil, spoil, tinfoil.
3. Look for words with the ____ pattern. . . . Touch them (wait). . . . Say one!	4. Look for a word that means. . . . Touch it (wait). . . . Say it!

(Continued)

Figure 6.22 (Continued)

T. Look for words with the *o-i* pattern. [Students scan.]	T. Look for the word that means dirt. [Students scan.]
T. Touch them. [Teacher waits, monitoring until she sees all students touching them.]	T. Touch it. [Teacher waits, monitoring until she sees all students touching it.]
T. Say one.	T. Say it.
S. Moist /spoil/tinfoil/join/soil!	S. Soil!
T. Look for words with the *o-y* pattern. [Students scan.]	T. Look for a word that is a kind of shellfish. You find pearls inside them. [Students scan.]
T. Touch them. [Teacher waits, monitoring until she sees all students touching them.]	T. Touch it. [Teacher waits, monitoring until she sees all students touching it.]
T. Take turns and read two to your elbow buddy.	T. Say it.
S. Cowboy, enjoy.	S. Oyster!

DECODABLE TEXT FOR PHONICS PRACTICE

Decodable text fosters literacy development by helping beginning readers build detailed and accurate replicas of patterns and words in neural circuitry (ILA Staff, 2019; Shaywitz & Shaywitz, 2020). These patterns and words are necessary if children are to become independent readers able to access a universe of words. For students who need more repetition and distributed practice, decodable text also provides extra phonics practice through carefully controlled and constructed sentences and paragraphs. Reading expert and author Wiley Blevins says that when it comes to teaching phonics, "the way to get that learning to stick is to apply it in connected text" (Schwartz, para. 10)—that is, decodable text.

Decodable text is not pattern or picture book text, nor is it leveled text. Pattern and picture book text supports young students through repetition, rhyming, picture cues, and simple sentence structure rather than through the phonic construction of the words. For example, Nancy Shaw's *Sheep in a Jeep* features a wide variety of phonic patterns (*go, yelp, push, grunt, shove, leap, splash, thud, shout, cheer*), and the words are presented within simple sentences that are paired with colorful, active illustrations. Meanwhile, leveled text supports students through predictable, repetitive sentence structure (among other ways). For example, the first four pages of a leveled reader might read like this: *Animals move in many ways. Birds fly through the sky. Fish swim through the water. Deer run through the fields.*

Decodable text, on the other hand, supports students by using a limited number of phonic patterns in its sentences. Directly connecting phonics instruction to reading, decodable text helps students "break the code" through repetition, distributed practice, a limited number of phonic elements, and a construction that consistently points students toward the strategies of "look at the letters," "look for patterns," and "sound out the word." This is why decodable sentences, paragraphs, and stories is an important part of many curriculums, such as Barton Reading and Wilson Reading, among others that aim to help students who have dyslexia.

When to Use and Where to Get

For those students who would benefit from more decodable text, time can be carved out of guided-reading lessons. For even more support, do repeated readings of decodable text (see echo and choral reading in the next section). If you have a majority of students who would benefit from explicitly practicing phonic patterns in sentences and paragraphs, piggyback the reading of decodable text onto the spelling-phonic lessons you present to the whole class.

The bulleted list that follows gives three examples of decodable text from published sources. The first, a snippet of a story, uses single-syllable, closed-syllable words. The second, also a story snippet, contains closed-syllable and vowel-team (*ee*) words. The third, a collection of sentences, uses words that contain consonant-*le* syllables. You can also create your own decodable sentences, à la the third example. Present them to students via smartboard slides, whiteboard writing, or photocopied handouts.

- *Jed had to trim the shrub and cut the grass for Mr. Smith. This was a big job. Lots of bugs bit Jed and it was hot. But at last the grass was cut . . .* (Wilson, 2009)
- *What is in the sack? Jack Green needs a sack. "That is odd. I can see a lump in the sack. What's in the sack?" "Is it a hen?" "Is it a duck?" . . . "No. It is a kitten. The kitten crept into the sack and fell asleep."* (SLDA-SA, 2020)
- *The little girl began to giggle; pass me a waffle and an apple; I saw a beetle in the middle of the sidewalk.* (Weakland, 2019)

Decodable text can be found in intervention programs, such as *Road to the Code*, in book sets available from publishers, and in free PDFs found online (see the For Further Study sidebar). The best ones expose young readers to "highly consistent and prolific patterns," make sense as stories, and build topical, background, and vocabulary knowledge (Schwartz, 2020).

In a pinch, you can create decodable text yourself. Stand-alone sentences are easier to write than entire stories, so I suggest starting there. When writing sentences, use sight words, words built from the focus of your current phonics-spelling lesson, and words containing patterns previously mastered. Also, don't worry about using the same word more than once. As noted by researcher Elfrieda Hiebert (Schwartz, 2020), decoding the same word several times helps students build strong links between the sound and spelling in their brain dictionaries, which can lead to more fluent reading. And your students will encounter many more words, authentic and rich in meaning, during their guided-reading and independent reading time.

Before we end, a word of caution is in order. Decodable sentences and books are not a stopping point, even for students who need more practice in phonics. Rather, they are a tool that exists in your toolbox of powerful instructional practices that help to prevent reading difficulties. Other types of text that serve as a tool for teaching at-risk students are ones that include natural language, a diversity of genres, and engaging stories (ILA Staff, 2019; Shanahan, 2018).

●●● FOR FURTHER STUDY

- A *Fresh Look at Phonics, Grades K–2: Common Causes of Failure and 7 Ingredients for Success*, written by Wiley Blevins and published by Corwin, is an excellent, widely used source of information on the explicit teaching of phonics, full of activities, routines, word lists, lessons, and more.
- The following are sources of decodable text for purchase:
    - Wilson Student Readers from the *Wilson Language* program
    - Spire Decodable Readers from the S.P.I.R.E. program
    - Flyleaf Publishing
    - Reading Genie books (available on Amazon)
    - Decodable sentences in *Super Speller Starter Sets*

- For free, decodable text from Australia, visit www.speld-sa.org.au/services/phonic-books.html.
- For a comprehensive list of decodable text, both free and available for purchase, visit the International Dyslexia Association of Ontario's website: www.idaontario.com/decodable-readers-and-text/.

Read, Read, Read

The activities, routines, and programs mentioned in this chapter help build the orthographically related skills of phonic decoding and spelling encoding. Many touch upon morphology, which also speaks to orthography. But the number-one way for a student, or anyone for that matter, to gain orthographic expertise is to read. Read, read, read! Researchers hypothesize there is a self-teaching component to reading, whereby at some point on a reader's path toward fluent reading, his phonology and decoding ability continue to develop without additional teaching (Share, 1999, 2011). Each bout of reading is an opportunity for a child to see more words in print, hear more words in his head, and build more word meanings. All of this leads to more words being stored in the brain dictionary through orthographic mapping, which, in turn, leads to more fluent reading. And so, the simple act of independent reading makes you a better reader (Kilpatrick, 2015; Share, 1999). There's a catch, though.

The positive feedback cycle of reading begetting more skills and more accomplished reading cannot occur if a child lacks a firm foundation in phonics and spelling. For readers who experience difficulties, self-teaching may not be occurring at peak levels. And for children with dyslexia, the self-teaching effect may not work effectively, if at all (Ehri, 2005a; Kilpatrick, 2015). Thus, to avoid or overcome a reading difficulty—and to reach a level of fluent reading where high degrees of self-teaching occur—some children will need more, perhaps significantly more, phonics-spelling practice than others.

I strongly encourage teachers to identify students who need more phonics-spelling-morphology instruction and then provide it, monitor its progress, and keep on teaching it until it becomes deeply rooted. Ultimately, however, orthographic skills are not increased through endless rounds of skill instruction. Rather, they are built through instruction that reflects the holistic nature of reading development. To this point, I'll give the last word to reading researcher Mark Seidenberg:

> Orthographic expertise is not acquired through the years of deliberate practice required to become an expert at playing chess or the tuba. We don't study orthographic patterns in order to be able to read; we gain orthographic expertise by reading. In the course of gathering all that spelling data, a person can also enjoy some books. (2017, p. 92)

CHAPTER 7

READING
GUIDED, REPEATED, INDEPENDENT

Reading . . . that fruitful miracle of a communication in the midst of solitude.

—Marcel Proust

One of my favorite books on the neuroscience of reading, *Proust and the Squid: The Story and Science of the Reading Brain* (Wolf, 2008), prominently features this chapter's opening quote. In just a few words, Proust brilliantly captures the personal reading experience: you, alone with a book, curled into the cushions of a couch or sitting quietly in a comfy chair, solitary yet in communion with every person, object, event and feeling evoked by the words you read. As you read, your thoughts intertwine with the book's settings and characters, connect passages to remembrances of friends and family, integrate personal experiences and knowledge, and perhaps even touch the spirit of the author himself. In the deepest throes of reading, you are transfixed and transported. That all of this arises from billions of electrical impulses and neurochemical interactions occurring on the time scale of milliseconds is almost unbelievable.

To be lost in a book is a magical and miraculous experience. But if we hope to foster that same experience in students, especially those who find reading difficult, we must set aside thoughts of magic and concentrate on the facts of the reading process. Thankfully, they are well known and readily available.

More Reading for Every Student

One well-known reading fact is the more you read, the better reader you become (Allington, 2014; Anderson et al., 1988; Brozo et al., 2008; Cipielewski & Stanovich, 1992). That more reading leads to better reading makes perfect sense. To become a better singer, sing a lot; to become a better skater, skate a lot. And to achieve more in shorter periods of time, take lessons from a knowledgeable instructor. We can apply the same logic to reading: For students to become competent readers, they must be taught essential skills and strategies by trained professionals and be given adequate time to practice (Allington, 1977, 2002).

For more than 30 years, reading researchers have said that giving students time to read is beneficial. In the words of Gambrell et al. (2011),

> It is clear that the amount of time spent reading is a critical consideration in reading development. We have long known that students who spend more time reading are better readers [Allington & McGill-Franzen, 2003; Anderson et al., 1988; Cunningham & Stanovich, 1998] and that students who have more experience with reading are better prepared than their counterparts with less experience [Allington, 1991; Neuman & Celano, 2001]. (p. 155)

Science tells us statistical learning plays an important part in our reading brain's pattern and word recognition process; this learning involves a kind of self-teaching that enables children to read more and more words even though the words are not directly and explicitly taught (Kilpatrick, 2015; Seidenberg, 2017; Share, 1999). Eventually, this self-teaching takes over, enabling fluent readers to build their brain dictionaries on their own. For me, this is one of the most important reasons to give students opportunities to read a variety of texts as often as possible. The more words they encounter, especially in settings such as guided-reading groups and supported independent reading time, the more chances their brains have to construct accurate word representations with regard to spelling, sound, and meaning.

Reading practices that give students extended amounts of time to read a variety of authentic, connected text translate into gains in fluency and vocabulary (Graves & Watts-Taffe, 2002; Liu & Zhang, 2018) and generally foster improved reading proficiency (Allington, 2009). Researchers Mol and Bus call the link between more reading and increased comprehension and spelling ability "an upward spiral of causality" (2011). For me, that's a fancy way to say one good thing leads to another. But if students are to accumulate these good things, they must have quality teachers, quality reading experiences in a variety of texts, and a volume of reading

(Topping et al., 2007). These quality reading experiences in volumes of text only occur when there is ample time. But how much?

Ivey and Fisher (2006) recommended the amount of time spent in the act of reading be greater than the amount devoted to instruction. For instance, if my reading block is 45 minutes long and I instruct my students for a total of 22 minutes, then those children should be reading for at least 23 minutes. Richard Allington (2006) wants more, suggesting that a minimum of 90 minutes be devoted to high-success reading activities every school day. This number excludes reading in tiny fits and spurts, such as when a student might complete a worksheet or scan a spelling list, but does include extended reading done in guided groups, independent time, content areas, and even a lunchtime book club. When thinking about a busy school day, a total of 90 minutes of uninterrupted reading time might strike you as an enormous number (it strikes me this way). But it is a necessary goal to work toward, for some young readers need a great deal of practice to master the complex skill of reading. In effect, they need to read, read, read.

Unfortunately, teachers can't rely on anyone outside the educational system to provide reading opportunities. Whereas some parents practice reading with their children, reinforce it at home, and set limits on screen time, others don't. There is also the issue of unequal access: Many parents want to provide reading and learning opportunities but are not in the position to do so. Regardless of the reasons, students are spending fewer and fewer hours reading extended text outside of the school setting (Pennington & Waxler, 2017; Wolf, 2018).

It's also unfortunate that some schools aren't programming enough extended reading opportunities. Brenner et al. (2009) found that school students spent, on average, only 20 percent of a 90-minute block reading any type of connected text. The bulk of the time was spent on activities such as teacher instruction, completing workbook pages, and classroom activities like playing word games. In another study, Brenner and Hiebert (2010) found that third-grade core-reading programs offered limited opportunities to read, specifically an average of 15 minutes per day, during which there was no specific mandate to have children read extensively out of books. Moving ahead a few years, a 2016 YouGov survey of over 4,000 teachers found only 36 percent of them programmed daily independent reading while 42 percent provided three or fewer opportunities a month (YouGov, 2016, p. 5).

Fortunately, even small increases in reading extended text can boost reading achievement. For example, Kuhn and Schwanenflugel (2009) found that classrooms of second-grade students who made significant gains in reading achievement had more reading time programmed than classrooms of students who did not. Amazingly, the gains were brought about by adding just seven minutes each day.

Knowing that even small increases in daily reading can lead to big gains in reading achievement, it makes sense to include as many extended-reading opportunities as possible in Tier 1 reading blocks, even as we also strive to give some children more direct and explicit instruction in phonology and orthography. In my book *Super Core* (2014), I suggest a minimum of 15 minutes for independent reading and 15 minutes for guided reading, which means at least 33 percent of a daily 90-minute reading block is given to encounters with connected, extended text. Once achieved, the challenge is to increase both numbers to 20, for an increase of five minutes in each practice leads to more than 26 extra hours of extended reading in a school year.

What follow are frameworks, routines, and activities that can help you give your students more opportunities for extended reading. We'll start with guided reading, move to independent, and examine repeated reading along the way.

IMPORTANT POINT

To become readers, students must practice with support and guidance from adults, as well as read on their own. But children also benefit when adults read to them. Parents and teachers have been reading out loud to young children since forever, and research supports the commonsense practice. One meta-analysis from 2011 is especially illuminating. Titled "A Synthesis of Read-Aloud Interventions on Early Reading Outcomes Among Preschool Through Third Graders at Risk for Reading Difficulties," the study generally points out that reading to students provides social and emotional benefits, positive impacts on language and literacy development, and an uptick in motivation to read (Swanson et al., 2011). It goes on to say that meta-analyses from prior decades provide support for reading aloud as an effective practice for helping children at risk for reading difficulties. Finally and most specifically, it states that instructional read-alouds, such as ones that use repeated reading; questioning before, during, and after reading; and/or extended vocabulary activities, have "significant, positive effects on children's language, phonological awareness, print concepts, comprehension, and vocabulary outcomes" (Swanson et al., 2011). If you'd like to revisit the instructional read-aloud, see Bringing It All Together: The Interactive Read-Aloud, which is the last section of Chapter 4.

Small-Group Guided Reading

The concept of guided reading was originally developed in New Zealand in the 1960s by Marie Clay and others (Lesley University, 2020). Later, after expanding upon Clay's ideas, Irene Fountas and Gay Su Pinnell wrote the 1996 book *Guided Reading: Responsive Teaching Across the Grades* and launched a teaching framework that swept America. Over the last 25 years, Fountas and Pinnell's original book has become something of a bible in the world of elementary school reading instruction, with many teachers closely following its methods. At the same time, other teachers begin with the framework's foundational ideas and then forge a path of their own.

Fundamental to guided reading is the idea that teachers work with small groups of students who are at similar reading levels. Assessment information and teacher observation contribute to the formation of the groups. In the small-group setting, students are given level-appropriate books to read, ones slightly above their independent reading level. The main emphasis is on *guiding* students as they use strategies to solve reading roadblocks and understand text more deeply.

During a guided-reading session, teachers model problem-solving strategies, such "read through each word," "look for a letter pattern," "think about the meaning," "use context," "make a connection," "go back and reread," and so forth. Then, as students read in their instructional-level text, teachers guide and coach the students, helping them to solidify the use of the skills they are learning. Through this process, students gain the reading skills they need to advance to higher-level texts (see Figure 7.1 for a glimpse of this in action).

I've included guided reading in this book because the small-group framework is an effective practice for preventing and lessening reading difficulties. It provides differentiation, scaffolded instruction, opportunities for formative assessment and progress monitoring, and a chance for students to read extended text. Any of these instructional elements is powerful in and of itself; in combination, they are especially effective. Also, the structure of guided reading and the books typically used within it support struggling beginning readers as they work toward accuracy, an especially important component of fluency. Simply put, when

Figure 7.1

Running a Guided-Reading Group

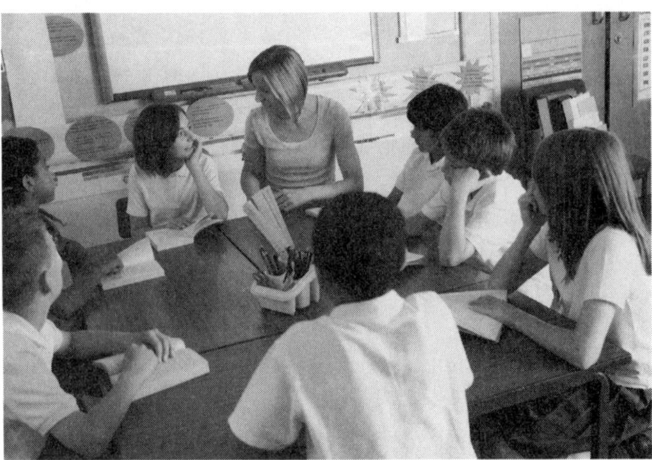

iStock.com/monkeybusinessimages

working with struggling beginning readers, aim for high accuracy (Rodgers et al., 2018).

Another reason guided reading is in this book is I have a hunch that a fair number of teachers, especially ones teaching second and third grade, don't use the framework much. I can't point to specific research that says this is true, but in my years of teaching in multiple elementary schools and in my extensive travels across the country, I have met and continue to meet primary grade teachers who do little to no guided reading. So I hope this section encourages teachers to get started on or go deeper into the practice.

THE BASICS: WHAT HAPPENS AND HOW IT UNFOLDS

It is beyond the scope of this book to teach you how to do guided reading. Also, although I have successfully run guided-reading groups in the primary grades (K–3), I am in no way an expert in the Fountas and Pinnell or *Reading Recovery* versions of it (sometimes written with capitals, as in Guided Reading). What follows, then, is a brief outline of traditional guided reading (à la Fountas and Pinnell), examples of lowercase guided reading that differs from the traditional, and a few tips I have picked up from masterful teachers.

Let's start with a basic outline of what happens in a traditional guided-reading group (Fountas & Pinnell, 2020; Lesley University, 2020):

- Students are grouped according to their reading achievement and their needs.
- The skill work that is the focus of the lesson is typically the same for each student in the small group.
- The teacher works with small groups of students, ideally three to six of them. Typically, the groups gather at a kidney-shaped table.
- Groups are flexible, meaning that students can be moved into one group or another based on either their reading level or their need for specific skill development (more on this in a moment). Flexibility also means groups are frequently adjusted based on ongoing assessment and observation. Some students will progress more quickly or slowly than others; some students will develop the need for different skills at different times.
- During the lesson, students read text slightly above their independent level.
- The teacher coaches and guides the students as they read, encouraging them to solve their reading roadblocks by employing strategies. The teacher also gathers assessment information, often in the form of a running record.
- The emphasis is on reading increasingly challenging books over time.

Here is the flow of a traditional guided-reading lesson:

- Students build fluency by rereading a previous text for several minutes.
- The teacher introduces the new text. Often, this involves a routine, such as this:
    - Point out and briefly discuss the book's front and back covers.
    - Look and discuss the pictures in the book (do a picture walk).
    - Guide students as they make predictions about the story.
    - Introduce new vocabulary words.

- Next, students read the text out loud. They do not take turns reading round-robin style. Rather, each student reads the whole text. Typically, the method is whisper-reading, in which children read (starting at staggered times) in a quiet voice. As a student reads, the teacher guides and coaches him or her. The teacher also gathers assessment information, often in the form of a running record.
- After the students have read their text and received guidance from the teacher, the teacher leads a discussion of the text. The discussion could involve asking and answering questions, talking about how reading roadblocks were solved, and/or giving the students two medals (pointing out what they did well) and a mission (what the teacher wants them to keep working on).

DIFFERENT DIRECTIONS

Earlier, I mentioned teachers who forge their own guided-reading path. The framework of ideas that has become guided reading exists beyond the Fountas and Pinnell programs. Once you deeply understand how the reading process works, you can bend and flex small-group instruction to fit the needs of your unique learners, as well as your own instructional style. A word of caution, though: Firmly ground yourself in the science and art of reading instruction before you bend and flex; otherwise something might break! Still, there is no ultimate way of teaching guided reading, just as there is no one way to teach reading itself. With that in mind, here are examples of variety within guided-reading instruction:

- Some teachers start with a minilesson that directly and explicitly describes and models the reading strategy they want their students to employ. An introduction to new text follows, perhaps using the routine described previously. After this, the strategy is described and modeled once more. Finally, the students begin to whisper-read their new text.
- Rather than using running records, teachers gather assessment data in other ways, such as oral-reading fluency probes and teacher-created checklists.
- For children who have or may have dyslexia, researcher Sally Shaywitz encourages teachers to use guided repeated oral-reading techniques (Shaywitz & Shaywitz, 2020). What better place to do this than in a guided-reading group? For more on repeated reading, see the next section of this chapter.

- Rather than reading levels, specific skills can determine group formation. For example, a group might focus on a language comprehension strategy, such as predicting and checking, and this group might contain readers on a variety of levels. Meanwhile, another group might be learning to use a phonic decoding strategy such as "read through the entire word." Years ago, my mother was a first-grade teacher who made use of this type of skill-based grouping. Figure 7.2 shows the type of guided-reading assignment chart she used: Before school started, she placed one of three colors next to students who needed instruction on a specific skill. For example, for those who needed practice with recognizing patterns in words, she placed a red card next to each name. Then during guided reading time, she called on the red group.
- As a reading interventionist and third-grade teacher, I regularly used direct and explicit phonics instruction, as well as decodable text, in some of my guided-reading groups. In third grade, because I ran 25-minute small-group sessions (concurrently with my coteacher), I could devote seven or eight minutes to pattern work prior to the main part of the session, which was comprehension-based. I also folded in more repeated readings.
- Some researchers and writers, such as Timothy Shanahan, Distinguished Professor Emeritus at the University of Illinois at Chicago, push back on the idea that students should use texts slightly above their reading level (i.e., instructional-level text) in Grades 2 and above, often advocating using more complex, upper-level texts (Shanahan, 2017a). This can be accomplished by giving students a variety of supports. It seems to me a guided-reading group is the perfect setting for trying out this idea.

Here's a quick story that speaks to the power of small-group instruction, motivation as a driver of skill acquisition, and the wisdom we find in reading research. One school year in early March, I had a third-grade guided-reading group of five students who were close to a beginning third-grade level. To a tee, the kids loved dogs, so when they saw multiple copies of *Balto and the Great Race* (by Elizabeth Cody Kimmel) on the bookrack, they were super excited. "Can we read it, Mr. Weakland?" they begged.

I was reticent because the book was 112 pages long and written on a fourth- or fifth-grade level, well above their instructional level.

Figure 7.2

Assignment Chart for Creating Skill-Based Guided-Reading Groups

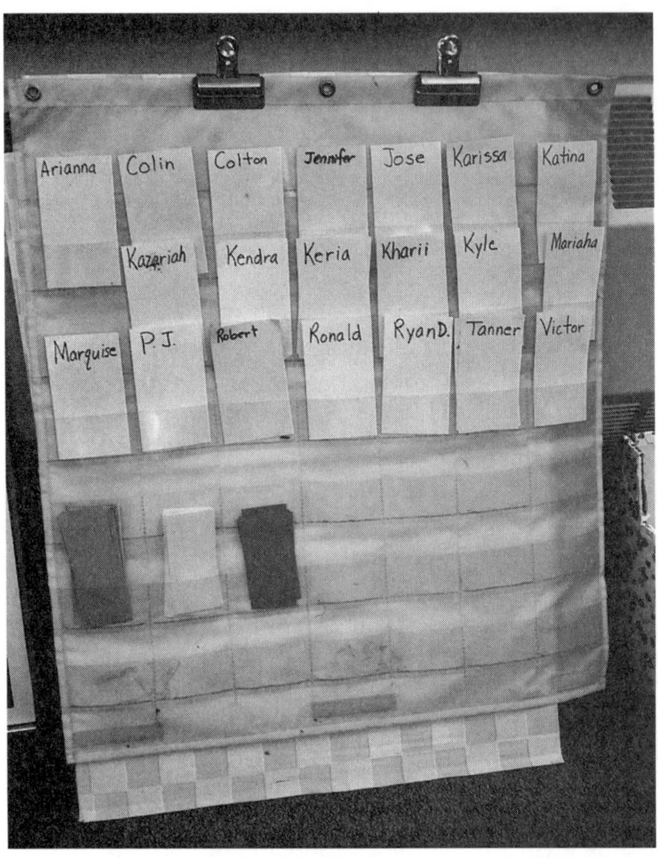

But because the students were motivated to read and because I could provide lots of support in their small group, I decided to give it a shot. In addition to strategy instruction, I did a fair amount of "teacher reads, you track along," as well as a lot of choral reading. As the weeks went by (it took us more than four weeks to read the book—an eternity in guided reading), their skill acquisition and fluency continued to rise. Also, they were exposed to a lot of vocabulary and gained a good deal of background knowledge, plus they experienced a wider variety of sentence structure than normal. Best of all, they finished a long chapter book, which brought a tremendous sense of accomplishment. "A hundred and twelve pages! I can't believe we read the whole book!" one exclaimed. Now if a comment like that doesn't make your teacher heart sing, I don't know what will.

FOR FURTHER STUDY ●●●

If you want to begin guided reading or become more skillful at using it, here are resources to explore. Also, I encourage you to find two teachers who are excellent at running guided-reading groups, watch them do their thing, and then do what they do!

- *Guided Reading: Responsive Teaching Across the Grades* by Irene Fountas and Gay Su Pinnell, (2016, 2nd ed.)
- *Who's Doing the Work* by Jan Burkins and Kim Yaris, 2016
- *The Next Step Forward in Guided Reading* by Jan Richardson, 2019
- *Guided Reading: Responsive Teaching in Grades K–2* at Lesley University Center for Reading Recovery and Literacy Collaborative (https://lesley.edu/center-for-reading-recovery-and-literacy-collaborative/guided-reading-responsive-teaching-in-grades-k-2)
- *Guided Reading for Struggling Readers* at Clemson University Reading Recovery Training Center (https://readingrecovery.clemson.edu/guided-reading-for-struggling-readers/)

TIPS FOR STARTING AND SCHEDULING

I suggest you do NOT start your guided-reading groups at the beginning of school. Rather, take some time, perhaps as long as four or five weeks, and teach students how to read independently. Ideas for how to do this are presented toward the end of this chapter. During this time, you'll be teaching writing, too. Both the *Kid Writing* and writers' workshop develop independent writing ability. When students can read independently for 15 to 20 minutes and do some independent writing, perhaps by the beginning or middle of October, you will have set the stage for the successful management of guided-reading groups.

The flexible nature of a guided-reading group is often discussed. What might not be mentioned is this, my second tip: The number of times you meet with each group is also flexible. In other words, in any given week you don't have to meet each group an equal number of times. In fact, meeting with a lower-achieving group more often than a higher-achieving group can be a way to prevent reading difficulties.

Let's say that through a variety of assessments, you have identified four distinct groups of readers in your classroom, ranging from low to high achieving. As an example, Figure 7.3 shows data on a diverse group of first graders I worked with in February and March of 2020. To retain their anonymity, I've changed their names. The number next to each student's name is a grade-level equivalent from Renaissance's Star Reading assessment. Although the groups have letter names, *A* to *D*, they also have color names. Colors allow for grouping that is less overtly hierarchical. They also easily transfer to color-coded book bins and book stickers (see the last section of this chapter).

Figure 7.3

First-Grade Classroom's Range of Readers

Lowest achieving ←			→ Highest achieving
Group A **(Blue)**	***Group B*** **(Green)**	***Group C*** **(Red)**	***Group D*** **(Yellow)**
Aryanna*	Lyon 1.2	Juel 2.0	Adian 3.6
Madison*	Cynthia 1.3	Hakeem 1.8	Emma 3.5
Bryson*	Zahari 1.3	Zoe 2.2	
Jose*	Miella 1.8	Caden 1.9	
Mahalie*	(lacks confidence)	Liam 2.0	

*All in Group A are beginning, preprimer readers near or at the end of kindergarten level.

The students in Group A, with reading levels almost a full year behind where they should be, need much more support and instruction if they are going to catch up. This can be provided by creating a schedule that allows you to teach Group A more often than Group D. Just as you shift your weight to balance your body as you ski or bike, shift your schedule to balance the needs of your students.

Figure 7.4 shows a schedule that reflects that balancing. Note that each guided-reading group meets for 15 minutes, there is time to see only one group on Monday and Friday, and whenever a group meets with the teacher, all the other students are busily engaged in independent reading and writing activities (more on this in the last section of this chapter). Figure 7.5 shows a second schedule, one that allows you to meet with Group D twice a week. This schedule could be rotated biweekly with Schedule #1.

Figure 7.4

Guided-Reading Schedule #1

Monday	Tuesday	Wednesday	Thursday	Friday
Group A (blue)	Group B (green) Group C (red)	Group D (yellow) Group A (blue)	Group B (green) Group C (red)	Group A (blue)

Figure 7.5

Guided-Reading Schedule #2

Monday	Tuesday	Wednesday	Thursday	Friday
Group A (blue)	Group D (yellow) Group B (green)	Group C (red) Group A (blue)	Group D (yellow) Group B (green)	Group A (blue)

Figure 7.6 tallies the effects of the two schedules. The result is students in Group A, significantly below reading benchmarks, receive twice the amount of guided-reading instruction as students in Groups C and D, who are solidly achieving or exceeding reading benchmarks. And speaking of Groups C and D, an asymmetrical schedule gives higher-achieving students more time to engage their reading circuitry through independent reading, where they will have many opportunities to increase their vocabulary, bolster their background knowledge, and strengthen their orthographic mapping circuits (via the self-teaching principle).

Appendix E provides more guided-reading schedules. Remember: Students who are at risk of developing reading difficulties (or who are already experiencing them) need more time with skillful teachers than students who are already strong readers.

Figure 7.6

Breakdown of Guided-Reading Instruction, Schedules 1 and 2

Every Two Weeks . . .	Group A	Group B	Group C	Group D
Number of times each group is seen	6	4	3	3
Number of minutes of guided reading given	90	60	45	45
Number of minutes available for independent reading/writing	150	180	195	195

Reading to Develop Fluency

Reading fluency—the ability to read accurately at an appropriate rate and with proper expression and phrasing—is essential to reading comprehension (LaBerge & Samuels, 1974; Stevens et al., 2017). Thus, it's best to use instructional practices that build all elements of fluency.

Importantly, fluency is more than rate or quickness of reading. My definition of fluency is this: reading the words of any text accurately, at a reasonable pace, and with expression and phrasing that sounds like someone talking. In "The Great Fluency Rush" that followed the 2000 release of the National Reading Panel's Report, fluency work was everywhere in schools, assessments like DIBELS and programs like Read Naturally were ubiquitous, and reading rate sometimes became synonymous with fluency. I like to say that "rate was overrated." In some schools, rate is still overrated! So I'm glad that researchers like Shaywitz and Shanahan, and organizations like the Iowa Reading Research Center (IRRC), remind us that it's important to build accuracy first, as well as not lose sight of expression and phrasing (IRRC, n.d.; Shanahan, 2017b; Shaywitz & Shaywitz, 2020). As the IRCC puts it, "Reading quality rather than reading speed."

One especially effective and efficient practice that builds students' reading fluency, especially accuracy, expression, and phrasing, is repeated reading. The activity provides less skilled readers with the opportunity to hear a model of fluent reading and then practice it in a way that minimizes errors. Additionally, reading aloud together, sometimes with the teacher, supports students who feel shy or nervous about reading out loud, lessens the stress of reading independently, and can help build self-confidence.

Using the practice of repeated reading typically leads to improved reading performance, especially for low-performing readers (Zawoyski et al., 2014), with the biggest payoffs being more accurate word reading, improved oral-reading fluency, and more reading comprehension (Shanahan, 2017b). Still, some schools and teachers don't make use of this powerful practice, which dyslexia researcher Sally Shaywitz (2020) has pointed out:

> The proven effectiveness of guided repeated oral reading to increase fluency is too often ignored. That is unacceptable. In fact, the evidence is so strong that I urge adoption of these programs as an integral part of every school reading curriculum throughout primary school. (p. 233)

Fortunately, it doesn't take much time and effort to understand and then adopt the practice in your reading block.

There are a variety of ways to do repeated reading. All versions, however, have a few key ingredients:

- **Oral reading**, as opposed to silent reading, so teachers can monitor word pronunciations, give feedback, and note errors
- **Teacher support**, provided when the teacher first models the passage and continuing if she reads along with the students
- **Feedback**, important because feedback gives readers input that helps them master specific words. This helps create the exact pronunciation and spelling of the words processed by and stored within neural circuitry (Shaywitz & Shaywitz, 2020).
- **Repetition**, that is, reading a passage multiple times in order to reach either a goal, such as a particular number of correct words read within a minute, WCPM, or a number or repetitions, such as three times in a row (Shanahan, 2017b).

Just as guided reading exists in capitalized and noncapitalized forms, so too does repeated reading. Here are variations on the theme, with the first being the capitalized one.

REPEATED READING

Repeated Reading is the specific (and thus capitalized) routine pioneered by reading researcher Jay Samuels. It has been shown to be effective at improving the oral-reading fluency of elementary students, including those with learning disabilities (Kim et al., 2017; Lee & Yoon, 2017; Stevens et al., 2017). According to Timothy Shanahan (2017b),

> Repeated Reading is a particular method . . . to develop decoding automaticity with struggling readers. In this approach, students are asked to read aloud short text passages (50–200 words) until they reach a criterion level of success (particular speed and accuracy goals). (para. 12)

Key components of capitalized *Repeated Reading* stretch beyond the previously mentioned ingredients of generic repeated reading to include instant error correction and peer mediation. If you would like to further explore the specific methodology of *Repeated Reading*, check out the Iowa Reading Researcher Center's blog listed in the For Further Reading section.

●●● FOR FURTHER READING

Here are resources to explore if you want to use Samuel's *Repeated Reading* method.

- "Repeated Reading With Goal Setting for Reading Fluency: Focusing on Reading Quality Rather Than Reading Speed" by Leah Zimmermann and Deborah K. Reed, 2019, https://iowareadingresearch.org/blog/repeated-reading-fluency
- "Everything You Wanted to Know About Repeated Reading" by Timothy Shanahan, 2017, www.readingrockets.org/blogs/shanahan-literacy/everything-you-wanted-know-about-repeated-reading
- "The Method of Repeated Readings" by S. J. Samuel in *The Reading Teacher*, February 1997.

Meanwhile, repeated reading of the uncapitalized kind takes a number of different forms. It can be young students reading a previously read book during independent reading time. It can be an activity in a guided-reading group. It can also be teacher-led choral and echo reading with a large group during poetry practice. Let's take a look at each.

CHORAL AND ECHO READING

Choral reading occurs when students read in unison with the teacher. Echo reading occurs when the teacher reads first and the students read the text back. Kindergarten kids typically echo one sentence. To determine the number of sentences for other grades, consider the demands of the text and the abilities of the students. If students need support and the sentences are relatively difficult (longer and/or with higher decoding demands), one sentence will do. But if sentences are shorter and easier to decode, pick two or three for echoing. Otherwise, students with good short-term memory will simply "parrot back" a sentence without ever reading it.

How To

Echo and choral reading can be used with groups of all sizes, from small to whole. When working with students who need a lot of support, use it regularly. Here's one possibility for what it might look like:

- In a guided-reading group, after students have whisper-read their text and you have identified passages that need extra fluency practice, use the *I Read, We Read, You Read* routine. The *I Read* provides the model of fluent reading, the *We Read* is a choral read, and the *You Read* is an echo read.
- Toward the end of the guided-reading session, ask students to go back into their text, find their two favorite sentences, and practice the sentences on their own for 30 seconds (possibly with paintbrush or whisper-phone reading).
- Finally, ask each student if he or she would like to read out loud. Some students will share and others will pass. Regardless, the result is that all students read selected sentences at least a half dozen times.

As an example of echo reading, let's imagine a guided reading group of five third-grade students who have just finished whisper-reading the text in Figure 7.7. Your teacher talk might sound like this:

Teacher: I saw and heard many of you using strategies to read the second and third paragraphs. I saw Brian reading all the way through his words and then rereading. I heard Chantal cross-checking for meaning. Let's go back and build fluency with the second paragraph. Everyone, point to the beginning of the second paragraph.

Students: [They point to the word *Other*.]

Teacher: We're going to do an *I Read, We Read, You Read.* I will read with a steady rate, with expression, and in smooth phrases. You track with your fingers as I read. [Teacher reads.] "Other items are more unusual. Metal daggers. . . ." [Teacher continues to the end.]

Go back to the beginning of the paragraph. [Students point to the word *Other*.]

Let's read that same passage together. Begin.

All: "Other items are more unusual. Metal daggers. . . ." [Teacher and students continue to the end.]

Teacher: Good effort. Go back to the beginning of the paragraph one last time. [They point to the word *Other*.] You read it. Use phrases and expression. Stay together. Ready? Begin.

Students: "Other items are more unusual. Metal daggers. . . ."

Teacher: I noticed how you broke some sentences into two smooth phrases. I heard you say, "A harp covered (pause) in glittering jewels."

Before we end, look over this page and find two sentences you would like to practice for fluency. [Students look.]

Point to your sentences so I can see the ones you picked. [Students point.]

Reread your sentences for 30 seconds. Do not stop practicing until the timer beeps. Ready? Begin. [Students track and read until the beeper goes off.]

OK. I saw everyone concentrating and reading. Good effort! Brian, would you like to share your two sentences?

Student: Pass.

Teacher: Chantal, how about you?

Student: "I looked up and saw a bear reaching down to grab me. Its mouth was open!"

Teacher: Thank you. You read smoothly and with expression. Did anyone else pick those two sentences?

Figure 7.7

Text for Repeated Reading

Props are the objects that actors use in a play or musical. The props room is crammed full of them. Chairs and sofas. Dishes and silverware. Pictures in wooden frames.

Other items are more unusual. Metal daggers. A harp covered in glittering jewels. A chest of polished wood holding a dozen golden eggs.

I dashed to the prop room to find something right for a detective. When I got there, I noticed the door was open. But no one was around. "Mr. Jamar?" I called.

The room was dark. I felt along the wall but couldn't find the light switch. "Mr. Jamar?" I called again. No reply.

I tiptoed in, carefully feeling my way around a grandfather clock and a suit of armor. In the darkness, I stumbled against a bench. Ka-thunk!

A metal sword fell to the floor, almost slicing my foot. I jerked backward, tripped, and stumbled against something furry. It was an enormous foot. With long black claws.

I looked up and saw a bear reaching down to grab me. Its mouth was open. White fangs gleamed in the darkness. . . .

Source: From *Bibi LeBreeze, Theater Detective* by Mark Weakland [Unpublished manuscript].

CONNECTIONS

These book sections make explicit and implicit connections to the practice of rereading:

Chapter 3

- Instant error correction (error-free learning)
- Repetition and distributed practice
- Direct and explicit instruction

Chapter 4

- Interactive read-aloud

Chapter 6

- Building orthographic skills through reading
- Decodable text

Chapter 7

- Guided reading
- Poetry reread

Reading Poems: Shared, Guided, and Independent

Playful, lyrical, musical, moving,

Hopeful, joyful, anguished, blue.

Concentrated yet expansive,

To the norm they may not hew.

Read in classrooms and on stages,

Through the ages, old and new.

Small but mighty, I applaud them, and

Wonder if you laud them, too.

—M. W.

WHY USE POEMS?

To me, poems share a lot with Yoda, pop-up books, and cans of Popeye's spinach: They take up little space but store tremendous wisdom, delightful surprise, and fortifying energy. Poems work beautifully within early-reading instruction because they lend themselves to the teaching and practicing of a variety of literacy elements, including fluency, phonic patterns, vocabulary building, speaking and listening, genre and author study, grammar and sentence structure study, asking and answering questions, and comprehension through close reading. Additionally, poems are relatively easy to find and manage, and they can be used for shared reading, guided reading, and independent reading. Finally, most children find poems engaging and enjoy reading and presenting them. I attribute this to the brevity, rhythms, and rhymes of poems, as well as their ability to evoke a wide variety of feelings and wonderment. Also, there's this, told to me by a parent: "My kids say they like reading and writing poems because poems break the rules."

When striving readers fluently read and then present a poem to others, they gain a real sense of accomplishment and success. During my years of working with low-achieving third graders, I presented maybe two poems a month. Now whenever

I teach in classrooms, I use three or four poems every two weeks. Presenting a variety of poems allows me to differentiate for reading levels, provides possibilities for classroom activities, gives students choice in what they read, and provides options when each student creates a personal poetry anthology (more on this in a bit).

If you need poems for teaching your primary grade readers, Figure 7.8 provides solid starting points.

Figure 7.8

Where to Find Poems for Kids

Poetry Anthologies

Naomi Shihab Nye	*A Maze Me: Poems for Girls*
Edward Lear	*A Book of Nonsense*
Shel Silverstein	*Where the Sidewalk Ends*
Jack Prelutsky	*Read-Aloud Poems for the Very Young*
Francisco X. Alarcón	*Belly Button of the Moon*
Robert Louis Stevenson	*A Child's Garden of Verses*
Nikki Giovanni	*Hip Hop Speaks to Children*
Steve Attewell	*Once, I Laughed My Socks Off*
Judith Viorst	*Sad Underwear and Other Complications*
Roald Dahl	*Revolting Rhymes*
Mary Ann Hoberman	*The Llama Who Had No Pajama*
Kwame Alexander	*Out of Wonder*

Poetry Websites

Lit2Go

https://etc.usf.edu/lit2go/59/a-childs-garden-of-verses-selected-poems/

The Children's Poetry Archive

https://childrens.poetryarchive.org

The Poetry Foundation

You can filter the search for children's poems: https://www.poetryfoundation.org/

Teaching Tip

I found this Renaissance classic in the Poetry Foundation's children's section. In mid-October, pass out the witchy-poo pointer fingers, model a good ghoul voice, and let your third graders have at it. By Halloween, some will be clamoring to recite this poem from memory!

Song of the Witches by William Shakespeare (from *Macbeth*)

Double, double toil and trouble;
Fire burn and caldron bubble.
Fillet of a fenny snake,
In the caldron boil and bake;
Eye of newt and toe of frog,
Wool of bat and tongue of dog,
Adder's fork and blind-worm's sting,
Lizard's leg and howlet's wing . . .
Double, double toil and trouble;
Fire burn and caldron bubble.

Between well-stocked websites and comprehensive print collections, you can amass dozens of poems for kids to read. If you want to use poems for shared reading, print them on poster-sized sheets or present them on smartboard slides. For guided and independent reading, copy poems on single sheets. Finally, be aware that under fair-use guidelines, it is fine to reproduce entire poems for teaching and to make them available to your students in all manner of media. But sharing downloaded poems with other teachers might be a copyright violation.

LOOSELY LEVELING POEMS

Gathering poems written on various levels gives you teaching flexibility. More specifically, leveled poems dovetail with these instructional best practices: choice, challenging text, shared reading, interactive read-alouds, small-group instruction, and supported independent reading.

Some poems come with a Lexile or grade level. For those that don't, you can type them into an ATOS website or Microsoft Word document to generate a grade level and/or readability score. But I find these scores can be misleading, sometimes egregiously so. That's why I roughly determine the level of a poem and its appropriateness for a particular group of students by using my teacher sense as I consider the following:

- Vocabulary load
- Sentence structure
- Complexity of concepts
- Total number of words
- Number of different phonic patterns presented

To illustrate, Figure 7.9 shows two poems I might present to second graders. Comparing them, I see that although my "Macaroni and Cheese" has a complex visual layout (the poem is written for two or more readers), it has half the number of words of "Bed in Summer" by Robert Louis Stevenson, fewer phonic patterns,

Figure 7.9

Two Second-Grade Poems

<table>
<tr><th>Bed in Summer
by Robert Louis Stevenson</th><th>Macaroni and Cheese
by Mark Weakland</th></tr>
<tr><td>In winter I get up at night
And dress by yellow candle-light.
In summer quite the other way,
I have to go to bed by day.

I have to go to bed and see
The birds still hopping on the tree,
Or hear the grown-up people's feet
Still going past me in the street.

And does it not seem hard to you,

When all the sky is clear and blue,
And I should like so much to play,
To have to go to bed by day?</td><td>Making macaroni and cheese
is a breeze.
It's as easy as one, two, three.
Step one: Macaroni
Step two: Add the cheese.
Step three: Serve yourself.
Hey! How about me?
Oh yeah . . .
Serve each other
Want some more?
Pretty please!</td></tr>
</table>

Source: From the collection *The Delicious Chocolate Donut (And Other Off-Kilter Poems).*

more repeated words, more contemporary language, and relatively simple subject matter. Thus, I think "Macaroni and Cheese" would be appropriate for readers who need more support. Meanwhile, the Stevenson poem would be best for shared reading: Its meaning is more complex, it would lead to more questioning and inferring, and some of my striving readers might find its length daunting. Finally, I would assign the Stevenson poem to my more advanced readers for independent reading, but I would give all my students the choice to read both.

Appendix B contains another example of leveled poems.

ROUTINE FOR TEACHING READING SKILLS THROUGH POEMS

Finding three poems of varying levels allows you to follow a three-day routine that incorporates a variety of practices, from applying comprehension strategies to noticing phonic patterns and rereading for fluency. I think teachers familiar with "shared reading" will find parts of this poetry routine to be that very thing, for it gives students a chance to join in the reading and thus see themselves as readers.

First Day (15 to 20 minutes)

- Using the upper-level poem, engage students in discussion around the title and preteach vocabulary words using direct and explicit instruction. All of this builds language comprehension (topic, background, vocabulary) before reading.
- Next, read the poem three times using *the I Read, We Read, You Read* method (direct and explicit instruction with gradual release). After the first read, point out any rhyming words and discuss any patterns.
- After *I Read, We Read, You Read*, discuss the poem using shared reading or interactive read-aloud techniques. Focus points for modeling and discussion might be text-to-text connections, thin and thick questions, visualizing, and so on. Read a section of the poem, do a think-out-loud (such as "I think the author is trying to . . ." or "I see that this sentence connects back to the beginning where . . ."), and ask questions, such as "Why did the author use this word," "What do you think this sentence means," and "What is the author trying to say here?"

Second Day (10 to 15 minutes)

- Using the midlevel and lower-level poems, talk about the titles and preteach vocabulary words. For some poems, you may want to show a picture or two (à la the slideshow mentioned in Chapter 4). Also, point out rhyming words and discuss their patterns.
- If a poem lends itself to movement, fold it into your instruction. Giving students opportunities to move is always a good idea!
- Next, read each poem three times using the *I Read, We Read, You Read* method.
- After the *You Read*, ask a comprehension question that centers on your comprehension skills for the week. For example, if I were focusing on text-to-text connections, I might ask, "What do these two poems have in common?" or "How do these two poems relate to the poem we read yesterday?"

Third Day (10 to 15 minutes)

- Have an appropriate number of three-hole punched copies of each poem ready. For example, in a class of 20 students you might have eight students reading the upper-level poem, six reading the midlevel, and six reading the lower. Also, have additional copies on hand in case students want to pick a second or third poem and put it in their individual poetry anthology.
- In a whole-group setting, keeping the pace brisk and using a poster or smartboard slide, read each poem using *I Read* and *We Read*. No need to do *You Read* because they'll have plenty of chances to do this in just a minute.
- Next, pass out individual poems for fluency practice. Students receive the poem that is most appropriate for their current achievement level.
- Using a quiet "1-inch" voice, students practice reading their poem at their desks for one minute. If a student says, "I'm done," or if he stops reading, say, "Practice it again. Time is not up yet." Prompt students to fine-tune expression, phrasing, and accuracy.
- Students pair up. Using a quiet "1-inch" voice, they take turns presenting their poem to each other. This lasts for two minutes. If students say, "We're done," or if they stop reading, prompt them as you did for solo reading.

- Students go back to their seats and read their poem one last time.
- Randomly call on two to three students. When called upon, they can either "pass" or present to the class.
- After each presentation, directly and explicitly describe any reading behavior you want to highlight and praise, such as effort, accuracy, phrasing, expression that demonstrated meaning, a strong voice, and the like.
- After each presentation, have the class give a round of applause or other cheer.

Figure 7.10

Poetry Practice

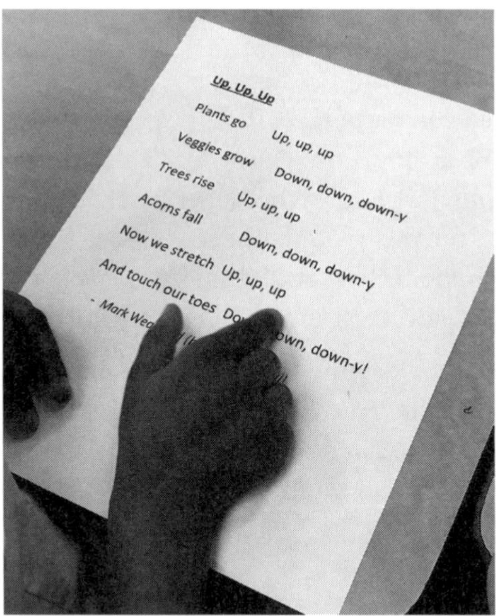

(b) iStock.com/SyhinStas

(c) iStock.com/PeopleImages

PERSONAL POETRY ANTHOLOGIES

Personal poetry anthologies grow and expand as the months go by, reflecting a child's reading preferences. Each poem in the anthology provides an opportunity for students to reread, build fluency, and share their reading with others.

Regardless of whether or not you use the aforementioned three-day routine, put the poem a child has read into a binder or folder with his or her name on it. I give students the option to take a second or even third poem, each typically at a different level of difficulty. Thus, after two months some children will have a dozen poems in their anthology while others may have only four or five. If your budget and/or storage space is limited, store poems in a two-pocket folder with or without fasteners. If you don't use fasteners, I suggest gradually stapling the poems into packets of six to eight (so papers don't go flying if the poems fall out).

Here's a list for students that provides options for poetry anthologies:

- During independent reading time, you can read . . .
  - At your desk or in the cozy chair (sign up)
  - With a partner on the carpet—read the entire poem

- With a partner—take turns and read every other sentence
- In a trio—take turns reading the sentences
- With a whisper-phone or paintbrush

- During share time . . .
  - Dramatically read a poem
  - Present a poem with buddies, using two or more voices (duo or trio)

Figure 7.11

Poems Gathered in an Anthology

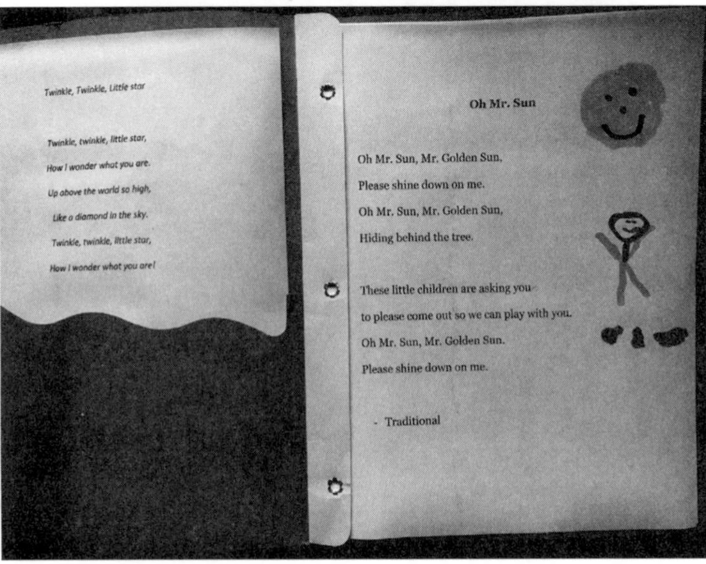

Teaching Tip

Fluent reading unfolds smoothly, with expression and in broad brushstrokes of phrasing. To drive the point home, introduce *Paintbrush Reading*. First, put out a container filled with small paintbrushes. Then, allow your students to take a paintbrush and reread a poem or passage by pulling the brush smoothly below the sentences (Figures 7.12a–b). It's a kinesthetic trick that keeps kids engaged as they reread. Encourage the reading of phrases, smoothly, in broad strokes. Read like a painter, not . . . like . . . a . . . pointer! The video linked from the QR code shows an example of *Paintbrush Reading*.

Video example of *Paintbrush Reading*: https://www.youtube.com/watch?v=birTbUgUgKI

Figure 7.12

Paintbrush Reading, Solo and Duos

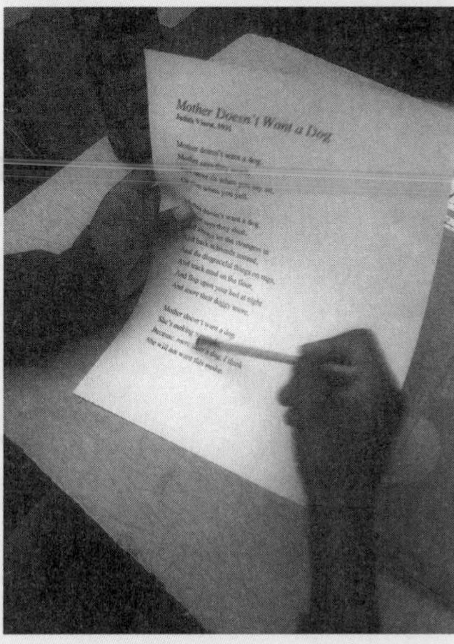

Supported Independent Reading

It's independent reading time, and students are hunched over desks reading early chapter books, sprawled on the floor gazing at picture books, and curled into the classroom's cozy chair practicing a poem, lips moving silently to the rhythm of the words. Sometimes, the reading experience is shared, as when two readers partner to read a big book about sea creatures. At other times, it is tech driven, with readers "flipping" through digital pages on an iPad or Chromebook.

Common to all of these types of reading is a state of reading *flow*. When students are caught up in flow, they are captivated by the text, enthralled with unfolding story lines, and engaged in a way that demands turning to the next page again and again.

How do we help students reach a state of reading flow? Fostering motivation is one way because intrinsic motivation has a positive effect on reading engagement. It also benefits reading achievement, comprehension, and how much text readers read (Guthrie et al., 1999; McGeown et al., 2015; Schiefele et al., 2016). Working with students, you can almost see the positive feedback loop in action: Success motivates children to read more, reading more helps them acquire skills, skill acquisition leads to greater reading ability, greater ability leads to more success . . . you get the idea. It's the best half of the Matthew Effect, whereby the rich keep getting richer.

When setting up independent reading routines that motivate, keep the following in mind:

- Reading an entire book, be it *Green Eggs and Ham* or *Make Way for Dyamonde Daniel*, is a significant accomplishment to a primary age child. Thus, regardless of size and style, **books** are motivating.
- **Choice** motivates humans of all ages. Just like us, children choose books that feature things they are interested in. Also, it's important to have choice in how you read: in a picture book, on an e-tablet, alone at a desk, with a partner on the carpet, in a house, with a mouse, in a box, with a fox . . .
- **A classroom culture that values and celebrates reading** can support students as they strive to become readers. This culture is built over time through books, organization, and routines.

Supported independent reading includes these components: uninterrupted time for students to deeply engage with reading, a wide variety of well-organized books that are easily accessible, and instruction and routines that help a teacher assess, guide, and build independent reading behaviors. Let's look at the specifics of each.

CREATING TIME FOR READING

Time: There is simply never enough of it. To create time for independent reading, I suggest deemphasizing or even removing instructional practices that are less than effective, including worksheets, workbooks, too much shared reading, and too much summative testing. I took this idea to heart when I reimagined a third-grade core-reading program to specifically help low-achieving readers. Initially, the 100-minute daily reading block had zero minutes for supported independent reading time. To be clear, when students were done with their work, they regularly grabbed a book off a bookshelf and paged through it for a few minutes, waiting for other students to finish. But this independent reading had no supportive organization or structure to it, and most students never got into reading flow. After major schedule revisions, however, students had 80 to 100 minutes a week to engage in supported independent reading. Appendix E has examples of first-, second-, and third-grade literacy block schedules that give time to guided and independent reading.

TEACHING STUDENTS TO BECOME INDEPENDENT READERS

At the beginning of the year, directly and explicitly show students how to think about books, find and choose books, and read them independently. Use think-alouds and modeling to demonstrate the thoughts and behaviors you want students to emulate. Perhaps you'll want to conduct a fishbowl in which students gather around and watch you and two selected students model quiet reading, prolonged reading, finger tracking, and a no-drama way to find a new book.

After a few minilessons that show independent reading behaviors, have the whole group practice independent reading. You may want to set an initial time goal for sustained reading, such as eight minutes. As students read, circulate and quietly point out and describe the positive behaviors they are exhibiting. Guide them away from behaviors that interfere with independent reading. Crouch by a reader and have a little conference—ask questions about what she is reading and how she is solving her reading roadblocks. As the days go by, set new goals for time spent reading. The key is to build stamina, not just for reading a book but for independent work itself. For example, in late September some first graders might be able to read for 16 minutes in one book while others might be able to read two books for eight minutes apiece. Either way, the result is the same: Students work independently for over 15 minutes.

I am not familiar with any studies that give an optimal length of time for primary grade children to independently read. But I've worked in kindergarten classrooms where students happily read on their own (in multiple books) for upwards of 20 minutes; my low-achieving third graders averaged 20 to 25 minutes of independent reading; and teachers interviewed for a Clemson University independent reading project said their kindergarten, first-, and second-grade students read independently for 20 to 25 minutes (Clemson University, 2019). Of course, most students must build up to these numbers, so start out small and keep the faith. To encourage stamina, some teachers post classroom graphs showing progress toward independent, reading, time goals. Figure 7.13 gives three ideas.

Figure 7.13

Graphs for Building Stamina

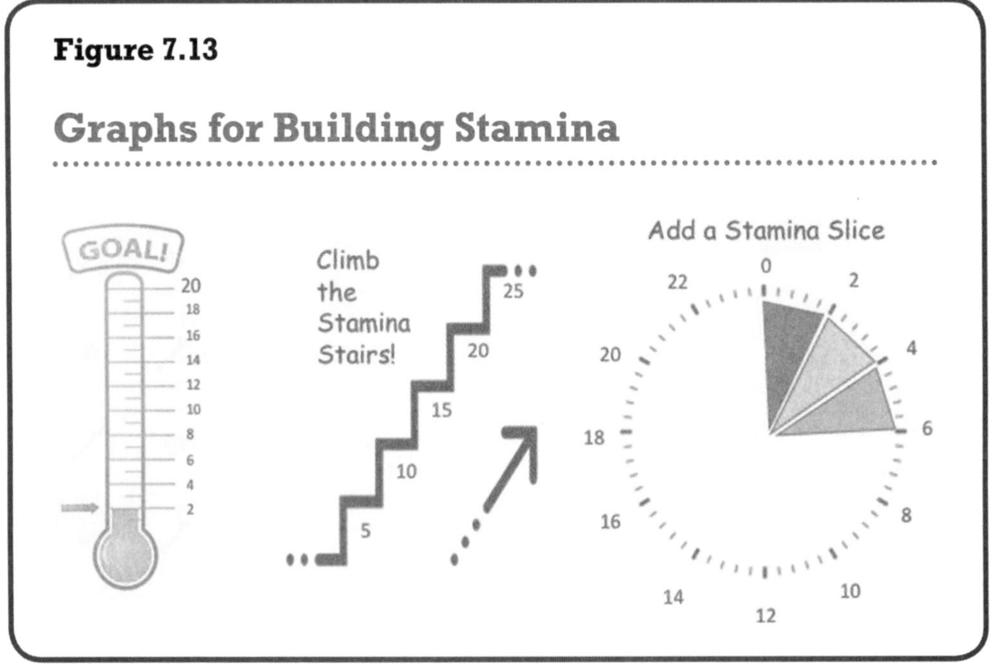

AN EFFECTIVE CLASSROOM LIBRARY

Classroom libraries play an important role in promoting literacy (NCTE, 2017). The research supporting that statement shows robust classroom libraries are a common feature of effective classrooms and can lead students to more motivation to read, increased knowledge of letters and sounds, and large jumps in time spent reading (Allington, 2011; Gambrell et al., 2007; Neumann, 1999).

In their comprehensive 2009 article "Building an Effective Classroom Library," Catapano, Fleming, and Elias gather advice from a multitude of reading experts and synthesize recommendations for classroom library features, including these tips:

- A minimum of 10 books for every child, with no fewer than 100 books total
- The possibility of 700 to 750 books in a primary grade classroom
- Books that vary across topic, genre, and levels, including "plenty that are easy enough for young students to sail through" during independent reading
- Books that are culturally relevant and diverse
- A collection that is gradually and carefully chosen because "it is more important to have high-quality books than to simply have a great number of books" (pp. 62–63)

Teaching Tip

Finding Books for Your Classroom Library

- Ask your administrator if money normally allocated for consumable workbooks can be redirected to the purchase of reading books. Keep your fingers crossed!
- Ask your custodial staff and administrators if they know of books tucked away in a closet, attic, or other out-of-the-way place.
- Post a request for books on social media. If you're lucky, you'll find a close-to-retiring teacher with a high-quality "ready to donate" library.
- Check out the website www.donorschoose.org. It empowers "public school teachers from across the country to request much needed materials."
- Survey your students and generate a list of preferred topics and authors. Then, ask your media specialist to pull 20 or 30 matching books. Put them into dedicated book bins, swapping out old ones for new every three weeks.

(Continued)

(Continued)

- Check thrift shops like Goodwill. Tell the staff you're creating a classroom library and maybe the shop will donate some books. Remember to be choosy: Pick quality over quantity.
- Ask your PTO to hold a book drive. As we speak, scores of little-used books are cluttering the homes of parents and grandparents.

CREATING A CULTURE OF READING: FEATURED BOOKS AND SELLING A BOOK

Before we get to specifics of displaying and organizing books, let's generally discuss how to build enthusiasm for reading. A good starting point is a prominent front-facing book display featuring a few carefully considered books. Take a few moments at the beginning of every week to "sell" two books to your class, telling students why you love each one (it's funny, the pictures are beautiful, the topic is fascinating). Place the books in your front-facing display and watch the kids flock to them! Later in the year, turn the routine into "teacher presents a book, student presents a book."

Figure 7.14

Front-Facing Book Display

Selling a book makes students really want to read it and helps create a classroom reading culture. What's especially fun to see is how primary age children are so easily influenced by your enthusiasm. I remember a kindergartener named Noah, a regular in one of my Title I reading groups. Noah thought every book I introduced was awesome. If I exclaimed, "Today, we are going to read *My Little Hen*!" he would cry, "Awesome!" If I gushed, "The title of this book is *Where We Work*!" he would yell, "Awesome!" There's no doubt that if I had passionately introduced *The Giant Boring Book of Gray Gravel*, Noah would have shouted "Awesome!"

IMPORTANT POINT

Book displays, unleveled browsing bins, and some independent book interaction time can be used even in preK. Giving very young students an opportunity to interact with picture books starts them on the journey of becoming readers and creates a culture of reading in your classroom. It also allows you to teach academic terms such as *book cover*, *title*, *words*, and *illustrations*. Finally, some preschool highfliers can actually recognize words or even read sentences, so let's give them opportunities to continue to practice and grow.

DISPLAYING BOOKS: UNLEVELED BROWSING BINS CATEGORIZED BY THEMES

Throughout this section, I've used the term *supported* independent reading. How is this different from plain old independent reading? Previously mentioned supports for reading, which are especially helpful to readers at risk for reading difficulties, include conferencing, setting incremental goals, modeling independent reading behaviors, and a well-organized classroom library full of a variety of high-quality books. Let's talk about that last item a bit more because organizing books in specific ways can make or break your independent reading routine.

I suggest you do NOT organize your books with spines facing out on bookshelves, as in a traditional public library. Even if your shelves are tidy and your books alphabetically filed, students may be overwhelmed when presented with dozens of choices, and the fuss of looking for a book can be distracting to others, especially if kids start to kibitz as they wander along the shelf. DO organize your books into bins easily accessible to all students and clearly marked as to their contents. Grouping books into small units (bins) makes it easier for young readers to find the category of book they are most interested in, minimizes noise and movement in your classroom, provides opportunities to do genre and author study, and creates more time for students to read (because they spend less time looking for books).

Books can be grouped by either reading level or theme. Each has its pros and cons; I am partial to the latter. When I first started teaching in elementary school, my first attempt at theme-based organizing involved just two bins: nonfiction and fiction. But at least I changed the content of each bin every other week. Although my method was better than a bookshelf, it had room for improvement.

Grouping books into many discrete themes or categories helps students quickly locate their specific interests—Star Wars, animals, early chapter books, dinosaurs, planets, Dr. Seuss, the Wimpy Kid, and so forth.

I like theme organization because I don't have to spend hours leveling books that don't have explicitly listed levels, nor do I have to translate one leveling system into another; for example, I typically think in terms of Developmental Reading Assessment-2 (DRA2) numbers, such as 4, 18, 24, and 40, not Fountas and Pinnell–Guided Reading levels, A, B, F, N). More important, if we consider bins from a learner's' perspective, theme-based bins avoid these potential problems:

- Students cannot find books that interest them in their assigned bins.
- Students feel embarrassed when choosing a book from a low-level bin.
- Readers never find challenging books, which they might read if they're highly motivated by the author, story, and/or subject matter.
- Conversely, readers never find and relax with easy books, ones below their independent level.

Finally, a word of caution on using leveling apps and readability formulas, which can give a false sense of whether or not a book is appropriate for a child. Without considering key aspects of a reader, such as background knowledge, developmental stage, or social pressures, readability formulas and their associated apps can easily miss the mark on matching a reader to a book. Consider *The Whipping Boy*, winner of the 1987 Newberry Award and authored by the wonderful Sid Fleischman. The book's Lexile

Figure 7.15

Books Categorized by Themes, Not Levels

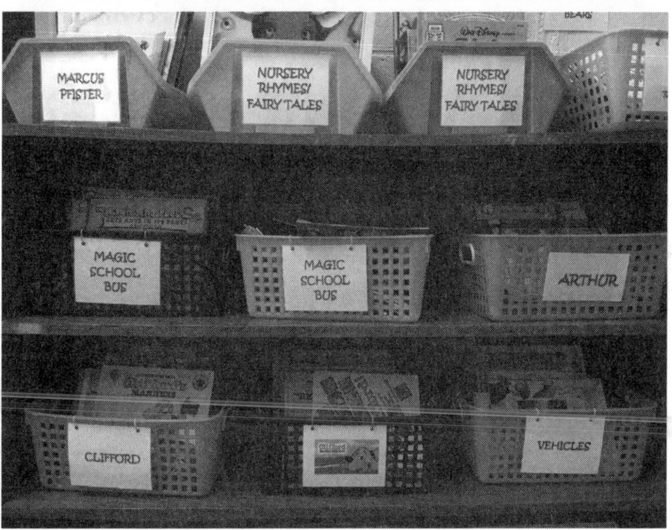

is listed as 570, which roughly translates as late-second grade (DRA2 24–28, guided reading L–M). I typed a random 200-word passage from the book into Microsoft Word and ran it through the program's readability program, which is calculated using sentence length and word length data. The Flesch Reading Ease score was 91.8 (meaning easier to read), and the Flesch-Kincaid grade level was 2.2 (early second grade). A second passage, given after the next paragraph, produced similar scores of 91.6 and 1.9.

Based on just the numbers, one might think *The Whipping Boy* would be an appropriate springtime chapter book for a typical second-grade reader and a cinch for a third. But the numbers fail to capture the book's rather intense emphasis on slang, unusual grammar, figurative language, and archaic vocabulary, all of which combine to make the text tricky to read and sometimes difficult to understand, as illustrated in this exchange between the book's main characters, a young prince and his whipping boy, Jemmy, who speaks first:

> "But ain't you afraid o' the dark? Everyone knows that! You won't even sleep without a lit candle."
>
> "Lies! Anyway, the moon's up, good and bright. Come on."
>
> Jemmy stared at him with dreadful astonishment. "The king'll have a gory-eyed fit!"
>
> "Positively."
>
> "He'll hunt us down. You'll get off light as a feather, but I'll be lucky if they don't whip me to the bone. More likely I'll be hung from the gallows. Scragged for sure!"

PICKING THE RIGHT BOOK THE "NO DRAMA" WAY

Because they are categorized by theme, browsing bins contain books on many reading levels, so you'll need to teach your students how to quickly choose one that is "just right." A simple two-step method is featured in the anchor chart shown in Figure 7.16. It asks students to open up a book, read any two pages, and then ask themselves, "How many words do I know" and "How much do I understand?"

A more specific method comes from one of my favorite books on organizing and running independent reading routines, Michelle J. Kelley and Nicki Clausen-Grace's *R5 in Your Classroom: A Guide to Differentiating Independent Reading and Developing Avid Readers* (International Reading Association, 2008). Here is an adaptation of their student-used book-choosing method:

- Go to a bin you are interested in. Choose a book.
- Read two or three short paragraphs from the book. If the book is short like a picture book, read two or three pages.

Figure 7.16

Two-Step Method for Picking a "Just Right" Book

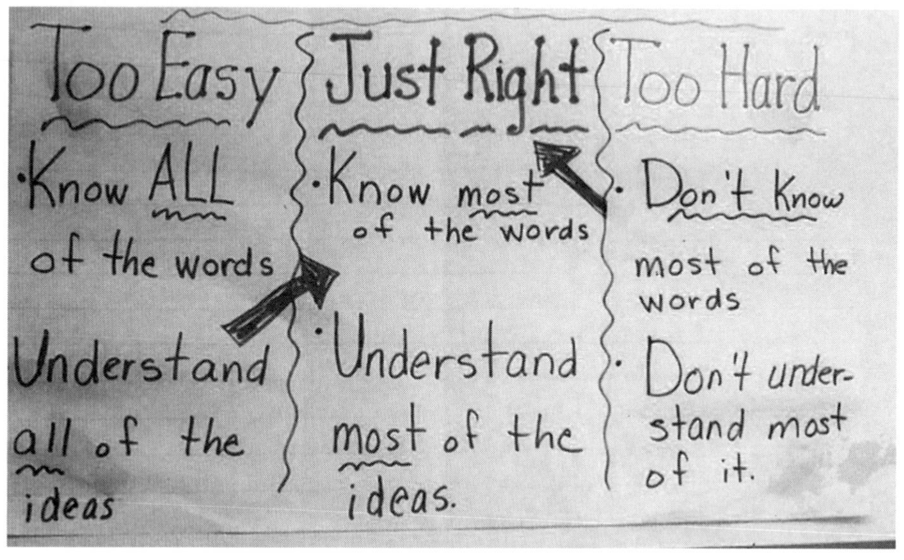

- Hold up one finger for each word you cannot read or you do not know.
- Think: Do you remember what you just read? If no, put the book back and get another book. If yes, count the fingers you have up.
    - 0–1 finger   This is an easy book for you.
    - 2–3 fingers   This book is just right. It's not too easy and not too hard.
    - 4–5 fingers   This book is challenging. Partner read this book.
    - 6 + fingers   This book is too hard. Put it back and try again next month.

DISPLAYING BINS: EZ SIX-BIN LEVELING METHOD

If you want the option of having students read books on or near their assessed levels and are looking for a way to level a lot of books in a short amount of time, consider the Six-Bin Method. Let's say you are a second-grade teacher who has inherited a classroom library of 100 books. None of the books has any type of level printed on it. An option for sorting them by levels of difficulty is this, which is shown graphically in Figure 7.17:

- Sort the books into two big piles—fiction and nonfiction.
- Set the nonfiction aside and use your teacher sense to quickly sort the fiction books into two levels, higher and lower. As you sort, keep in mind vocabulary, word count, sentence structure, concept complexity, and so forth.
- Next, sort the lower pile into two piles: low and high. Do the same for the higher pile, making lower and higher piles. Combine the two middle piles (the higher low and the lower high) and voilà, you have three piles: low, middle, and high.
- Repeat the process for your nonfiction books. The result is that you have six bins of books: low, middle, and high fiction and nonfiction. Label the book bins *Fiction* and *Nonfiction* and add one of three colors, such as blue, green, and orange. You can then steer your students toward a bin appropriate to their reading ability and interest, such as the blue fiction bin or the orange nonfiction bin.

Figure 7.17

Easy Way to Sort Books Into Six Leveled Bins

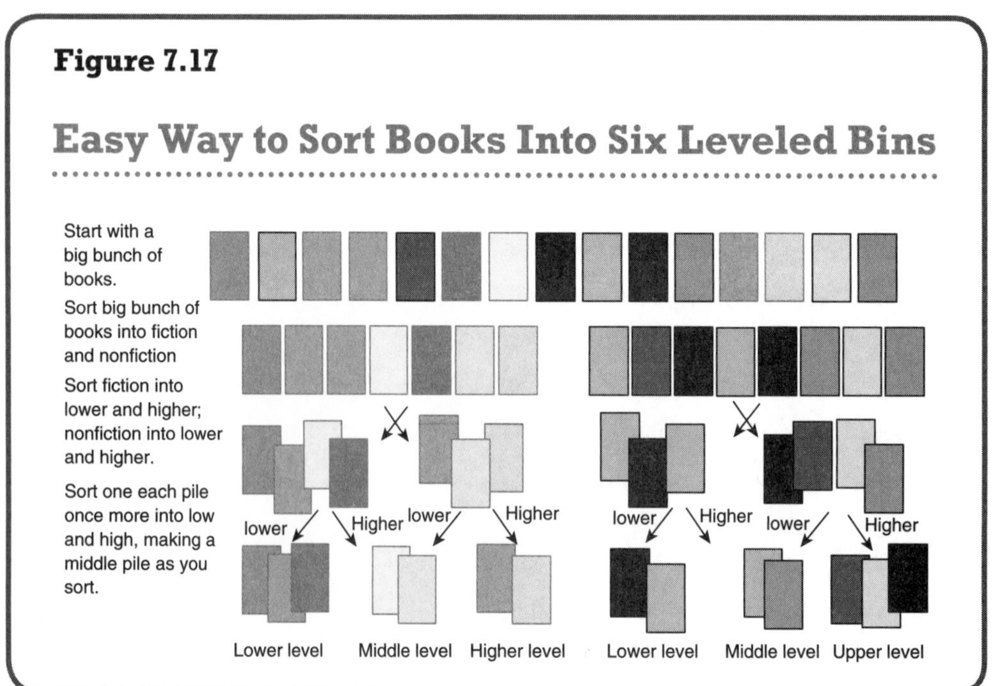
Start with a big bunch of books.
Sort big bunch of books into fiction and nonfiction
Sort fiction into lower and higher; nonfiction into lower and higher.
Sort one each pile once more into low and high, making a middle pile as you sort.
lower
Higher
lower
Higher
lower
Higher
lower
Higher
Lower level
Middle level
Higher level
Lower level
Middle level
Upper level

IMPORTANT POINT

To avoid overtly or implicitly labeling students as "high, middle, low," use colors on leveled books bins rather than numbers or letters. Red, orange, yellow, green, blue, indigo, and violet give you seven discrete levels that also connect to elementary science and art curricula (ROY G BIV). Colored stickers applied to each book's back cover make it easy for students and teachers to return and sort books into their correct bins. Also, consider switching the colors on your leveled bins every nine weeks and then assigning your students a new color. Finally, a true commitment to flexible grouping, whereby students are not locked into one group for the entire year, will help avoid labeling, too.

PERSONAL BOOK BAGS AND ENVELOPES

In one of my classrooms, to lessen the amount of time students were moving around looking for books, I used an expandable file folder and a book-choosing routine. Every Monday at the start of the reading block, my coteacher and I had our third-grade readers remove finished or unwanted books from their expandable files and place them in a bin. Later, I could sort these books back to where they belonged. Next, the students browsed the room for 5 or 10 minutes, picking books and placing them into their files. When independent reading time rolled around, they simply picked up their file and pulled out the book they wanted to read. If they found they didn't like the book, they put it back into their file until Monday and chose one of the four remaining books.

Katrina Kimmel, a talented kindergarten and first-grade teacher I've worked with, uses little drawstring bags as "book bags" (see Figure 7.18). Originally, the strings slid over the back of student chairs, but an easier method is hanging the books from magnetic hooks attached to the sides of each student's desk. When it is independent reading time right after recess, children remove the bags, pull out their books, and read, read, read. During their 15 minutes of dedicated and supported independent reading, Mrs. Kimmel conferences with a few students, sharing an interest in what they are reading, helping them navigate their reading roadblocks, and asking a few questions about their books.

Figure 7.18

Moving Books From Bins to Bags

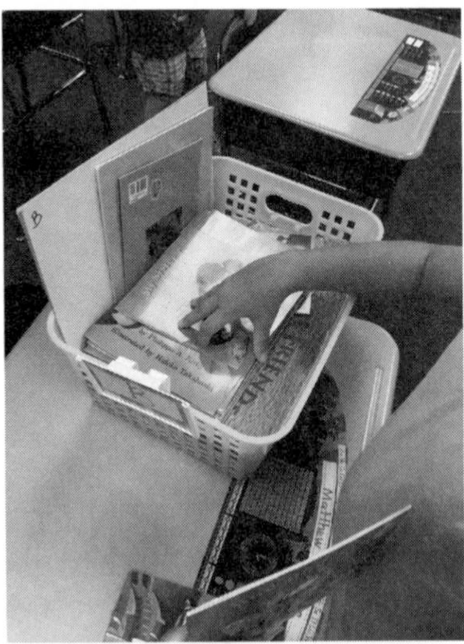

THE *I CAN LIST*

The *I Can List* (originated by Debbie Diller) is a tool that supports independent readers through their options for independent reading and writing. It's a must for running guided-reading groups because while you are working with a small group, the rest of your students need to be deeply engaged with independent work. I found the *I Can List* much easier to manage than literacy centers: There were few materials to create or store, the activities were authentic, and the focus was firmly on reading and writing. But you don't need to run guided-reading groups to use an *I Can List*. It can simply be an organizer for stand-alone independent reading time.

I suggest starting with an *I Can List* that presents these four activities, ordered from less student choice to more (see Figure 7.19). If you don't like the idea of assigning a leveled book (found in an assigned color bin), simply leave item #2 off your list.

1. Reread your guided-reading book.
2. Read a book from your color bin.
3. Read a poem or poems in your poetry anthology.
4. Read books you pick.

Figure 7.19

***I Can List* With First Four Reading Activities**

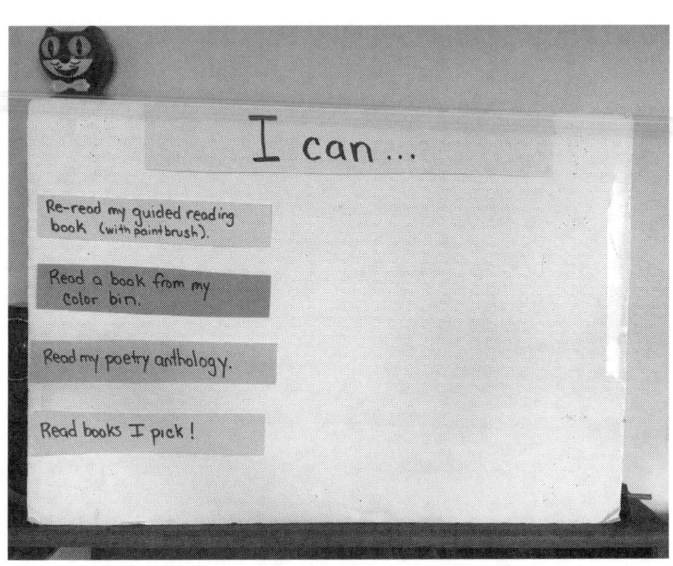

First, explicitly and directly teach what each activity involves and then have the students practice it while you monitor and guide them. Do a little wrap-up at the end of your practice session and praise students for what they did well—for example, "I saw Javon finish his poem and then immediately go to a book bin and pick out a book. And I watched Halley read every word in her guided-reading book."

Once your students are secure in these four activities, teach them another and add it to the list. For example, show them what appropriate buddy reading looks like, give them some time to practice buddy reading where you coach and guide them, and then add the activity to your *I Can List*. You may prefer to use a pocket chart for your list because it allows for an ever-accumulating string of activities. As the weeks go on, add independent writing activities, too. Important note: These activities are not grade specific. You can use an *I Can List* from kindergarten to third grade and beyond.

The *I Can List* is extremely flexible in its use. You can allow children to pick any activity off the list, give fewer choices by denoting "open" or "closed" options with clothespins (see Figure 7.20), or even assign one option to the entire class, which must be completed before students go on to pick activities of their choice. Also, the list comes in handy when you're unexpectedly confronted with a schedule change

Figure 7.20

I Can List With 11 Activities, Some of Them Open

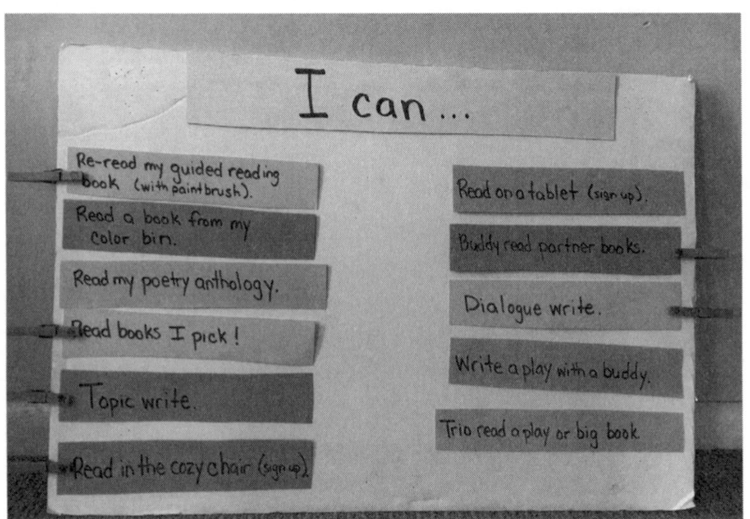

or classroom interruption. When this happens, just have your class work off the list, each child picking an activity to do. Figure 7.21a–f shows some examples of the *I Can List* in action.

Figure 7.21

The *I Can List* in Action

Read my poetry (a)

Buddy reading books (b)

Read a big book in a trio (c)

Reread guided-reading book with a witchy-poo finger (d)

Read a book I pick (e)

Topic writing (f)

a

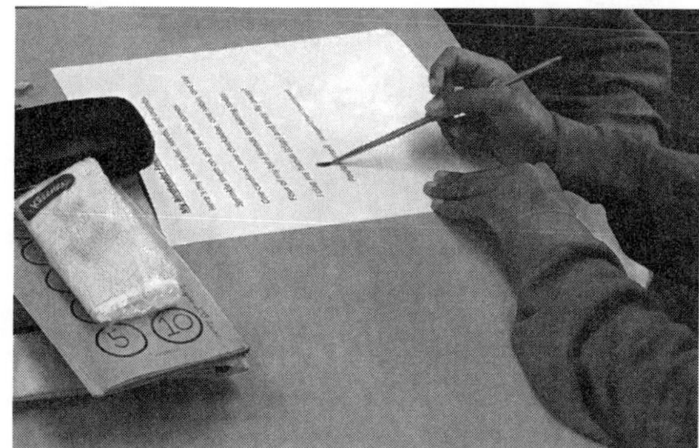

b

(Continued)

Figure 7.21 (Continued)

c

d

e

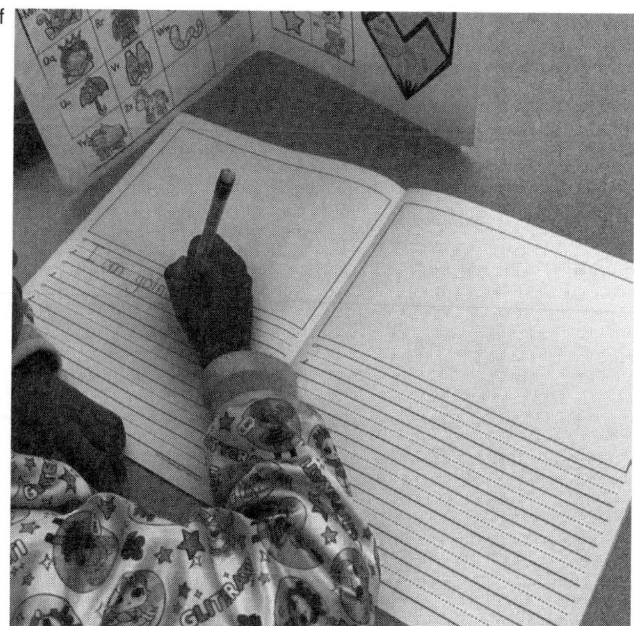

iStock.com/Wavebreakmedia

There are many benefits to supported independent reading. Educationally speaking, the most important one is building and strengthening the two Simple View of Reading variables: word recognition and language comprehension. But even more, independent reading is great for the teacher heart, for it is tremendously satisfying to look out from a guided-reading table and see students immersed in reading on their own, communing in glorious solitude.

FOR FURTHER STUDY ●●●

Here are resources for exploring and learning more about supported independent reading routines:

- *No More Independent Reading Without Support* by Debbie Miller and Barbara Moss, 2013
- *Independent Reading: Practical Strategies for Grades K–3* by Denise Morgan, Maryann Mraz, Nancy Padak, and Timothy Rasinski, 2008
- *The Book Whisperer: Awakening the Inner Reader in Every Child* by Donalyn Miller, 2009

(Continued)

(Continued)

- *Creating a Classroom Library* by Mandy Gregory (https://www.readingrockets.org/article/creating-classroom-library)
- *Learning in Wonderland: Library Organization for the Primary Teacher* (https://www.learninginwonderland.com/2018/01/library-organization-for-primary-teacher.html)
- *Independent Reading Time Handbook*, a free PDF from the Collaborative Classroom (https://www.collaborativeclassroom.org/wp-content/uploads/2017/12/asklibraries_handbook_asl-irthbk.pdf)
- *Independent Reading Time* module, free online professional development through Clemson University (https://readingrecovery.clemson.edu/independent-reading/overall-structure/)

WHAT'S NEXT?

As many as 20 percent of all American children experience significant problems in learning how to read (Drummond, n.d.; Hurford et al., 2016; Petretto & Masala, 2017). While it is true the practices specifically presented and generally referenced in this book can reduce reading difficulties, they are not a panacea. Despite our best efforts, some students will struggle to read, write, and spell, and their problems may be severe and persistent. The reasons for this are many.

Learning to read is difficult for children born with an intellectual disability such as Down syndrome, Fragile X, or autism (Special Olympics, 2020). For others, developmental conditions such as Tourette's syndrome, hyperactivity with attention deficit disorder, and dyslexia make learning to read a challenge (Raskind et al., 2013). Consider this: The prevalence of dyslexia is 4 percent to 17 percent of the general population, meaning millions of students who exhibit reading difficulties may be at a permanent, although not insurmountable, reading disadvantage (Penesetti, 2018; Yale Center, 2020).

There are societal factors at work, too. Parental drug abuse and environmental toxins like lead can cause neurological impairments, leading to learning difficulties. Also and unfortunately, the United States has great social and economic inequality.

Poverty, homelessness, and low socioeconomic status impact children greatly, and through no fault of their own, some come to school not ready to learn. Others are at a disadvantage because they lack access to libraries, the internet, preschool, well-funded elementary schools, safe and nurturing neighborhoods, and general experiences that build background knowledge and vocabulary. For all these reasons—inequity, poverty, dyslexia, cognitive and behavioral disabilities—some students will develop reading difficulties, even when general education teachers are teaching reading in the best ways possible.

Today, another terrible reason has been added. As I write this conclusion, a pandemic has settled over the world. In my state of Pennsylvania, schools closed in March 2020, pivoted to online learning in April, and continued with a mixture of remote learning and in-class instruction through the 2020–2021 school year. So—despite the great efforts of teachers and administrators—the education of millions of children has been greatly disrupted, and this disruption will continue for some time, rippling into the future, affecting the learning of all boys and girls, some much more than others. Additionally, it seems certain that the economic fallout from the pandemic will create even greater inequality and social disturbances in years to come. And finally, the teaching profession itself will be affected.

There is always hope, however, and it springs eternal because many people in the world are good-hearted and determined. Education is a noble calling, and highly capable and deeply caring people heed the call year after year, joining the ranks of teachers, working to make the world a better place through education. Equally important, the educational community knows a lot about how to prevent reading difficulties from happening in the first place, as well as how to mitigate them if they develop. While there is no magic fairy dust that wipes away reading problems, there is a general body of know-how and wisdom that speaks directly to what teachers and school systems can effectively do. That's what this book is all about.

In many ways, we are living in a golden age of reading knowledge. Over the last 50 years, the world of reading has seen myriad waves of research ebb and flow. The result, however, is not erosion. Rather, it is beach building. In this analogy, *what reading is and how to teach it effectively* is reliably firm land, and the land is growing in length, breadth, and depth, becoming more stable over time. Across the many decades, reading researchers and cognitive scientists have labored to discover the transactional nature of the reading experience, the importance of making meaning and using metacognition, the value of quality children's literature and authentic reading and writing experiences, the significance of forming letter–sound associations, the critical nature of mastering the alphabetic code, the essential workings of the neural circuitry that give rise to reading, and, very important, the types of instruction that best connects and strengthens the foundational reading circuit of meaning, sound, and spelling.

In this book, I have tried to not only lay out some of this knowledge but also connect it to classroom practices and then present, describe, and explain the practices that are most effective in the prevention of reading difficulties. These practices are informed by and aligned with scientific knowledge. I find it tremendously exciting to know primary grade teachers have at their disposal many routines, activities, materials, and teaching techniques that can increase the number of students who become successful readers, writers, and spellers and conversely decrease the number who develop persistent reading difficulties. These instructional practices help all students to learn but are especially effective for children who are at risk of reading difficulties due to poverty, unequal access, intellectual or behavioral disabilities, and/or differences in brain wiring.

To recap, here are five things we can do to prevent reading difficulties. Each category of practice, laid out in chapters of this book, encompasses myriad activities, materials, routines, and frameworks.

- **Instruct with teaching techniques that are especially effective at engaging students, presenting content, minimizing errors, fostering deep thinking, and moving patterns and words into the brain's dictionary**. These techniques include but are not limited to direct and explicit instruction, sense activation (multisensory), instant error correction, repetition and distributed practice, and wait time.
- **Build language comprehension**, a term that includes background knowledge and topical knowledge, vocabulary knowledge, the understanding of concepts of print and genre, grammar and syntax, and more. Opportunities that build language comprehension include rich classroom discussions;

interactive read-alouds; vocabulary routines and activities; hands-on activities paired with conversation; the use of online images, short video clips, and technology that provides interactivity and immersion; and, of course, lots and lots of reading (and writing, too).

- **Develop advanced phonemic awareness and analysis.** This can be accomplished by consistently and determinedly teaching basic to advanced phonological activities, starting before kindergarten and continuing for as long as needed, in a variety of ways, in short bouts of instruction that are distributed over time, to a point where all students can masterfully analyze and manipulate phonemes.
- **Offer many opportunities to learn, practice, and master orthography, the beating heart of the fundamental reading process.** Holistically thought of as phonics-spelling-morphology, orthography can be taught and boosted through a variety of activities, routines, and even frameworks that give students opportunities to learn letter–sound associations, master phonic and spelling patterns for both decoding and encoding, and eventually store whole words in their brain dictionaries.
- **Program more opportunities to read.** This means we continue to try to reduce busywork, minimize summative testing, weed out ineffective practices, trim back the bells-and-whistles of core reading programs, and promote and use integrative, synergistic teaching, all in order to give students more time to read extensively in text at their instructional level, at their independent level, and even at a level that challenges them.

We know a great deal about what reading practices work best; the challenge is to implement what we know. Implementing is an art, a complex act that involves not one ideological truth but a number of truths guided by knowledge of students and instincts developed over time. Science gives us facts but doesn't tell us what to *do* with them. For that, we need information melded with critical thinking and a caring heart. If we can scale this melding to millions of teachers in thousands of classrooms across the country, we might transform reading instruction and society itself. My trust in science, teachers, and the fundamental goodness of human nature is great—and I choose to optimistically believe in a future full of hardworking educators helping students gain a firm foundation in reading, writing, and spelling.

APPENDIX A

GUIDED-READING SCHEDULES

Guided-Reading Schedule #3

Each guided-reading group is given a 20-minute block of time; only one group is seen on Monday and Friday.

Monday	Tuesday	Wednesday	Thursday	Friday
Group A	Group B Group C	Group D Group A	Group B Group C	Group A

Per Week	A	B	C	D
Number of times each group is seen	3	2	2	1
Number of minutes given to guided reading	60	40	40	20
Number of minutes available for independent reading/writing	100	120	120	140

Guided-Reading Schedule #4

Guided-reading AM groups are each given a 15-minute block of time; an additional afternoon group is seen.

	Monday	Tuesday	Wednesday	Thursday	Friday
AM	Group A	Group C Group D	Group B Group A	Group A Group B	Group A
PM	Group B	Group A	Group D	Group C	Group B

Per Week	A	B	C	D
Number of times each group is seen	5	4	2	2
Number of minutes given to guided reading	75	60	30	30
Number of minutes available for independent reading/writing	120	135	165	165

APPENDIX B

EXAMPLE OF THREE LEVELED THEME-RELATED POEMS

Upper Level	Middle Level
Seeds Go, Seeds Grow —by Mark Weakland	**My Birdfeeder Friends** —adapted from the traditional by Paula Purnell
Seeds go, seeds grow *In garden beds we till and sow.* *With sun, soil, water, air,* *Flowers blossom everywhere.* *Soon tiny plants stretch up in shoots,* *They grow to give us leaves and fruits.* *And mighty trees in forest green,* *Spring from small seeds, once barely seen.*	*Here's my bird feeder, seeds, and crumbs.* *Sprinkle them on and see who comes.* *One cardinal, one chickadee, one robin, one jay.* *Four of my bird friends are eating today.* *I clap my hands (clap) and they fly away!*

Lower Level

Up, Up, Up

—adapted from the traditional by Mark Weakland

Plants go	*Up, up, up*
Veggies grow	*Down, down, down-y*
Trees rise	*Up, up, up*
Acorns fall	*Down, down, down-y*
Now we stretch	*Up, up, up*
And touch our toes	*Down, down, down-y!*

APPENDIX C

SECOND-GRADE AND THIRD-GRADE MORPHEME-BASED WORD LADDERS

Second Grade Word Bank

Prefix/Suffix	Meaning	Words
un-	Not or opposite	unlock, unsafe
re-	Again or back	relock, redo, reread, rewrite, return
dis-	Not or opposite	dislike, distrust
-er	Person	teacher, preacher, writer, baker, maker
-er	Comparison	older, bolder, colder, bigger, madder, sadder
-est	Superlative	oldest, boldest, coldest, tallest, smallest

Word Ladder Sentences for Reading and Spelling

Unlock the door and restock the shelves.

He's the oldest and baldest man.

Read like a teacher.

Ben is the biggest and best baker in town.

It is wise to lock the door.

Word Ladders

restock	baldest	teacher	biggest	lock
stock	bald	preacher	bigger	unlock
stocking	scald	preach	big	undone
rocking	scold	beach	bag	unlace
rocked	bold	bead	bake	unsafe
rock	bolder	lead	baker	unwise
lock	boldest	leader	biker	wise
unlock	coldest	reader	bike	
	oldest	reading	bin	
	older	reread	bit	
	old	read	best	
			Ben	

Third Grade Word Bank

Suffix	Meaning	Words
-ful	Full of	painful, beautiful
-less	Without	careless, helpless
-ly	Characteristic of	badly, friendly, quickly
-y	Characterized, like	cloudy, fishy

Word Ladder Sentences for Reading and Spelling

A duck stuck in the muck can get sick quickly.

Gain his trust by carefully dusting.

Can you turn harmful into helpful?

Word Ladders

quickly	carefully	helpful
prickly	careful	helpless
sickly	careless	painless
sick	care	painful
stick	dare	pain
stuck	dust	chain
muck	dusting	charm
duck	trusting	charmless
	trust	harmless
		harmful

APPENDIX D

LETTER-SOUND GRIDS

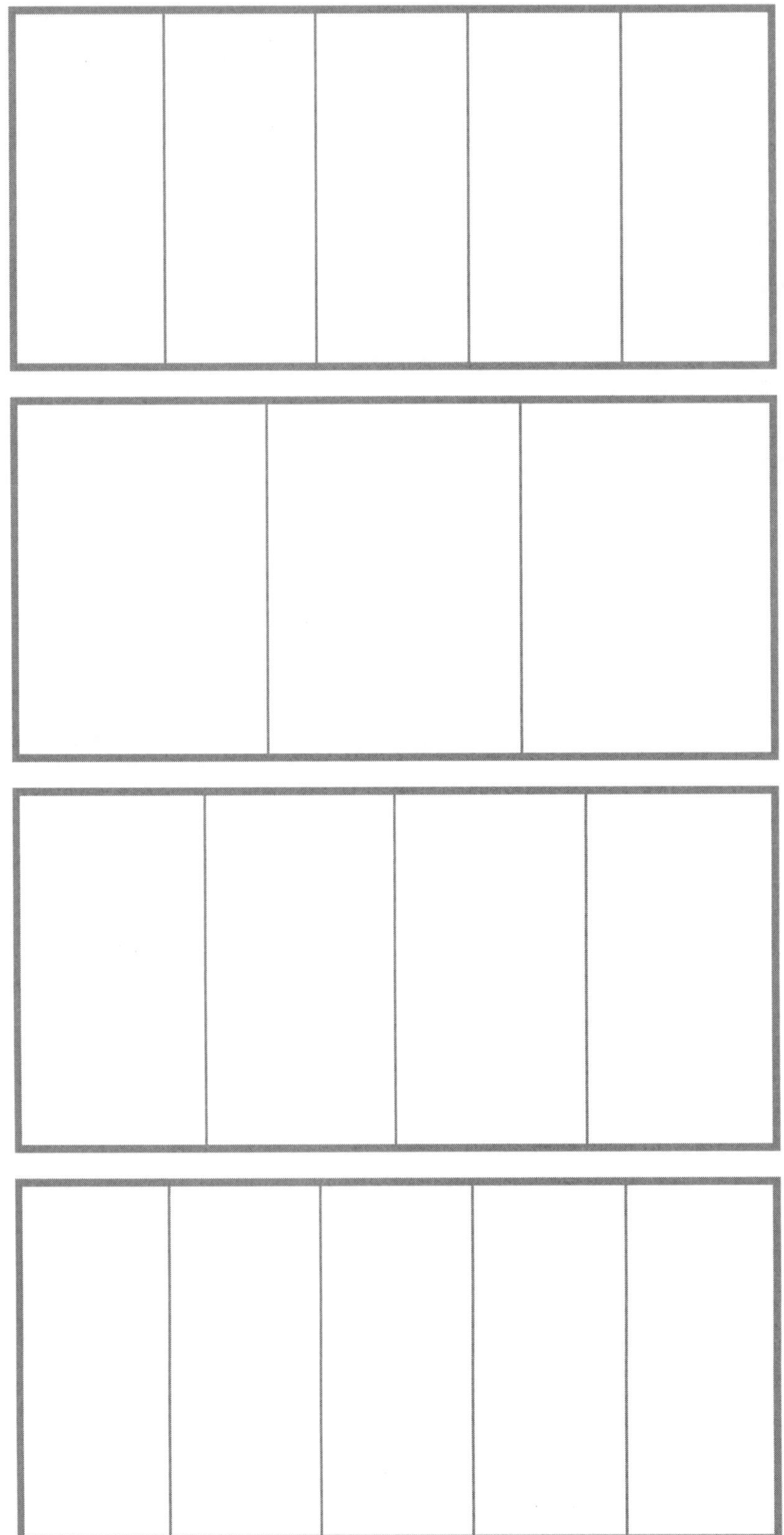

APPENDIX E

EXAMPLES OF FIVE-DAY SCHEDULES

First- or Second-Grade Five-Day Schedule, 120 Minutes

	5	10	20	30	40	50	60	70	80	90	100	110	120
Day 1	**Phonemic Awareness** **Phonics** **Spelling**		**Language comprehension** (including background knowledge [BK], vocabulary, sight words)			**Writing** (including letter formation, grammar, spelling, and phonics)				**Language comprehension, shared reading**		**Phonemic** **Phonics** **Spelling**	
	5	10	20	30	40	50	60	70	80	90	100	110	120
Day 2	**Phonemic Awareness** **Phonics** **Spelling**		**Language comprehension** (including BK, vocabulary, comprehension strategies), **shared reading**			**Writing** (including letter formation, grammar, spelling, and phonics)			**Guided reading, independent reading and writing**			**Phonemic** **Phonics** **Spelling**	**Read-aloud**
	5	10	20	30	40	50	60	70	80	90	100	110	120
Day 3	**Phonemic Awareness** **Phonics** **Spelling**		**Writing** (including letter formation, grammar, spelling, and phonics)			**Guided reading** (two to three groups; including assessment, elements of language comprehension, word work as needed), independent reading and writing					**Phonemic** **Phonics** **Spelling**		**Read-aloud**
	5	10	20	30	40	50	60	70	80	90	100	110	120
Day 4	**Phonemic Awareness** **Phonics** **Spelling**		**Writing** (including letter formation, grammar, spelling, and phonics)			**Guided reading** (two to three groups; including assessment, elements of language comprehension, word work as needed), independent reading and writing					**Phonemic** **Phonics** **Spelling**		**Read-aloud**
	5	10	20	30	40	50	60	70	80	90	100	110	120
Day 5	**Phonemic Awareness** **Phonics** **Spelling**		**Writing** (including letter formation, grammar, spelling, and phonics)			**Guided reading** (two to three groups; including assessment, elements of language comprehension, word work as needed), independent reading and writing					**Assessment**		**Read-aloud**

Note: Independent reading occurs while teacher is running guided-reading groups.

Second- or Third-Grade Five-Day Schedule, 90 Minutes

	5	10		20		30		40		50		60		70		80		90
Day 1	**Phonemic Awareness** **Phonics-Spelling-Morphology**			**Language comprehension** (including background knowledge, vocabulary) , **shared reading**						**Writing** (integrated grammar and spelling; include traits of writing, possibly in a workshop format)						**Phonics** **Spelling** **Morphology**		
	5	10		20		30		40		50		60		70		80		90
Day 2	**Phonemic Awareness** **Phonics-Spelling-Morphology**			**Language comprehension** (including BK, vocabulary, comp. strategies), **shared reading**				**Writing** (integrated grammar and spelling; include traits of writing, possibly in a workshop format)						**Phonics** **Spelling** **Morphology**		**Independent whole-group reading/read-aloud**		
	5	10		20		30		40		50		60		70		80		90
Day 3	**Phonemic Awareness** **Phonics-Spelling-Morphology**				**Writing** (handwriting)			**Guided reading** (two groups; including assessment, elements of language comprehension, word work as needed**), independent reading and writing**								**Independent whole-group reading/read-aloud**		
	5	10		20		30		40		50		60		70		80		90
Day 4	**Phonemic Awareness** **Phonics-Spelling-Morphology**			**Language comprehension** (including BK, vocabulary, comp. strategies), **shared reading**				**Guided reading** (two groups; including assessment, elements of language comprehension, word work as needed), **independent reading and writing**						**Phonics** **Spelling** **Morphology**		**Independent whole-group reading/read-aloud**		
	5	10		20		30		40		50		60		70		80		90
Day 5	**Whole-Group Assessment**				**Writing** (handwriting)			**Guided reading** (two groups; including assessment, elements of language comprehension, word work as needed), **independent reading and writing**								**Independent whole-group reading/read-aloud**		

Note: Independent reading occurs as stand-alone time and while teacher is running guided-reading groups. It also happens at the end of Days 2, 3, 4, and 5, when the whole group independently reads for 10 to 15 minutes (this time also has the option for a teacher read-aloud).

Third-Grade Five-Day Time Chart, 70 Minutes

	5	10		20		30		40		50		60		70
Day 1	**Phonics** **Spelling** **Morphology**				**Language comprehension** (including BK, vocabulary, comp. strategies), **shared reading**									**Read-aloud**
	5	10		20		30		40		50		60		70
Day 2	**Phonics** **Spelling** **Morphology**			**Writing** (handwriting and/or grammar)		**Guided reading** (two groups; including assessment, elements of language comprehension, word work as needed), **independent reading and writing**								**Read-aloud**
	5	10		20		30		40		50		60		70
Day 3	**Phonics** **Spelling** **Morphology**			**Writing** (integrated grammar and spelling; include traits of writing, possibly in a workshop format)						**Guided reading** (one group; including assessment, elements of language comprehension, word work as needed), **independent reading and writing**				**Read-aloud**
	5	10		20		30		40		50		60		70
Day 4	**Phonics** **Spelling** **Morphology**				**Language comprehension** (including BK, vocabulary, comp. strategies), **shared reading**					**Guided reading** (one group; including assessment, elements of language comprehension, word work as needed), **independent reading and writing**				**Read-aloud**
	5	10		20		30		40		50		60		70
Day 5	**Whole-Group Assessment**			**Writing** (integrated grammar and spelling; include traits of writing, possibly in a workshop format)						**Guided reading** (one or two groups; including assessment, elements of language comprehension, word work as needed), **independent reading and writing**				

Note: Independent reading occurs while teacher is running guided-reading groups.

APPENDIX F

SIMPLE VIEW OF READING GRAPH

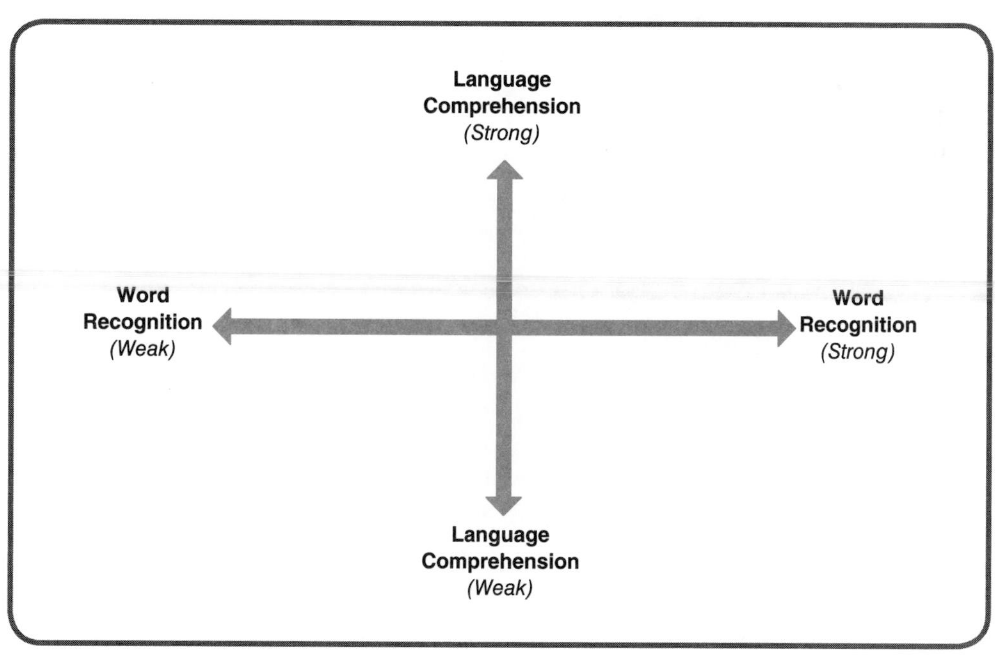

REFERENCES

Adams, M. (1998). The three-cueing system. In F. Lehr & J. Osborn (Eds.), *Literacy for all issues in teaching and learning* (pp. 73–99). Guilford Press.

Adlof, S., Perfetti, C., & Catts, H. (2011). Developmental changes in reading comprehension: Implications for assessment and instruction. In S. J. Samuels & A. E. Farstrup (Eds.), *What research has to say about reading instruction* (4th ed., (pp. 186–214). International Reading Association.

Allington, R. (2011). *What at risk readers need: What students need to learn.* ASCD.

Allington, R. (2014). How reading volume affects both reading fluency and reading achievement. *International Electronic Journal of Elementary Education, 7*(1), 13–26.

Allington, R. L. (1977). If they don't read much, how they ever gonna get good? *Journal of Adolescent & Adult Literacy, 21*(1), 57–61.

Allington, R. L. (2002). What I've learned about effective reading instruction from a decade of studying exemplary elementary classroom teachers. *Phi Delta Kappan, 83*(10), 740–747.

Allington, R. L. (2006). Fluency: Still waiting after all these years. In S. J. Samuels & A. E. Farstrup (Eds.), *What research has to say about fluency instruction* (pp. 94–105). International Reading Association.

Allington, R. L. (2009). If they don't read much . . . 30 years later. In E. H. Hiebert (Ed.), *Reading more, reading better* (pp. 30–54). Guilford Press.

Anderson, R. C., Wilson, P. T., & Fielding, L. G. (1988). Growth in reading and how children spend their time outside of school. *Reading Research Quarterly, 23*, 285–303.

Archer, A. L., & Hughes, C. A. (2011). *Explicit instruction: Effective and efficient teaching.* Guilford Press.

Beck, I. L., McKeown, M., & Kucan, L. (2002). Choosing words to teach. In *Bringing words to life: Robust vocabulary instruction* (pp. 15–30). Guilford Press.

Beck, I. L., McKeown, M., & Kucan, L. (2008). Creating robust vocabulary: Frequently asked questions and extended examples. Guilford Press.

Benjamin, A. S., & Tullis, J. (2010). What makes distributed practice effective? *Cognitive Psychology, 61*(3). 228–247.

Berninger, V. W., & Amtmann, D. (2003). Preventing written expression disabilities through early and continuing assessment and intervention for handwriting and/or spelling problems: Research into practice. In H. L. Swanson, K. R. Harris, & S. Graham (Eds.), *Handbook of learning disabilities* (pp. 345–363). Guilford Press.

Blevins, W. (2016). A *fresh look at phonics, Grades K–2: Common causes of failure and 7 ingredients for success.* Corwin.

Bradley, L., & Bryant, P. (1983). Categorizing sounds and learning to read—A causal connection. *Nature, 30*(1), 419–421.

Brenner, D., Hiebert, E. H., & Tompkins, R. (2009). How much and what are third graders reading? Reading in core programs. In E. H. Hiebert (Ed.), *Reading more, reading better* (pp. 118–140). Guilford Press.

Brozo, W. G., Shiel, G., & Topping, K. (2008). Engagement in reading: Lessons learned from three PISA countries. *Journal of Adolescent and Adult Literacy, 51*(4), 304–315.

Burkins, J., & Yaris, K. (2018). From a presentation at the 2018 SDE National Convention.

Carnine, D. W., Silbert, J., & Kameenui, E. J. (1997). *Direct instruction reading* (3rd ed.). Merrill/Prentice-Hall.

Castles, A., Rastle, K., & Nation, K. (2018). Ending the reading wars: Reading acquisition from novice to expert. *Psychological Science in the Public Interest, 19*(1), 5–51.

Catapano, S., Fleming, J., & Elias, M. (2009). Building an effective classroom library. *Journal of Language and Literacy Education, 5*(1), 59–73.

Catts, H., Adlof, S., & Weismer, S. (2006). Language deficits in poor comprehenders: A case for the simple view of reading. *Journal of Speech, Language, and Hearing Research, 49*, 278–293.

Catts, H., Hogan, T. P., & Fey, M. E. (2003). Subgrouping poor readers on the basis of individual differences in reading-related abilities. *Journal of Learning Disabilities, 36*(2), 151–164.

Cipielewski, J., & Stanovich, K. E. (1992). Predicting growth in reading ability from children's exposure to print. *Journal of Experimental Child Psychology, 54*, 74–89.

Clemson University Reading Recovery. (n.d.). *Guided reading for struggling readers.* https://readingrecovery.clemson.edu/guided-reading-for-struggling-readers/

Coppola, S. (2014). Building background knowledge. *The Reading Teacher, 68*(2), 145–148.

Deci, E. (2014). Five research-based tips for providing students with meaningful feedback. *Edutopia.* https://www.edutopia.org/blog/tips-providing-students-meaningful-feedback-marianne-stenger

Dehaene, S. (2009). *Reading in the brain: The new science of how we read.* Penguin Books.

Drummond, K. (n.d.). About reading disabilities, learning disabilities, and reading difficulties. *Reading Rockets.* https://www.readingrockets.org/article/about-reading-disabilities-learning-disabilities-and-reading-difficulties

Ehri, L. (2000). Learning to read and learning to spell: Two sides of a coin. *Topics in Language Disorders, 20*(3), 19–36.

Ehri, L., & McCormick, S. (2013). Phases of word learning: Implications for instruction with delayed and disabled readers. In D. Alvermann, N. Unrau, & R. B. Ruddell (Eds.), *Theoretical models and processes of reading.* International Reading Association.

Ehri, L. C. (1998). Grapheme-phoneme knowledge is essential for learning to read words in English. In J. L. Metsala & L. C. Ehri (Eds.), *Word recognition in beginning literacy* (pp. 3–40). Erlbaum.

Ehri, L. C. (2005a). Development of sight word reading: Phases and findings. In M. J. Snowling & C. Hulme (Eds.), *The science of reading: A handbook* (pp. 135–154). Blackwell.

Ehri, L. C. (2005b). Learning to read words: Theory, findings, and issues. *Scientific Studies of Reading, 9*, 167–188.

Ehri, L. C. (2017). Orthographic mapping and literacy development revisited. In K. Cain, D. L. Compton, & R. K. Parrila (Eds.), *Theories of reading development* (pp. 169–190). John Benjamins.

Feldgus, E., Cardonick, I., & Gentry, R. (2017). *Kid writing in the 21st century: A systematic approach to phonics, spelling, and writing workshop.* Hameray.

Foorman, B., Schatschneider, C., Eakin, M., Fletcher, J., Moats, L., & Francis, D. (2006). The impact of instructional practices in grades 1 and 2 on reading and spelling achievement in high poverty schools. *Contemporary Educational Psychology, 31*(1), 1–29.

Foorman, B., & Torgesen, J. (2001). Critical elements of classroom and small-group instruction promote reading success in all children. *Learning Disabilities Research & Practice, 16*(4), 203–212.

Fountas, I., & Pinnell, G. S. (1996). *Guided reading: Responsive teaching across the grades.* Heinemann.

Gambrell, L., Morrow, L. M., & Pressley, M. (Eds.). (2007). *Best practices in literacy instruction*. Guilford Press.

Gambrell, L. B., Marinak, B. A., Brooker, H. R., & McCrea-Andrews, H. J. (2011). The importance of independent reading. In S. J. Samuels & A. E. Farstrup (Eds.), *What research has to say about reading instruction* (4th ed., pp. 143–158). International Reading Association.

Gentry, J. R., & Graham, S. (2010). *Creating better readers and writers: The importance of direct, systematic spelling and handwriting instruction in improving academic performance*. Saperstein.

Gentry, R., & Ouellette, G. (2019). *Brain words: How the science of reading informs teaching*. Stenhouse.

Glezer, L., Kim, J., Rule, J., Jiang, X., & Riesenhuber, M. (2015). Adding words to the brain's visual dictionary: Novel word learning selectively sharpens orthographic representations in the VWFA. *Journal of Neuroscience, 35*(12), 4965–4972.

Gough, P. B., & Tunmer, W. E. (1986). Decoding, reading and reading disability. *Remedial and Special Education, 7*, 6–10.

Graham, S. (2009–2010). Want to improve children's writing? Don't neglect their handwriting. *American Educator*, Winter, 20–40. https://www.aft.org/sites/default/files/periodicals/graham.pdf

Graham, S. (2019). Changing how writing is taught. *Review of Research in Education, 43*(1), 277–303.

Graves, M., & Watts-Taffe, S. (2002). The place of word consciousness in a research-based vocabulary program. In S. J. Samuels & A. E. Farstrup (Eds.), *What research has to say about reading instruction* (3rd ed., pp. 370–389). International Reading Association.

Guthrie, J., Wigfield, A., Metsala, J., & Cox, K. (1999). Motivational and cognitive predictors of text comprehension and reading amount. *Scientific Studies of Reading, 3*(3), 231–256. https://doi.org/10.1207/s1532799xssr0303_3

Harlaar, N., Cutting, L., Deater-Deckard, K., DeThorne, L. S., Justice, L. M., Schatschneider, C., Thompson, L. A., & Petrill, S. A. (2010). Predicting individual differences in reading comprehension: A twin study. *Annals of Dyslexia, 60*, 265–288.

Hart, B., & Risley, T. R. (1995). *Meaningful differences in the everyday experience of young American children*. Paul H. Brookes.

Hattan, C. (2019). Prompting rural students' use of background knowledge and experience to support comprehension of unfamiliar content. *Reading Research Quarterly, 54*(4), 451–455.

Heibert, E. H. (2020). The core vocabulary: The foundation of proficient comprehension. *The Reading Teacher, 73*(6), 757–768.

Heibert, E. H., Goodwin, A. P, & Cervetti, C. N. (2018). Core vocabulary: Its morphological content and presence in exemplar texts. *Reading Research Quarterly, 53*(1), 29–49.

Hindman, A. H., & Wasik, B. A. (2018). Why wait? The importance of wait time in developing young students' language and vocabulary skills. *The Reading Teacher, 72*(3), 369–378.

Hoover, W., & Gough, P. (1990). The simple view of reading. *Reading and Writing: An Interdisciplinary Journal, 2*, 127–160.

Hruby, G., & Goswami, U. (2013). Educational neuroscience for reading researchers. In D. Alvermann, N. Unrau, & R. B. Ruddell (Eds.), *Theoretical models and processes of reading* (pp. 558–588). International Reading Association.

Hurford, D. P., Hurford, J. D., Head, K. L., Keiper, M. M., Nitcher, S. P., & Renner, L. (2016). The dyslexia dilemma: A history of ignorance, complacency and resistance in colleges of education. *Journal of Childhood & Development Disorders, 2*(3), 26.

ILA Staff. (2019). What research really says about teaching reading (even beyond ILA 2019). *International Literacy Association.* https://www.literacyworldwide.org/blog/literacy-daily/2019/10/22/recapping-what-research-says?utm_source=TW-10222019&utm_medium=email&utm_campaign=ThisWeek&utm_content=Story-1

International Dyslexia Association. (2015). *Fact sheet: Dyslexia and the brain.* Author.

International Literacy Association. (2016). Dyslexia [Research advisory]. Author.

Iowa Reading Research Center. (n.d.). *Oral reading fluency error correction procedure.* https://iowareadingresearch.org/sites/iowareadingresearch.org/files/oral_reading_fluency_error_correction_procedure.pdf

Ivey, G., & Fisher, D. (2006). *Creating literacy-rich schools for adolescents.* Association for Supervision and Curriculum Development.

Jolly Phonics. (2018). *A programme that grows with your children.* https://www.jollylearning.co.uk/jolly-phonics/

Jones, C. D., & Reutzel, D. R. (2012). Enhancing alphabet knowledge instruction: Research implications and practical strategies for early childhood educators. *Early Childhood Education Journal, 41*(2), 81–89.

Joshi, R. M., Binks, E., Hougen, M., Dahlgren, M. E., Ocker-Dean, E., & Smith, D. (2009a). Why elementary teachers might be inadequately prepared to teach reading. *Journal of Learning Disabilities, 42*(5), 392–402.

Joshi, R. M., Binks, E., Hougen, M., Dean, E. O., Graham, L., & Smith, D. (2009b). The role of teacher education programs in preparing teachers for implementing evidence-based reading practices. In S. Rosenfield & V. Berninger (Eds.), *Implementing evidence-based academic interventions in school settings* (pp. 605–625). Oxford University Press.

Kame'enui, E. J., Simmons, D. C., Baker, S., Chard, D. J., Dickson, S. V., Gunn, B., Smith, S. B., Sprick, M., & Lin, S. J. (1997).

Effective strategies for teaching beginning reading. In E. J. Kame'enui, & D. W. Carnine (Eds.), *Effective teaching strategies that accommodate diverse learners*. Merrill.

Kelly, M. & Clausen-Grace, N. (2008). *R5 in your classroom: A guide to differentiating independent reading and developing avid readers*. International Reading Association.

Kendeou, P., Savage, R., & van den Brock, P. (2009). Revisiting the simple view of reading. *The British Journal of Educational Psychology, 79*, 353–370.

Kilpatrick, D. (2015). *Essentials of assessing, preventing, and overcoming reading difficulties*. John Wiley & Sons.

Kim, G., Guo, Q., Liu, Y., Peng, Y., & Yang, L. (2019). Multiple pathways by which compounding morphological awareness is related to reading comprehension: Evidence from Chinese second graders. *Reading Research Quarterly, 55*(2), 193–212.

Kim, M. K., Bryant, D. P., Bryant, B. R., & Park, Y. (2017). A synthesis of interventions for improving oral reading fluency of elementary students with learning disabilities. *Preventing School Failure: Alternative Education for Children and Youth, 61*, 116–125.

Kuhn, M. R., & Schwanenflugel, P. J. (2009). Time, engagement, and support: Lessons from a 4-year fluency intervention. In E. H. Hiebert (Ed.), *Reading more, reading better* (pp. 141–160). Guilford Press.

LaBerge, D., & Samuels, S. J. (1974). Towards a theory of automatic information processing in reading. *Cognitive Psychology, 6*, 293–323.

Language and Reading Research Consortium. (2015). Learning to read: Should we keep things simple? *Reading Research Quarterly, 50*(2), 151–169.

Lee, J., & Yoon, S. Y. (2017). The effects of repeated reading on reading fluency for students with reading disabilities. *Journal of Learning Disabilities, 50*, 213–224.

Lesley University. (2020). *Guided reading's 20th anniversary*. https://lesley.edu/article/guided-readings-20th-anniversary

Liu, J., & Zhang, J. (2018). The effects of extensive reading on English vocabulary learning: A meta-analysis. *English Language Teaching, 11*(6).

Loewus, L. (2019). Data: How reading is really being taught. *Education Week: Getting Reading Right, 39*(15), 3–5.

MacKay, R., & Teale, W. (2015). *No more teaching a letter a week (Not this but that)*. Heinemann.

McArthur, G., & Castles, A. (2017). Helping children with reading difficulties: Some things we have learned so far. *npj Science of Learning, 2*(7).

McGeown, S., Johnston, R. S., Walker, J., Howatson, K., Stockburn, A., & Dufton, P. (2015). The relationship between young children's enjoyment of learning to read, reading attitudes, confidence and attainment. *Educational Research, 57*(4). https://doi.org/10.1080/00131881.2015.1091234

McGilchrist, I. (2019a). One head, two brains: How the brain's hemispheres shape the world we see. *NPR.* www.npr.org/templates/transcript/transcript.php?storyId=690656459

McGilchrist, I. (2019b). *The master and his emissary: The divided brain and the making of the western world.* Yale University Press.

McKeown, M. G., Beck, I. L., Omanson, R. C., & Pople, M. T. (1985). Some effects of the nature and frequency of vocabulary instruction on the knowledge and use of words. *Reading Research Quarterly, 20*(5), 522–535.

Moats, L. (2005). How spelling supports reading: And why it is more regular and predictable than you think. *American Educator, 29*(4), 14–22.

Moats, L. C. (2020). *Teaching reading is rocket science, 2020: What expert teachers of reading should know and be able to do.* American Federation of Teachers.

Moats, L. C., Dakin, K., & Joshi, M. (Eds.). (2012). *Expert perspectives on interventions for reading.* International Dyslexia Association.

Mol, S. E., & Bus, A. G. (2011). To read or not to read: A meta-analysis of print exposure from infancy to early adulthood. *Psychological Bulletin, 137*(2), 267–296. https://doi.org/10.1037/a0021890

Munger, K. A., & Blachman, B. A. (2013). Taking a "simple view" of the dynamic indicators of basic early literacy skills as a predictor of multiple measures of third-grade reading comprehension. *Psychology in the Schools, 50*(7).

Muter, V., Hulme, C., Snowling, M. J., & Stevenson, J. (2004). Phonemes, rimes, vocabulary, and grammatical skills as foundations of early literacy development: Evidence from a longitudinal study. *Developmental Psychology, 40*(5), 665–681.

Nation, K. (2008). Learning to read words. *Quarterly Journal of Experimental Psychology, 61*(8), 1121–1133.

National Assessment of Educational Progress (NAEP). (2019). NAEP report card: 2019 NAEP reading assessment. https://www.nationsreportcard.gov/highlights/reading/2019

National Early Literacy Panel. (2008). *Developing early literacy: Report of the National Early Literacy Panel.* National Institute for Literacy.

National Institute of Child Health and Human Development, NIH, DHHS. (2000). *Report of the national reading panel: Teaching children to read: Reports of the subgroups* (00-4754). U.S. Government Printing Office.

NCTE. (2017). *Statement on classroom libraries.* https://ncte.org/statement/classroom-libraries/

Neuman, S., Kaefer, T., & Pinkham, A. (2014). Building background knowledge. *Reading Rockets*. https://www.readingrockets.org/article/building-background-knowledge

Neuman, S. B. (1999). Books make a difference: A study of access to literacy. *Reading Research Quarterly, 34*(3), 286–311. https://doi.org/10.1598/RRQ.34.3.3

Opitz, B., Ferdinand, N., & Mecklinger, A. (2011). Timing matters: The impact of immediate and delayed feedback on artificial language learning. *Frontiers of Human Neuroscience, 5*(8).

O'Reilly, T., Wang, Z., & Sabatini, J. (2019). How much knowledge is too little? When a lack of knowledge becomes a barrier to comprehension. *Psychological Science, 30*(90), 1344–1351. https://doi.org/10.1177/0956797619862276

Ozernov-Palchik, O., Norton, E. S., Sideridis, G., Beach, S., Wolf, M., Gabrieli, J. D., & Gaab, N. (2017). Longitudinal stability of pre-reading skill profiles of kindergarten children: Implications for early screening and theories of reading. *Developmental Science, 20*(5).

Paige, D. D. (2020). Phonics instruction: K–2. In *Comparing reading research to program design: An examination of teachers college units of study* (pp. 10–16). Student Achievement Partners.

Patrick, C., Manyak, P. C., Baumann, J. F., & Manyak, A.-M. (2018). Morphological analysis instruction in the elementary grades: Which morphemes to teach and how to teach them. *The Reading Teacher, 72*(3), 289–300.

Penesetti, D. (2018). What is specific learning disorder? *APA*. https://www.psychiatry.org/patients-families/specific-learning-disorder/what-is-specific-learning-disorder

Pennington, M., & Waxler, R. (2017). *Why reading books still matters: The power of literature in digital times*. Routledge.

Petretto, D., & Masala, C. (2017). Dyslexia and specific learning disorders: New international diagnostic criteria. *Journal of Child Development Disorders, 3*(4), 19.

Phillips, B. M., & Piasta, S. B. (2013). Phonological awareness and alphabet knowledge: Key precursors and instructional targets to promote reading success. In T. Shanahan & C. J. Lonigan (Eds.), *Literacy in preschool and kindergarten children: The national early literacy panel and beyond* (pp. 95–116). Paul H. Brookes.

Pressley, M., & Allington, R. (2014). *Reading instruction that works, fourth edition: The case for balanced teaching*. Guilford Press.

Quinn, M., Gerde, H., & Bingham, G. (2016). Help me where I am: Scaffolding writing in preschool classrooms. *The Reading Teacher, 70*(3), 353–357.

Raskind, W. H., Peter, B., Richards, T., Eckert, M. M., & Berninger, V. W. (2013). The genetics of reading disabilities: From phenotypes to candidate genes. *Frontiers in Psychology, 3*, 601.

Rastle, K. (2018). The place of morphology in learning to read in English. Cortex. Advance online publication. https://doi.org/10.1016/j.cortex.2018.02.008.

Reutzel, D. R. (2015). Early literacy research: Findings primary-grade teachers will want to know. *The Reading Teacher, 69*(1), 14–24.

Ripoll Salceda, J. C., Alonso, G. A., & Casilla-Earls, A. P. (2104). The simple view of reading in elementary school: A systematic review. *Revista de Logopedia, Foniatria y Audiologia, 34*(1), 17–31.

Rodgers, E., D'Agostino, J., Kelly, R., & Mikita, C. (2018). Oral reading accuracy: Findings and implications from recent research. *The Reading Teacher, 72*(2), 149–157.

Rosenshine, B. (2012). Principles of instruction: Research-based strategies that all teachers should know. *American Educator, 36*(1), 12–19.

Rowe, M. B. (1974). Wait-time and rewards as instructional variables, their influence on language, logic, and fate control: Part one—Wait time. *Journal of Research in Science Teaching, 11*(2), 81–94. https://doi.org/10.1002/tea.3660110202.

Rowe, M. B. (1986). Wait time: Slowing down may be a way of speeding up! *Journal of Teacher Education, 37*(1), 43–50. https://doi.org/10.1177/002248718603700110.

Samuels, S. J., & Wu, Y.-C. (2003). *The effects of immediate feedback on reading achievement.* http://www.epsteineducation.com/home/articles/file/research/immediate_feedback.pdf

Scarborough, H. S. (2001). Connecting early language and literacy to later reading (dis)abilities: Evidence, theory, and practice. In S. Neuman & D. Dickinson (Eds.), *Handbook for research in early literacy* (pp. 97–110). Guilford Press.

Schiefele, U., Stutz, F., & Schaffner, E. (2016). Longitudinal relations between reading motivation and reading comprehension in the early elementary grades. *Learning and Individual Differences, 51,* 49–58.

Schwartz, S. (2020, March 13). "Decodable" books: Boring, useful, or both? *Education Week.* https://www.edweek.org/ew/articles/2020/03/12/decodable-books-boring-useful-or-both.html

Sedita, J. (2018). Background knowledge and reading comprehension. *Literacy Lines.* https://keystoliteracy.com/blog/background-knowledge-and-reading-comprehension/

Seidenberg, M. (2017). *Language at the speed of sight: How we read, why so many can't, and what we can do about it.* Basic Books.

Shanahan, T. (2017a, July 10). Language at the speed of sight—On cueing systems, phonemes, speed reading, and sequences of learning. *Reading Rockets.* https://www.readingrockets.org/blogs/shanahan-literacy/language-speed-sight-cueing-systems-phonemes-speed-reading-and-sequences

Shanahan, T. (2017b, August 4). Everything you wanted to know about repeated reading. *Reading Rockets.* https://www.reading

rockets.org/blogs/shanahan-literacy/everything-you-wanted-know-about-repeated-reading

Shanahan, T. (2018). *Shanahan on literacy: Should we teach with decodable text?* https://shanahanonliteracy.com/blog/should-we-teach-with-decodable-text

Shapiro, L. R., & Solity, J. (2008). Delivering phonological and phonics training within whole-class teaching. *British Journal of Educational Psychology, 78*(4), 597–620. https://doi.org/10.1348/000709908X293850.

Share, D. (1999). Phonological recoding and orthographic learning: A direct test of the self-teaching hypothesis. *Journal of Experimental Child Psychology, 72*(2), 95–129.

Share, D. (2011). On the role of phonology in reading acquisition: The self-teaching hypothesis. In S. A. Brady, D. Braze, & C. A. Fowler (Eds.), *Explaining individual differences in reading: Theory and evidence* (pp. 45–68). Psychology Press.

Shaw, N. (1988). *Sheep in a Jeep.* HMH Books for Young Readers.

Shaywitz, S. E. (2003) *Overcoming dyslexia: A new and complete science-based program for reading problems at any level.* Knopf.

Shaywitz, S., & Shaywitz, J. (2020). *Overcoming dyslexia: Second edition, completely revised and updated.* Knopf.

Snow, C., & Strucker, J. (1999). *Lessons from preventing reading difficulties in young children for adult learning and literacy: Review of adult learning and literacy, Vol. 1.* https://files.eric.ed.gov/fulltext/ED508704.pdf

Special Olympics. (2020). Intellectual disabilities. https://www.specialolympics.org/about/intellectual-disabilities

Specific Learning Difficulties Association of Southern Australia. (n.d.). *SPELD SA phonic books.* https://www.speld-sa.org.au/services/phonic-books.html

Stahl, R. J. (1994). Using "think-time" and "wait-time" skillfully in the classroom. *ERIC Digest.* https://files.eric.ed.gov/fulltext/ED370885.pdf

Stanovich, K. E., & Siegel, L. S. (1994). Phenotypic performance profile of children with reading disabilities: A regression-based test of the phonological-core variable-difference model. *Journal of Educational Psychology, 86*, 24–53.

Stevens, E. A., Walker, M. A., & Vaughn, S. (2017). The effects of reading fluency interventions on the reading fluency and reading comprehension performance of elementary students with learning disabilities: A synthesis of the research from 2001 to 2014. *Journal of Learning Disabilities, 50*, 576–590.

Sutherland, S. (2015). What happens in the brain when we read? *Scientific American Mind, 26*(4), 14. https://www.scientificamerican.com/article/when-we-read-we-recognize-words-as-pictures-and-hear-them-spoken-aloud/

Swanson, E., Wanzek, J., Petscher, Y., Vaughn, S., Heckert, J., Cavanaugh, C., Kraft, G., & Tackett, K. (2011). A synthesis of read-aloud interventions on early reading outcomes among preschool through third graders at risk for reading difficulties. *Journal of Learning Disabilities*, *44*, 258–275.

Topping, K. J., Samuels, J., & Paul, T. (2007). Does practice make perfect? Independent reading quantity, quality and student achievement. *Learning and Instruction*, *17*(3), 253–264. https://doi:10.1016/j.learninstruc.2007.02.002

Torgesen, J. K., Rashotte, C. A., Alexander, A., Alexander, J., & MacPhee, K. (2003). Progress toward understanding the instructional conditions necessary for remediating reading difficulties in older children. In B. R. Foorman (Ed.), *Preventing and remediating reading difficulties: Bringing science to scale* (pp. 275–297). York Press.

Vellutino, F. R., Scanlon, D. M., & Lyon, G. R. (2000). Differentiating between difficult-to-remediate and readily remediated poor readers: More evidence against the IQ-achievement discrepancy definition of reading disability. *Journal of Learning Disabilities*, *33*(3), 223–238.

Walther, M. (2019). *The ramped-up read aloud*. Corwin.

Weakland, M. (2011). *Bubbles float, bubbles pop*. Capstone Press.

Weakland, M. (2014). *Super core: Turbocharging your basal reading program with more reading, writing, and word work*. International Reading Association.

Weakland, M. (2019). *Super speller starter sets*. Stenhouse.

Webb, S. (2007). The effects of repetition on vocabulary knowledge. *Applied Linguistics*, *28*, 46–65. As cited in Richards, M. (2009). *Developing academic vocabulary independently (DAVI): A usability study*. Graduate Theses and Dissertations. Paper 11160.

Werker, J., & Tees, R. (1999). Influences on infant speech processing: Toward a new synthesis. *Annual Review of Psychology*, *50*, 509–535.

Werker, J., & Tees, R. (2002). Cross-language speech perception: Evidence of perceptual reorganization during the first year of life. *Infant Behavior and Development*, *25*(1), 121–133.

Wilson, B. (2009). *Wilson student reader 2*. Wilson Language Training.

Wolf, M. (2008). *Proust and the squid: The story and science of the reading brain*. Harper Perennial.

Wolf, M. (2018). *Reader, come home: The reading brain in a digital world*. Harper Collins.

Wright, D., & Ehri, L. (2007). Beginners remember orthography when they learn to read words: The case of doubled letters. *Applied Psycholinguistics*, *28*, 115–133.

Wylie, R., & Durrell, D. (1970). Teaching vowels through phonograms. *Elementary English*, *47*, 787–791.

The Yale Center for Dyslexia & Creativity. (2020). What is dyslexia? https://dyslexia.yale.edu/dyslexia/what-is-dyslexia/

Yonchevaa, Y. N., Wise, J., & McCandliss, B. (2015). Hemispheric specialization for visual words is shaped by attention to sublexical units during initial learning. *Brain and Language, 145/146*, 23–33. doi.org/10.1016/j.bandl.2015.04.001

You Gov. (2016). *Teacher & principal school report: Focus on literacy.* Scholastic. https://www.scholastic.com/content/dam/tpr-downloads/Scholastic-Teacher-and-Principal-School-Report-Literacy.pdf

Zawoyski, A., Ardoin, S., & Binder, K. (2014). Using eye tracking to observe differential effects of repeated readings for second-grade students as a function of achievement level. *Reading Research Quarterly, 50*(2), 171–184.

INDEX